Legal Discourse across Languages and Cultures

Linguistic Insights

Studies in Language and Communication

Edited by Maurizio Gotti,
University of Bergamo

Volume 117

PETER LANG
Bern · Berlin · Bruxelles · Frankfurt am Main · New York · Oxford · Wien

Maurizio Gotti & Christopher Williams (eds)

Legal Discourse across Languages and Cultures

PETER LANG
Bern · Berlin · Bruxelles · Frankfurt am Main · New York · Oxford · Wien

Bibliographic information published by Die Deutsche Nationalbibliothek
Die Deutsche Nationalbibliothek lists this publication in the Deutsche Nationalbibliografie; detailed bibliographic data is available on the Internet at ‹http://dnb.d-nb.de›.

British Library and Library of Congress Cataloguing-in-Publication Data:
A catalogue record for this book is available from *The British Library*, Great Britain.

Library of Congress Cataloging-in-Publication Data

Legal discourse across languages and cultures /
Maurizio Gotti & Christopher Williams (eds).
p. cm. – (Linguistic insights ; v. 117)
Includes bibliographical references and index.
ISBN 978-3-0343-0425-2 (alk. paper)
1. Law–Language–Cross-cultural studies. 2. Culture and law. I. Gotti, Maurizio.
II. Williams, Christopher.
K213.L3989 2010
340'.14–dc22

2010019811

This volume is part of a national research project on *Tension and Change in English Domain-Specific Genres* supported by the Italian Ministry of Education (COFIN Grant No. 2007JCY9Y9) and is published under the auspices of the University of Bergamo, Dipartimento di Lingue, Letterature e Culture Comparate.

ISSN 1424-8689
ISBN 978-3-0343-0425-2

Hochfeldstrasse 32, CH-3012 Bern, Switzerland
info@peterlang.com, www.peterlang.com, www.peterlang.net

Printed in Switzerland

Contents

Legal Discourse across Cultures

MAURIZIO GOTTI / CHRISTOPHER WILLIAMS

Introduction

1. Legal discourse across languages and cultures

The starting point for this volume was the International Conference hosted by CERLIS University of Bergamo between 18 and 20 June 2009 on 'Researching Language and the Law: Intercultural Perspectives'. The conference had aroused considerable curiosity, and a lively, fruitful debate had emerged among scholars from a variety of academic backgrounds whose interests converged on themes relating to intercultural legal linguistics.

Legal language seen from cross-cultural perspectives brings together two areas of research that have burgeoned in recent years, i.e. legal linguistics and intercultural studies. It is almost half a century since the American scholar David Mellinkoff published his groundbreaking work *The Language of the Law* (1963), which was to prove so influential in stigmatizing the vagaries of English legal language. Since then – and especially over the last 15 years or so – a large number of publications have been devoted to analysing various aspects of legal language: for example, within the space of a single decade several volumes in the Peter Lang *Linguistic Insights* series have been devoted to legal language alone. Besides works dealing with legal language in more general terms (e.g. Tiersma 1999) there are now flourishing areas of expertise in specialized fields of legal linguistics, such as forensic linguistics (e.g. Olsson 2008), legal translation (e.g. Šarčević 2000), comparative legal linguistics (e.g. Mattila 2006), or plain legal language (e.g. Asprey 2010).

There has also been a growth of interest in intercultural studies in recent years, partly as a result of globalization and of the rapid spread and penetration of information technology in contemporary society which, on the one hand, has led to a kind of homogenization of cultural values while, on the other, by bringing 'the world' into people's living rooms and offices at the click of a mouse, it is arguable that people's awareness of linguistic diversity and of cultural difference has actually been heightened.

The chapters constituting this volume reflect this rapidly changing, multifaceted world in which legal institutions and cultural/ national identities interact, at times by reshaping the past, as when colonizers of old (e.g. the white settlers in Australia), having imposed their laws and values on a native population long ago, attempt to redress the balance by readjusting (up to a point) the legal framework and hence the lexis used by legal drafters and theorists. In other cases it may be a question of defining the threats posed by present society: in the wake of the terrorist attacks of 11th September 2001 we discover, for example, how the US Supreme Court constructs the category of 'terrorist' with respect to how this is done by the European Court of Human Rights. Elsewhere we can read of how nations are getting ready to meet the future: it is no coincidence that three of the chapters in this book focus on the legal-linguistic problems facing Croatia, a country preparing for entry into the European Union (EU). And, as can be seen in this volume, within the EU itself the language debate still rages. On the one hand the aim is to ensure total equivalence and dignity among all of the official languages of the EU; on the other there is the (tantalizing yet highly controversial) prospect of creating a pan-European legal language – i.e. English – so as to ensure greater harmonization in certain areas of European law.

All 14 chapters in this volume are based on papers that were presented at the 2009 conference held in Bergamo, though several of them have been substantially revised. Within the broad thematic leitmotif of this volume – namely legal discourse across languages and cultures – it has been possible to identify two major strands: legal discourse across languages on the one hand, and legal discourse across cultures on the other. Of course, labels of this kind are adopted partly as a matter of convenience, and it could be argued that any paper dealing with legal discourse across languages inevitably has to do with legal discourse across cultures. But a closer inspection of the papers comprising each of these two strands reveals that there is a coherent logic behind the choice of labels. All seven chapters in the section entitled 'Legal Discourse Across Languages' are concerned with legal topics where more than one language is at stake, whereas all seven chapters in the section entitled 'Legal Discourse Across Cultures' are concerned with legal topics where English is the sole – or the main – language taken into consideration but where cultural differences within the English-speaking world (or within countries where English is the predominantly spoken language) are brought to the fore. Each of the 14 chapters is briefly illustrated below.

2. Contents of the volume

2.1. Legal discourse across languages

The first part of the volume deals with the realization of legal concepts through various languages. This is the common reality that is experienced not only in pluricultural countries which need to draft provisions in the various tongues officially recognized within them, but also of many international organizations that have adopted a multilingual policy. This is the case, for example, of the EU, which considers all the national tongues of its member states as the official languages of the Union. This plurilingual policy often gives rise to cases of terminological inconsistency and incoherence in EU directives, which sometimes pose a threat to cross-border transactions. This problem has sparked a lively debate on the crucial role of language in the harmonization process and the need for a pan-European legal language as a precondition for greater convergence in areas of private law. In her chapter SUSAN ŠARČEVIĆ analyses the new approach to language in the Draft Common Frame of Reference (DCFR), published in 2008 by the Academic Network of Excellence 'Common Principles of European Contract Law' as a model for a Common Frame of Reference to be adopted by European authorities. The DCFR proposes a common terminology, definitions of key concepts and model rules for a

European contract law and other areas of private law. Although today the unifying language is English, this pan-European legal language is not intended to promote a process of Anglification, but rather to provide a meta-language with a common terminology and legal concepts at EU level, which will be translated into all EU languages.

COLIN ROBERTSON takes a personal look at the work of legal-linguistic revision of legislative texts of the Council of the European Union, an important process where the aim is to maintain semantic equivalence between language versions and guarantee the quality of the texts. The chapter first addresses the human context and the qualifications required to work as lawyer-linguists. Next it considers the EU linguistic regime and the way in which this imposes an obligation to produce multilingual legislative texts and what that means in practice. In particular, the author examines the process of constructing EU legislative texts from a pragmatic point of view and places the work of legal-linguistic revision in a 'production-line' context. The heart of the chapter is a presentation of four viewpoints – legal, linguistic, policy and action – for the purposes of practical revision work, and shows how their integration is needed to give a broad view of the overall draft text to be revised and finalized in readiness for adoption, signature and publication.

The translation of EU terminology is also the main topic of MARTINA BAJČIĆ's chapter, which illustrates how the creation of adequate equivalents in the various languages of the EU calls for both creative skills and, more importantly, knowledge of the law. This is particularly visible in the recent experience of new and prospective member states where linguists and lawyers are confronted with difficulties when searching for terms in their respective languages to render the same meaning of an EU term. In particular, the author focuses on the problems relating to the search for adequate equivalents in Croatian for EU legal terminology and provides examples from social policy directives concerning the provision of minimum terms and conditions which member states must apply to workers posted to their territory from another member state. In the absence of a standardized translation, the author discusses the most important relevant terms in English, French, German and Slovene and compares them to the proposed Croatian equivalents.

The strict relationship existing between the community of users and the meaning representation of legal discourse is dealt with also in the following chapter, which investigates how national genre norms affect the way legal concepts are verbalized in legislative texts. JAN ROALD and SUNNIVA WHITTAKER adopt Norwegian and French legislative texts on public procurement as the empirical basis of the study. Although the texts are based on the same EU directive (though not itself an EU member, Norway is obliged to enact EU legislation in certain areas) and thereby cover the same subject matter, the transposition of the directive into the respective national legislation is shown to require an adaptation to the discursive norms governing the genre. The French text displays considerable variation in the terms used; in the Norwegian text, on the other hand, the same terms tend to be adopted throughout the text and their meaning in the text is context-dependent. The analysis highlights various factors that may explain this difference, such as the length of the texts, the rhetorical traditions and coreferencing devices.

LELIJA SOČANAC analyses the impact of major legal languages – Latin, French, German and English – on Croatian scholarly articles and uses both quantitative and qualitative methods to establish the main sources of linguistic transference. The analysis is based on a corpus of law articles published in the periods that have marked certain transition points in recent Croatian history, starting from 1950 to the present. The various types of language-contact phenomena – single-word lexical transfers, multiple transfers, hybrid forms, code-switching – are described for each of the major donor languages. In addition, the chapter concentrates on particular areas of law in which the major legal languages have left their impact, and the author explains the potential motives for this linguistic transference.

In the following chapter SILVIA CACCHIANI and CHIARA PREITE concentrate on the meaning description of a few borrowings across English and French desk law dictionaries in paper format: *Oxford Dictionary of Law*, 2006 [*ODL*] and *Longman Dictionary of Law*, 2007 [*LDL*] for English; *Vocabulaire juridique*, 2007 [*VJ*] for French. The prefaces and informative blurbs of these dictionaries suggest similar purpose and target user groups in the same situations of use; however, in reality they do not seem to translate into similar meaning representations. The authors therefore adapt Wiegand's (1977) actional-semantic theory of dictionary form in order to detail and motivate variation in meaning description across English and French dictionaries. Their analysis shows that *ODL* and *LDL* focus on disciplinary knowledge and provide a comprehensive treatment of lemmas within encyclopaedic dictionary entries characterized by an initial condensed meaning paraphrase, subsequent extensive meaning descriptions, and cross-references to the relevant disciplines. By contrast, *VJ* favours non-condensed items, provides comments on form and etymology and keeps explanations to a minimum within additions to the meaning paraphrase. The reason for this seems to lie precisely in different trade-offs between legal practitioners and lexicographers, which result in different assumptions on what best fulfils the users' needs: *ODL* and *LDL* were compiled by professionals who benefited from the expertise of lexicographers. By contrast, *VJ* is the product of the joint efforts of linguists and law professionals within the framework of legal linguistics. As such, *VJ* has a multiple focus on language, which translates into an interest in form and language use and, consequently, results in a departure from the main emphasis on the encyclopaedic and disciplinary knowledge which is a distinctive feature of *ODL* and *LDL*.

The next chapter concentrates on the teaching of legal English in Croatia. The growing process of globalization and Croatia's upcoming accession to the European Union have determined the increase in the importance of cross-cultural legal communication skills for practising professionals. SNJEŽANA HUSINEC identifies divergent culture-specific terminology as one of the major issues in teaching the language of law for cross-cultural communication. This is rendered particularly problematic by the presence of different legal traditions and the asymmetry of legal systems. The significance of this asymmetry and its consequences for the process of legal language teaching can be seen in practical terms: the English common law legal system differs considerably from the Croatian civil law legal system. Therefore, whereas the participants of legal English courses expect to be taught matching equivalents which would enable them to communicate more efficiently in their international contacts, they are confronted with only a partial overlap of legal systems and the relativity of concepts. To overcome this difficulty, the teaching of language cannot be separated from the teaching of content. In the author's experience, the adoption of comparative legal analysis has proved very useful as a basis for discussing the appropriateness of usage of certain legal terms as near or approximate equivalents.

2.2. Legal discourse across cultures

The second part of the volume comprises investigations of various issues concerning the link between law, language and culture. JANET AINSWORTH's study examines the role of language ideology in driving legal doctrine in American employment discrimination law. In particular, she analyses the legal validity of rules adopted by some American employers requiring that employees speak exclusively in English on the job. These so-called 'English only' policies have been accused of violating American laws prohibiting discrimination against workers based on their ethnicity or national origin. These accusations, however, have found a chilly reception in American courts for their claims of discrimination. In part, this is due to the ideologically-based belief by lawyers and judges that all languages are commensurate with one another as means of interpersonal communication. According to this assumption, bilingual employees are not disadvantaged by being required to express themselves in English alone as, by definition, they can fully communicate in either language. The author, however, demonstrates how the courts' reasoning in these cases fails to account for the linguistic research on multilingual cross-cultural communication. By ignoring the cognitive aspects of bilingual code-switching, the law erroneously assumes that employees are making deliberate and unnecessary choices about their manner of expressing themselves on the job, and fails to understand the degree to which code-switching by bilinguals serves as a rich resource for encoding identity and meaning. The analysis of a few cases exposes the breadth of linguistic ideological hegemony in the law, and suggests the need for explicit legal recognition of language rights as a civil rights issue in order to protect workers from identity-based discrimination in employment.

WILLIAM BROMWICH's chapter also deals with divergences in employment issues deriving from cross-cultural differentiations. In particular, it examines the institutional constraints on discourse processes in cases in Employment Tribunals in the UK, at the European Union Civil Service Tribunal in Luxembourg, and at the International Labour Organization Administrative Tribunal (ILOAT) in Geneva. Although in each case the pragmatic function is the presentation of complaints by employees against their employers with a view to obtaining compensation or reinstatement, the procedural rules shaping the discourse are strikingly different, with consequent variation in generic structure and lexical content. The chapter highlights the fact that Employment Tribunals in the UK, standing firmly in the common law tradition, provide for courtroom hearings in which the parties present oral evidence, following the classic sequence of *examination-in-chief* and *cross-examination*. However, at the European Union Civil Service Tribunal and the ILOAT the proceedings reflect the civil law tradition, even in cases in which the working language is English. As a result, the discourse is structured in a manner entirely different from the proceedings in the UK, with claims presented and argumentation developed almost exclusively on the basis of written documents, in a genre chain consisting of the *complaint*, the *defendant's reply*, the *complainant's rejoinder*, the *defendant's surrejoinder*, and then the *judgment*. This enables the Tribunal to deal with cases entirely on the basis of documentary evidence, with applications for hearings seldom allowed. The examination of the terminology in the Tribunals – one national, one supranational, one international – also reveals significant differences, as the parties seek to comply with the institutional constraints prevailing in each system.

The following two chapters likewise examine the conduct of different judging authorities operating in different cultural contexts. GIORGIA RIBONI examines decisions taken by the Supreme Court of the United States and by the European Court of Human Rights after the events of 11th September 2001 in order to investigate the way people accused of carrying out terrorist attacks are represented on both sides of the Atlantic. Her analysis shows that in both American and European decisions findings underline a preoccupation with the definition of status of the individual, but whereas the European Court of Human Rights frequently uses the term 'person', the Supreme Court relies more on the notion of 'citizenship'. In the decisions of the

Supreme Court terrorism is represented as an external danger which threatens American citizenry and territory and has to be fought against by waging war. The European approach to terrorism is shown to be different as it mainly relies on international cooperation and the strict application of the law. The investigation of the ways the Supreme Court and the European Court of Human Rights discursively construct the figure of the terrorist thus contributes to highlighting the differences existing between the legal cultures on each side of the Atlantic.

DAVIDE MAZZI discusses the importance of argumentation in the judicial process and in particular examines the centrality of counterfactual conditionals (CTFs) in House of Lords and US Supreme Court judgments. According to Nivelle and Van Belle (2007), the study of CTFs is of particular interest in that these forms shed light on an overall key feature of argumentative discourse, i.e. the expression of causation. In order to test the validity of this theory, this chapter explores the textual functions of CTFs within two corpora representative of the Common Law legal tradition. The results of this analysis show that the pervasiveness of CTFs is common to both courts: more specifically, CTFs appear to express or criticize causation in a number of key contexts of judicial argumentation, i.e. the evaluation of previous judicial decisions, judicial procedures and the overall interpretation and categorization of facts.

IGNACIO VÁZQUEZ ORTA's chapter is also related to the analysis of argumentation in the judicial process. The purpose of his investigation is to explore the way judges reason and negotiate their decisions by focusing on, firstly, the specific forms of negotiating alternative positions, and secondly, how texts (or rather judges as writers) negotiate past decisions, integrate these texts into their own and align themselves with these past decisions. Central to these arguments is the idea of dialogue and negotiation. In a judgment, the writer enters into a number of dialogues with previous texts: with the evidence, argument and submissions made by the litigants in court, with the decision which is being appealed against, and with similar decisions in the past (precedent). And finally, a writer may enter into a dialogue with his/her colleagues on the bench who may decide a case differently. By analysing judgments of appellate courts in the common law system, the author demonstrates that they may play a very important role from a discursive point of view: they contain the rules as they have been declared by the judges on a case-by-case basis and are therefore a primary source of law; moreover, they provide a public account of the judges' reasoning processes. This makes judgments important texts also in legal education.

Issues of property and land rights as applied to indigenous groups in Australia have received increasing attention in recent years as recognition of continuing dispossession and injustices to indigenous groups has led to the movement to incorporate more indigenous concepts into Anglo-Australian Law. How successful such attempts may be depends not only on political will and public acceptance but also on whether the differing conceptualizations of abstract ideas such as property and ownership can be made compatible. In his chapter THOMAS CHRISTIANSEN examines this issue from the perspective of cognitive grammar (Langacker 1987) by looking at reference works on indigenous Australian languages in order to gauge how far a general concept of possession is grammaticalized and lexicalized. The author finds that, while a notion of possession exists in many Aboriginal languages broadly in line with the conceptual archetype identified in English, there is evidence that the part such a concept plays in culture is less important than it is in English-speaking societies – judging by the number of different terms and frequency of the same in wordlists. The chapter then examines the clusters formed by a selection of words pertaining to property and possession in a corpus of the Australian *Indigenous Law Bulletin* compared to a reference corpus of texts from the US *Harvard Law Review*. From this, it transpires that the concept of property in Anglo-Australian legal discourse is more multifarious than in US law, where it is treated as a given entity used to categorize or qualify other concepts but not itself categorized or qualified. This leads to the conclusion that there are evident attempts in Australian legal discourse to incorporate indigenous groups' conceptualizations of possession and property which are less individualistic, more communal, and stem from a less anthropocentric world view.

ISMAEL ARINAS PELLÓN's analysis shows how patents can be considered hybrid texts with features of legal and scientific languages. Indeed, these documents adopt an 'all-inclusiveness' communicative strategy typical of legal texts (Bhatia 1993), although motivated by different reasons: laws and contracts try to cover as many contingencies as possible, whereas patents try to claim as much intellectual property as possible. The analysis of the needs of those working or studying in research areas shows that patents are both a very important source of scientific information for researchers and an expected outcome of many research processes. Having thus justified the need to research the genre of patents, this chapter then proceeds to identify the typical move structure of a 2.5 million token corpus of US patents. To reach his purpose, the author adopts an analytical method which complements Swales' (1990) and Bhatia's (1993) genre approaches with Paltridge's (1997) concept of prototypicality.

3. Concluding remarks

As illustrated in this brief overview, the analyses collected in this foray into intercultural legal linguistics highlight the influence that cultural elements play in differentiating legal texts in various contexts. Indeed, legal terminology can be so culture-bound (for a variety of historical, sociological, political or jurisprudential reasons) that a satisfactory translation of all the legal terms of a text from one context to another is at times impossible. Examples abound of linguistic and cultural discrepancies in texts relating to the process of harmonization between different legal systems when trying to build a common legal framework: this task is much more complex than the simple rendering of common normative documents in all the languages of the countries involved, because this newly created framework is meant to be interpreted within the contexts of a diversity of individual legal systems and tongues. Generally speaking, these harmonizing efforts and initiatives have not been able to solve all the problems of discrepancy, as the final texts may sometimes be conditioned by the different rhetorical traditions pertaining to the cultural systems involved.

Various chapters in this volume have provided valuable evidence of how in the translation process there is often an addition to and/or alteration of the semantic value of the original, with translators bringing their own experience, knowledge and attitudes to the text being translated. Texts which are the result of a translation or a re-writing process have often been shown to contain significant traces of adaptation of the text to the legal and socio-cultural traits of the national target users. In spite of the desire to make legal texts and terminology equivalent at an international level, differentiations in the construction of legal discourse often remain.

These issues are fundamental in the study of the link between language, culture and the law and they represent challenges and opportunities that confront scholars researching into these matters. It is hoped that this volume will contribute to further debate and reflection, while enhancing our understanding of such linguistic, legal and cultural phenomena.

Acknowledgements

We would like to thank a number of colleagues who have contributed to this volume in a variety of ways. Their invaluable assistance has helped to make the compilation of this volume a stimulating and rewarding experience. Special thanks go to: Douglass Bellis, Vijay Bhatia, Marta Chroma, Marina Dossena, Diane Edelman, Lyspeth Ford, Peter Goodrich, Massimiliano Granieri, Peter Gray, Lita Lundquist, John Morley, Boris Pritchard, Susan Šarčević, Natalie Stoljar, and John Swales.

References

Asprey, Michelle 2010 [1992]. *Plain Language for Lawyers*. Annandale, NSW: The Federation Press.

Bhatia, Vijay K. 1993. *Analysing Genre: Language Use in Professional Settings*. London: Longman.

Langacker, Ronald 1987. *Foundations of Cognitive Grammar.* Vol. I. Stanford: Stanford University Press.

Mattila, Heikki 2006. *Comparative Legal Linguistics.* Aldershot, UK: Ashgate.

Mellinkoff, David 1963. *The Language of the Law.* Boston: Little, Brown & Co.

Nivelle, Nele / Van Belle, William 2007. The Use of Counterfactual Conditionals Expressing Causation in Legal Discourse. In van Eemeren, Frans H. / Blair, J. Anthony / Willard, Charles A. / Garssen, Bart (eds) *Proceedings of the Sixth Conference of the International Society for the Study of Argumentation.* Amsterdam: SicSat, 989-996.

Olsson, John 2008 [2004]. *Forensic Linguistics.* London: Continuum International Publishing Group.

Paltridge, Brian 1997. *Genre, Frames and Writing in Research Settings.* Amsterdam: John Benjamins.

Šarčević, Susan 2000. *New Approach to Legal Translation.* The Hague: Kluwer Law International.

Swales, John 1990. *Genre Analysis.* Cambridge: Cambridge University Press.

Tiersma, Peter 1999. *Legal Language.* Chicago: Chicago University Press.

Wiegand, Herbert Ernst 1977. Einige grundlegende semantisch-pragmatische Aspekte von Wörterbucheinträgen. Ein Beitrag zur praktischen Lexikologie. *Kopenhagener Beiträge zur Germanistischen Linguistik* 12, 59-149.

Legal Discourse across Languages

SUSAN ŠARČEVIĆ

Creating a Pan-European Legal Language

1. Introduction

Since the link between language, law and cultural identity is traditionally the strongest in private law, it is not surprising that the greatest resistance to the harmonization of European law has been in core areas of private law relating to contract law. In a Communication of 2001,[1] the European Commission recognized that the co-existence of different national contract laws hinders the internal market's ability to function, and for the first time it acknowledged that terminological inconsistency and incoherence in directives and their national transposing instruments pose a threat to cross-border transactions. This sparked, among other things, a lively debate among legal scholars on the crucial role of language in the harmonization process and the need for a pan-European legal language as a precondition for greater convergence in areas of private law.

On the political front, the Commission responded in 2003 with an Action Plan for a more Coherent European Contract Law,[2] in which it called on the legal academic community to intensify its ongoing research activities with a view to creating a Common Frame of Reference (CFR) which would propose a common terminology and rules in the area of European contract law. In its follow-up Communi-

1 Communication from the Commission to the Council and the European Parliament on European Contract Law (OJ C 255 of 13.9.2001).

2 Communication from the Commission to the European Parliament and the Council, 'An Action Plan for a more coherent European Contract Law' (OJ C 63 of 15.3.2003).

cation of 2004,[3] the Commission confirmed that the CFR should contain definitions, fundamental principles and model rules to enhance the quality and consistency of the existing *acquis* and possibly serve as an optional instrument for further convergence of European private law. In 2005, the Academic Network of Excellence "Common Principles of European Contract Law" (CoPECL) was established under the EU Sixth Framework Research Programme and commissioned with the task of drawing up a Draft Common Frame of Reference (hereinafter: DCFR) (see von Bar 2005: 19-20; 2008b: 5).[4]

This chapter examines basic terminological problems in the present *acquis* and the new approach to language in the 'academic' DCFR, which was published in 2008 as a model for a 'political' Common Frame of Reference (CFR) to be completed by the Commission and adopted during 2010.[5] Although it remains to be seen whether and to what extent the CFR will be used in future EU legislation, Professor Christian von Bar, chairman of the Study Group on a European Civil Code, is optimistic that it will eventually lead to the creation of a new *ius commune europaeum* (von Bar 2005: 17; on the *ius commune*-debate see Smits 2007: 219-230). This reference to the common law of continental Europe formed by the reception of Roman law in the 17th and 18th centuries raises questions as to the feasibility of such an ambitious project under the present conditions. Namely, at that time lawyers in large parts of continental Europe were all part of one unified culture and used the same legal language, i.e. Latin.

---

3 Communication from the Commission to the European Parliament and the Council, 'European Contract Law and the revision of the *acquis*: the way forward' (OJ C 14 of 20.01.2005).

4 See website of the joint network on Common Principles of European Contract Law, today the joint network on European Private Law at <http://www.copecl.org>.

5 An interim outline edition of the Draft Common Frame of Reference (DCFR), *Principles, Definitions and Model Rules of European Private Law*, was published by Sellier European Law Publishers in 2008; the full edition with comments and comparative notes in six volumes followed in October 2009. The Commission is currently assessing the DCFR and will consult the other institutions before adopting a political CFR in 2010. See the Commission's Communication of 10.06.2009, SEC(2009) 767.

Today the common drafting language of the DCFR is English; however, the new pan-European legal language is not intended to be a process of Anglification. Therefore, the project can be successful only if the EU policy of multilingualism is upheld, and to that end high quality translations are required. My main purpose is to examine whether the CFR could eventually serve as the basis for a future pan-European legal language, a meta-language with common legal concepts at EU level.

2. Bridging legal, language and cultural barriers in Europe

The catalyst for the largest research project in European private law is usually regarded as the 1989 resolution of the European Parliament calling for the elaboration of a European Civil Code,[6] which resulted in the formation of the Study Group on a European Civil Code in 1999.[7] By that time, comparative lawyers had already commenced the debate on whether the convergence of private law is desirable and feasible in Europe. Some scholars, such as Pierre Legrand, a Canadian comparativist trained in both the civil law and common law traditions, flatly denied that such convergence is possible, mainly due to the absence of a common European legal culture and language (1996: 61-62; his tone has since mellowed but not his stance, cf. Legrand 2008: 198-218). Challenging Legrand's pessimism, some European lawyers have confirmed that a new European legal culture is gradually emerging despite national cultural and linguistic diversity (Hesselink 2001; Weigand 2008; see divergent views in Wilhelmsson/Paunio/ Pohjolainen 2007). Others have suggested that before Brussels imposes further legislative action in private law, attempts should be made to create a common legal language in Europe, which would

6 26 May 1989 (OJ C I56, 26.06.1989, at 400).

7 The predecessor to the Study Group, the Lando Commission on European Contract Law, was constituted in 1982 and published three volumes of the Principles of European Contract Law (PECL) (see note 13 below).

facilitate the free movement of legal ideas and doctrines, eventually leading to a European legal thinking (Weigand 2008), culture and identity (Pozzo 2003; López-Rodríguez 2003/04; Heutger 2004). Mentioned earlier by the Italian comparativist Rodolfo Sacco of Turin (1996), the idea of creating a common legal language in Europe found support among legal scholars who strongly believe that a common legal language in Europe cannot be a *lingua franca* such as English but must be a neutral meta-language with common legal concepts detached from their national laws, legal languages and cultures (Campana 1999).[8]

The new emphasis on bridging legal, language and cultural barriers in Europe found resonance among European lawyers who recognized the important role of language in the harmonization process. In particular, the Research Group on the Existing EC Private Law, officially dubbed the Acquis Group in 2002, focused its research from 2002 to 2006 on a "Uniform Terminology for European Private Law".[9] Head of the Acquis Group, Professor Gianmaria Ajani of the University of Turin, called the need to develop coherent terminological usage "a crucial step" in the "long march" of the European Union towards the harmonization of private law (2007: 493; cf. Ajani/Ebers 2005: 15). As he realized, the heart of the problem is not just incoherent terminological usage but rather the lack of uniform concepts at EU level. In this sense, Viola Heutger stressed that "legal harmonisation can be attained only by standardizing legal terms within the European Union" (Heutger 2003: 2; cf. Ajani/Ebers 2005: 17).

8 Cf. van Hoecke/Warrington (1998: 525), who regard the development of some conceptual legal meta-language as "a necessary condition for a real development of comparative law". A linguist, Anne Lise Kjær, joined the debate on the possibility and desirability of developing a common European legal language. Discussing the topic outside the framework of a European private law, she rejects the creation of a meta-language, calling instead for a European legal discourse across languages as a means of promoting a "common understanding" between lawyers of different legal systems (2004: 396; cf. 2008: 153-156).

9 See results of studies of the research network in Schulze/Ajani (2003) and Ajani/Ebers (2005). In May 2005 the Acquis Group became part of the Joint Network on European Private Law. For current activities, see their website at <www.acquis-group.org>.

What Heutger meant is the standardization of legal concepts, which she clarified by calling for "clear definitions, concepts and principles for specific use" (2004: 3). A strong advocate for a pan-European legal language, she claims that "it would probably [be easier] to create a common pan-European legal language than to synchronise the use of one language and its legal terminology in different national states" (2003: 6; also 2004: 2). Encouraging interdisciplinary studies in law and linguistics, Heutger warns that "European integration cannot proceed without paying attention to linguistic matters" (2004: 4; 2008: 6).

3. Terminological problems in the present *acquis*

In accordance with the Union's unique policy of multilingualism, Community acts are drafted in either English or French and then translated into all the other official languages, currently a total of 23. EU law is sometimes described as an independent legal order with its own autonomous conceptual system (de Groot 1999: 14), thus implying that EU legal terms share a common system of reference in the sense that EU terms in the 23 official languages derive their meaning from a common conceptual system at EU level. Unfortunately, this is not yet the case (Šarčević 2006; Kjær 2007; cf. Prechal/van Roermund 2008). EU law is still developing and is very much dependent on the terms and conceptual systems of the national legal systems of the Member States. As a result, it is more appropriate to speak about a system of multiple references (cf. Kjær 2007: 80-82), in which EU terms are often interpreted by national courts in accordance with their own national concepts.

Multiple references are common in private law where fragments of contract law, such as consumer protection law, have been harmonized by means of directives, which are binding only as to the result to be achieved, leaving the choice of form and method of implementation to the national authorities (Art. 249(3) EC). Since the earlier consumer protection directives aimed at achieving minimum harmonization, national legislators were allowed to transpose the directives by using terms of their national legal systems (see Šarčević/Čikara 2009: 200; cf. Pasa 2007: 7-8), thus resulting in multiple references which pose a threat to the uniform application of EU law and the principle of equality.

3.1. Lack of definitions or vague definitions for EU concepts

Multiple references occur especially when the EU legislator fails to define the specific meaning and scope of application of a EU term or provides unclear, vague or inconsistent definitions, 'forcing' national judges to interpret the term in accordance with their national law, a practice which inevitably leads to different results in the Member States. Deeply rooted in the legal culture and history of each state, private law terminology has different meanings and usages and is sometimes classified differently in different national legal systems (cf. Pozzo 2003: 756-763; 2006: 7-12; Ajani speaks of legal taxonomy, 2003: 349-353). This is also true in regard to legal terms belonging to the common core of all legal systems, such as *contract*, *consumer* and *damage*. For instance, a type of damage which qualifies for compensation in one national legal system is not necessarily recognized as such in another, although the legal systems are closely related and even the same language is spoken, as in Austria and Germany (Heutger 2003: 7; 2008: 12). As for EU law, the term *damage* is defined differently in the defective products Directive (85/374/EEC) and the self-employed commercial agents Directive (86/653/EEC). More recently, the environmental liability Directive (2004/35/EC) provides a non-technical definition of *damage* which fails to specify clear criteria for its usage (Pozzo 2006: 14), thus enabling the national courts to interpret the term in accordance with their national law, at least until the European Court of Justice (hereinafter: the ECJ) provides a clear definition for the purpose of the Directive.

This was done, for example, in regard to the Package Tour Directive (90/314/EEC), which failed to specify what types of damage are covered, but referred to "damage other than personal injury", thus raising the question whether non-material damage caused by "spoiled holidays" must also be compensated under the Directive. In *Simone Leitner v TUI Deutschland GmbH & Co. KG,* the Austrian court of first instance awarded the claimant damages only for physical pain and suffering, arguing that, contrary to German law, Austrian law has no express provision providing compensation for non-material damage caused by the loss of enjoyment of one's holidays. However, on appeal, the *Landesgericht* Linz requested the European Court of Justice to issue a preliminary ruling on the interpretation of Article 5 of the Package Tour Directive. In its preliminary ruling of 12 March 2002,[10] the ECJ held that *damage* in the Directive must be given an autonomous, 'European' legal meaning – and in this context *damage* is to be interpreted as including non-material damage caused by loss of enjoyment of one's holidays (see also von Bar 2008a: 32, no. 25).

3.2. Use of national terms to transpose general clauses

Another practice now considered controversial is the use of a national term to transpose a general clause of a directive. Formulated in abstract, often neutral language that is easily translatable, general clauses are frequently used in directives to serve as a reference to general principles or standards which exist in most national systems of the Member States but are regulated in different ways and are usually designated by different terms (see Pasa 2007: 12-15; Šarčević/Čikara 2009: 206-207). A good example is the requirement of *good faith* as a criterion for assessing the unfair character of consumer contracts in Article 3 of Directive 93/13/EEC on unfair terms in consumer contracts, which is based largely on the German concept of *Treu und Glauben* in § 242 BGB but is also present in most of the continental civil law systems, for example, *bonne foi* in Article 1134 Code civil, *buona fede* in Articles 1337 and 1375 Codice civile and *buona fede* in Article 1.258 Codigo civil (see Mance 2007: 94, no. 45; Pasa 2007: 12).

Although the principle of good faith is derived from common sources in Roman law, there are significant differences in how the notion is interpreted by national case-law and legal scholars even in

10 Case C-168/00 [2002] ECR I-2631.

the civil law countries (see Hesselink: 2004: 472-496). On the other hand, English contract law does not recognize a general legal requirement of good faith, as a result of which the UK was 'forced' to introduce the concept in its national transposing statute for the purpose of the Directive[11] (see Teubner 1998: 11-32; Mance 2007: 94; Whittaker 2008: 58-59). Since the principle of good faith does not have one single meaning, the EU legislator attempted to provide a test or standard for determining when consumer contract terms are contrary to the principle of good faith by including a grey list in the Annex of specific situations in which consumer contract terms may be deemed unfair. However, this proved to be highly ineffective as the list is not only non-binding but also non-exhaustive (see López-Rodríguez 2003/04: 1204; Pasa 2007: 14-16).

Later the Commission changed its strategy and introduced the first detailed directives requiring maximum harmonization in consumer protection. Nevertheless, Directive 2005/29/EC on unfair commercial practices also contains general clauses drawing on a "code of conduct" based on "honest market practices" and/or "the general practice of good faith". In an attempt to achieve maximum harmonization, national legislators are required to faithfully reproduce the words of the detailed provisions as closely as possible when transposing such directives and incorporate word-for-word the long black (= binding) list of aggressive and misleading commercial practices in the Annex which are deemed unfair in all circumstances (on difficulties of implementing maximum harmonization, see Lurger 2007: 185, 195-196). As stated in Recital (18) of the Unfair Commercial Practices Directive, the objective is to remove internal market barriers by replacing Member States' divergent general clauses, thus putting pressure on the ECJ to introduce an autonomous interpretation of good faith that would eventually lead to a consistently applicable criterion for determining which commercial practices qualify as aggressive and

11 Directive 93/13/EEC was transposed in the UK by the Unfair Terms in Consumer Contracts Regulations 1994, which was later superseded by the Regulations 1999. Teubner (1998: 11-32) refers to the requirement of good faith in consumer contracts in English law as a "legal irritant" causing new divergences which endanger the unity of the private law system.

misleading for the purpose of the Directive. Whether this is possible and desirable has recently been challenged by cultural experts who stress the need to take account of variations of consumer culture in Europe (Wilhelmsson 2007: 265-268).

3.3. Terminological inconsistency

Another shortcoming of the *acquis* is the EU legislator's use of different terms to express the same concept within the same directive and in other directives. Terminological inconsistency on the part of the EU legislator results in multiple references causing incoherency, leading to legal uncertainty and inevitable linguistic diversity in the translations (Šarčević 2006: 128). For example, Art. 4 of the Doorstep Selling Directive (85/577/EEC) governs the *right of cancellation* whereby the consumer is released from all his obligations; however, the term *right of renunciation* is used in Article 7 to express the same concept, although the term *renounce* has a special usage indicating the possibility of renouncing a right or interest, for instance, when someone renounces an inheritance (*Black's Law Dictionary* 2000: 1041). In the same token, the French version uses the terms *droit de resilier le contrat* and *droit de renunciation,* the German version *Widerrufsrecht* and *Rücktrittsrecht* (cf. Pozzo 2006: 14-16). In Article 5 of the Timeshare Directive 94/47/EC, the verbs *withdraw* and *cancel* are used as synonyms in tandem with *right to withdraw* and *right of cancellation* (*droit de resiliation, droit de se retracter / das Recht vom Vertrag zurückzutreten, das Rücktrittsrecht*). The EU term *right of withdrawal* (*le droit de retractation / das Widerrufsrecht*) finally appears by itself in Article 4 of the Distance Selling Directive 97/7/EC and has been used consistently thereafter by EU drafters (Šarčević/Čikara 2009: 204-206), although the time period allowed for withdrawal differs in almost every directive on consumer protection.

Another flagrant inconsistency is the use of different terms and definitions in respect of the parties to a consumer contract. Although one party is always a consumer, the term is defined differently for the purpose of each directive (see Denkinger 2007: 261), causing confusion and encouraging litigation. The other party is always a professional; however, instead of using the generic term *professional* in the English texts of the directives, as in some French texts, more specific terms are used, such as *trader*, *seller*, *supplier*, *vendor* and *retailer,* thus resulting in considerable terminological diversity in the various language versions of the relevant directives.

3.4. Use of polysemous terms without clear definitions

Multiple references are intensified by the use of polysemous terms which appear in different contexts of EU law but have not been clearly defined. Sometimes the terms are EU internationalisms which are also used in some or all of the national legal systems of the Member States but with different meanings. In such situations problems arise when national judges fail to recognize the term as an EU internationalism and interpret it in accordance with its national usage and meaning, as a result of which it takes on the role of a false friend. For example, depending on its EU or national context, the term *guarantee* (*garantie, garanzia, Garantie*) can mean:

> warranty, legal rights, extra rights of a buyer in case of defective goods added to the buyer's legal rights, a security, a pure consumer guarantee, or a confirmation that something will not change. (Heutger 2008: 9-10)

This list of terminological problems in the *acquis* is by no means exhaustive, nor is it intended to be. In the following parts we turn our attention to the DCFR to investigate whether the new approach to language could perhaps succeed in creating an autonomous European conceptual system and whether the final CFR could serve as a basis for a future pan-European legal language in private law.

4. Draft Common Frame of Reference (DCFR)

Seventeen European universities and research institutions participated in the Network of Excellence; however, most of the work was carried out by the Study Group for a European Civil Code and the Acquis Group, while the Project Group 'Restatement of European Insurance Contract Law' worked separately.[12] These drafting groups were joined by various evaluation teams which dealt with economic and jurisprudential questions (the Tilburg Law and Economics Center; the Association Henri Capitant), developed databases (the Database Group), prepared case studies on the basis of the rules developed by the drafting teams (Common Core Group) and organized conferences (The Academy of European Law) (see complete list of academic contributors in von Bar 2008a: 41-48). In addition, the Commission engaged stakeholders with technical expertise representing a diversity of legal traditions and economic interests to provide detailed feedback and to challenge the academic researchers.

As reflected in its title – *Principles, Definitions and Model Rules of European Private Law* – the scope of the DCFR gradually grew to cover not just contractual obligations but all obligations, thus causing fear among many common law lawyers (and also civil lawyers) that the intention is to introduce a civil code in disguise, which was denied by von Bar despite the name of his Study Group (von Bar 2005: 21; 2008b: 3). As a type of restatement, the bulk of the DCFR consists of seven Books of model rules proposing solutions to legal problems based on an extensive comparative analysis of Community law and the national laws of the Member States in areas of contract law (including pre-contractual negotiations, the entire life of a contract and specific contracts), *negotiorum gestio*, torts and unjust enrichment. As regards substance, the DCFR is said to be a "blend" of

---

12 The Insurance Group submitted the Principles of European Insurance Contract Law (PEICL) to the Commission separately; hence they are not included in the interim edition of the DCFR. The final text of the PEICL of 1 August 2009 and a number of translations are available at the project website: <www.uibk.ac.at/zivilrecht/restatement>.

the present *acquis* and the "best" solutions of the national legal systems of the Member States. Our main concern in this chapter is not substance but rather the new approach to language in the DCFR, at the level of both the term and the concept.

4.1. New approach to language in the DCFR

While the drafting language of the DCFR is English, this is not the English of the common law. The main actors are civil law lawyers, non-native speakers of English from different legal backgrounds and cultures, who have made painstaking efforts to draft the DCFR in plain and clear language, thereby achieving the goal of transparency. Most importantly, a conscious effort has been made to avoid technical terms of English law, making it clear that the terms are not to be defined in accordance with English legal concepts. In essence, the goal is to create a new meta-language that is detached from English law and culture. According to Heutger (2008: 3), a member of the working group on Sales Law, several instruments served as models for English terminology: the Principles of European Contract Law (PECL), the UNIDROIT Principles of International Commercial Contracts, the Convention of the International Sale of Goods (CISG), the relative EU Directives and even the English translation of the Dutch Civil Code.

As regards term formation, priority is given to neutral terms and descriptive paraphrases "which can be readily translated without carrying unwanted baggage with them" (von Bar 2008a: 23). For example, torts (delicts) are described as "non-contractual liability arising out of damage caused to another". The injured party is referred to as "a person who has suffered legally relevant damage" and the tortfeasor as "a person who caused the damage" (DCFR 2008: VI.-1:01). The rule on *force majeure* is simply called *event beyond control* (DCFR 2008: VI.-5:302). There is a special Book on *unjustified enrichment*, known in the common law as *unjust enrichment*. Here the basic rule provides that "a person who obtains an unjustified enrichment which is attributable to another's disadvantage is obliged to that other to reverse the enrichment" (DCFR 2008: VII.-1:101). Again the parties are designated by neutral terms: *the enriched person* and *the disadvantaged person*; the technical collocation *to make restitution* is replaced by *to reverse the enrichment*, and *restitution* is referred to as *disenrichment*. Furthermore, an entire Book is devoted to the continental civil law institution of *negotiorum gestio* (*Geschäftungsführung ohne Auftrag*), an institution unknown in the common law, which is referred to in the DCFR as *benevolent intervention in another's affairs* (DCFR 2008: Book V).

During the course of work, the Study Groups were asked to draw up a list of key terms of European private law based on the *acquis* and the new model rules. Prepared by Professor Erich Clive of the University of Edinburgh, the terminology list is published together with definitions in Annex 1 of the DCFR (2008: 331-344) (hereinafter: the Glossary). As the drafters later conceded, the Glossary helped them to achieve terminological consistency and coherency in their own drafting (von Bar 2008b: 7). Special efforts were made to eliminate the terminological inconsistency that plagued earlier consumer directives. For example, the Glossary provides a uniform definition of *consumer* (see DCFR 2008: 335). Furthermore, the terms *withdraw* and a *right to withdraw* are used consistently and the definition of *withdraw* provides a uniform period (usually 14 days)

> within which the entitled party [...] may exercise his right to withdraw from a contract [...] without having to give any reason for so doing and without incurring any liability for non-performance of the obligations. (DCFR 2008: 344)

The definitions, which are crucial for the success of the DCFR, have "the function of suggestions for the development of a uniform European legal terminology" (von Bar 2008a: 9). As such, care was taken to formulate them in clear language which sets out the meanings and restricts their scope of application. The substance of the definitions is derived partly from the *acquis*, but predominantly from the model rules. Therefore, when some scholars suggested that the Glossary could do the job of establishing uniform concepts, the view prevailed that the definitions cannot be separated from the model rules. As emphasized in the General Provisions, the definitions in the Glossary apply "for all the purposes of the rules unless the context otherwise requires" (DCFR 2008: I.-I:103(1)). Accordingly, the definitions are essential for the model rules, and the model rules for the definitions. As Professor Beale explained, if he were asked to define when a contract is concluded, he could do so only "by laying down a set of rules to govern the topic" (2006: 8). From the linguistic point of view, the model rules often define the extensional meaning of a given term by enumerating situations in which it is to be applied or not applied (cf. Šarčević 2000: 239).

4.2. Disputable conceptual innovations

The structure of the DCFR follows the civil law system of the law of obligations, as a result of which the key terms are *contract* and *obligation*. In light of the differing national approaches to the concept of contract, it was particularly difficult to agree on a definition of contract (Mance 2007: 96-97). As a compromise, contract is defined in the Glossary as

> an agreement which gives rise to [...] a binding legal relationship or which has, or is intended to have, some other legal effect. It is a bilateral or multilateral juridical act. (DCFR 2008: 330)

While common law lawyers do not object to the main part of the definition, they have criticized the incorporation of the civil law concept of *Rechtsgeschäft* and the artificial neologism chosen to denote it – *juridical act* (Whittaker 2008: 78). This institution, which is used in varying extents in continental Europe, is unknown in English law and is usually translated as *transaction*.

Another conceptual innovation criticized by common law lawyers is the use of the continental civil law concepts of *debtor* and *creditor* to identify the parties to contracts (other than consumer contracts) and to obligations in general. This is a consequence of the DCFR's concern with obligations rather than merely contracts. In this sense, *debtor* is defined as "a person who bears an obligation" and *creditor* as "a person holding the right to performance of an obligation, whether monetary or non-monetary" (DCFR 2008: 330). The qualification "whether monetary or non-monetary" has been added, making it clear that the usage is not restricted to an obligation to pay money, especially one arising from a loan of money, as is the case in English law. Nonetheless, this broad usage of the terms *debtor* and *creditor* is potentially misleading to common law lawyers (see Whittaker 2008: 10, 115-116).

One conceptual innovation which both common and civil law lawyers could find problematic is the technical distinction between *obligation* and *duty*, a relationship which is crucial to the understanding of a number of model rules. As defined in the Glossary, an obligation is "a duty to perform which one party to a legal relationship, the debtor, owes to another party, the creditor" (DCFR 2008: 338). As for the term *duty*, for our purpose it suffices to say that

> a person has a 'duty' to do something if the person is bound to do it or expected to do it according to an applicable normative standard of conduct [...]. There is not necessarily a sanction for breach of a duty. All obligations are duties, but not all duties are obligations. (DCFR 2008: 332)

This distinction is important because numerous rules are restricted to obligations and do not apply to duties, such as the rules governing "non-performance of contractual obligations" and the remedies which sanction it. However, it is sometimes difficult to distinguish between them, especially if the term *obligation* or *duty* does not appear in the heading or text of the rule. In such cases, one must examine the language of the given context, noting that a duty is usually expressed in terms of being 'bound' or 'expected' to do something according to a standard of conduct, while an obligation is expressed by the verb *oblige* or, most frequently, by the modal *must*.

In accordance with the practice of plain English, the DCFR drafters use *must* instead of *shall* to express obligations, although this is contrary to the usual EU drafting practice (Šarčević 2007: 47). The definition of *must* in the Glossary alerts readers to this special usage:

> 'Must', when used of a person (e.g., 'the lessor must'), means that the person has an obligation, unless otherwise indicated. 'Must', when used of a thing (e.g., 'the goods must'), indicates a requirement. (DCFR 2008: 337)

From the above definition it follows that *must* is used to express requirements as well. While this is the usual drafting practice in common law countries, it may cause some confusion for civil law lawyers. However, the main problem is the occasional use of *must* to express duties in the model rules, making it difficult to determine whether the provision lays down a duty or an obligation if this is not clear from the particular context (Whittaker 2008: 116-118).

Another disputable innovation is the introduction of the concept of *accountability* in the Book on torts. Although the title of the Book refers to "non-contractual liability", the majority of the provisions do not set out when "liability" will be imposed, nor do they refer to "liability" much at all. Instead, they set out the "grounds of accountability", such as "accountability for damage caused by defective products" and "accountability for damage caused by employees and representatives", giving the false impression that *liability* and *accountability* are used as synonyms. However, there is one provision in which both terms are used, thus implying that a distinction exists, although this remains unclear:

> Liability for damage for the causation of which a person is accountable under VI.-3:204 cannot be restricted or excluded. (DCFR 2008:VI.-5:401(3))

Since the term *accountability* is defined neither in the Glossary nor in the model rules, the only explanation to clarify the relationship between these two central concepts is in a brief note in the Comments to be published in the full edition of the DCFR. There it is explained that

> the expression *grounds of accountability* is used [...] as an umbrella term embracing both the *potential for liability* on account of intentionally causing damage or negligence on the one hand and the *potential for liability* on account of responsibility for a source of danger on the other. (cited in Whittaker 2008: 163)

Simplifying the matter, it can be said that the expression *grounds of accountability* means 'the potential for liability', as distinct from *liability* itself, i.e. where a person *is* liable. According to Professor Whittaker, such a distinction is unnecessary as other national laws (including English law) "are happy to set out grounds of liability without prejudging whether liability is actually imposed". In his opinion, preference should be given to a unified terminology which has the "advantage of simplicity and familiarity" (2008: 164).

4.3. Key concepts defined too broadly; failure to concretize vague principles and concepts

While the DCFR drafters took care to define key terms, English lawyers insist that some definitions are formulated too broadly to be used as uniform definitions which apply not only to consumer but also to commercial contracts, the latter of which are not regulated by the present *acquis*. An example is the all-inclusive nature of the concept of *loss*, which includes not only economic but also non-economic loss, thus explicitly including "pain and suffering and impairment of the quality of life" (DCFR 2008: 337). Since numerous provisions concerning pre-contractual liabilities (Book II) and liability for non-performance of contractual obligations (Book III) impose liability simply for "loss" without any restriction as to the type of harm to be recovered, it appears that a person is entitled to recover damages in respect of "non-economic loss" in such cases as well. The DCFR drafters have apparently drawn this generalization from the ECJ's ruling in *Leitner*, although this decision was based on a specific context and was intended solely for the purpose of that particular Directive (see above at 3.1.).

Moreover, the term *loss* is related to the terms *damage* and *injury*, both of which are used liberally in the DCFR. In fact, *damage* is even broader than *loss* as it includes both *loss* and *injury,* attributing considerable substantive breadth to these key concepts. Some English lawyers find this unjustified, especially because it creates considerable interpretational uncertainty in regard to commercial contracts (Whittaker 2008: 113). As for *injury*, there is no definition either in the Glossary or in the model rules.

Another problem which has not been adequately resolved, at least from the perspective of common law lawyers, is the central role of the general principle of *good faith* and the indeterminate concept of *good faith and fair dealing*, both of which allow significant judicial discretion to the point that the courts are even empowered to amend a contract after a change of circumstances (House of Lords Committee's Report 2009: 13). As defined in the Glossary, *good faith and fair dealing* "refers to an objective standard of conduct", whereas *good faith* on its own "may refer to a subjective mental attitude, often characterized by an absence of knowledge of something which, if known, would adversely affect the morality of what is done" (DCFR 2008: 334). In accordance with the distinction between a subjective and objective understanding of these concepts in the continental civil laws, *good faith* requires a subjectively moral behaviour in the sense of honesty, whereas *good faith and fair dealing* sets a standard of conduct to be imposed by the rules of the DCFR or by the courts. Without going into detail, it suffices to say that the rules relating to *good faith and fair dealing* in the DCFR are too abstract and cover a large area of the life of the contract (Whittaker 2008: 156). Contrary to the objective of laying down specific rules to "concretize" the requirement of good faith in specific contexts (see Hesselink 2004: 474-496), the widespread use of blanket provisions relating to good faith seems to imply that it is not only a general but rather a fundamental principle (as suggested by von Bar 2008a: 17), thus elevating it to the category of an abstract basic value which could always be invoked as a basis for further judicial intervention.

For their part, civil law lawyers strongly object to the 'excessive' use of the concept of *reasonableness* in the DCFR. In many ways this is the common law's closest counter-part to good faith as it allows the courts to hold a person (or a term of a contract) to an external (objective) standard (Whittaker 2008: 156). According to the definition,

> what is *reasonable* is to be objectively ascertained, having regard to the nature and purpose of what is being done, to the circumstances of the case and to any relevant usages and practices. (DCFR 2008: 340)

In the eyes of civil law lawyers, this open-ended definition gives judges too much discretion in relation to contracts, thus creating too high a degree of legal uncertainty. The term is said to appear in the text of the DCFR over 400 times in its various forms ([un]reasonable/ y) (see Wagner 2009: 5-6, 40).

Despite criticism by both common and civil law lawyers, members of the Study Groups are hopeful that the future political CFR will achieve its goals of establishing "basic principles for a uniform law" and "a new *lingua franca* for all European lawyers" (Takoff 2009: 1). While the term *lingua franca* is misleading, Professor Takoff's remark confirms the high expectations that the political CFR could eventually lead to the creation of a pan-European legal language.

5. Could the final CFR Serve as a Basis for a Future Pan-European Legal Language?

The DCFR is a trans-systemic instrument formulated in a meta-language which is intentionally detached from national legal languages, laws and cultures to the greatest extent possible. Drafted in neutral English, the final CFR will be translated into the other 22 EU official languages. The quality of the translations will be crucial not only for the success of the CFR but also for its potential to serve as a basis for a future pan-European legal language in private law. For this reason, the DCFR drafters have made conscious efforts to follow the EU drafting guideline on respecting multilingualism (*Joint Practical Guide* 2003: Guideline 5). First, they consistently avoid technical terms, choosing neutral terms which are easily translatable. Secondly, they use "simple, clear and direct" sentence structures with the aim of avoiding any "inaccuracies, approximations or real mistranslations in one or more of the other Community languages" (see Šarčević 2007: 49; Kjær 2007: 83). In the end, however, the quality of the translations of the final CFR will depend on the competence and choices of the individual translators or translation teams. Quite obviously, the translators will not be able to consult English law for guidance as to the intended meaning of the neutral terminology of the DCFR. In fact, some of the neutral English terms "stray quite a long way from the English used by English lawyers, especially in England and Wales" (Whittaker 2008: 96), and a number of transnational neologisms have been created to express civil law concepts and new concepts. Therefore, it is essential that the translators have a genuine understanding of the way the terminology and concepts of the DCFR relate to each other and to their own national laws.

As to the translation strategy, it is important that the translators attempt to 'imitate' the CFR by using neutral and descriptive language which best conveys the sense of the concepts and legal phrases in the DCFR, instead of conveying the sense of the rules by using technical terminology of their own national systems. Although this risks the creation of translations which are not always readily understood by national lawyers, in my opinion, it is the only strategy which could achieve the goal of creating a uniform terminology in all official languages, which could eventually serve as a basis for a future pan-European language. Not surprisingly, this is the main strategy used in earlier translations of the Principles of European Contract Law (PECL),[13] which have been revised and incorporated to a large extent into the DCFR.

To date, translations or commentaries of the entire DCFR or individual Books have been made in various languages by the drafters themselves or colleagues in the project who are familiar with the intended meaning and usage of the English terms. For example, the first three Books of the French *Cadre commun de reference pour le droit europeén des contrats* are available online, as is a Czech translation – *Návrh spolecého referencniho rámce* – of the entire DCFR (without the Glossary).[14] Commentaries of individual Books of the German *Gemeinsamer Referenzrahmen* (*Entwurf eines gemeinsamen Referenzrahmens für europäisches Vertragsrecht*) have been pub-

13 See list of translations of the Principles of European Contract Law, Parts I, II and III in von Bar (2008a: 7, n. 2).

14 See links at the website of the Study Group on a European Civil Code at <www.sgecc.net>. The Czech Republic held the presidency of the EU for the first half of 2009.

lished in Sellier's series on European private law. Work on the German translation of the entire DCFR is in progress.

Obviously there are numerous translation problems, some of which could affect the understanding of certain basic terms and, in turn, application of the relevant model rules. For example, the question arises as to how the new technical difference between *obligation* and *duty* will be expressed in the other languages. In French the corresponding terms are *obligation* and *devoir* and in Czech *závazek* and *povinnost.* However, it is questionable whether all EU languages possess sufficient words which express basically the same (deontic) idea, but can be used in these two technical ways. In such cases, translators will have to create neologisms which are transparent and will be accepted by users. Another potential pitfall for translators is the inconsistent use of *must* in the English text to express both obligations and duties (see above at 4.2). While this is not the place to discuss specific translation problems, one should be aware of the important role of translation in creating a common terminology and concepts for a future pan-European legal language.

At present, the role of the final CFR has not yet been specified; however, as stated by the Commission in its Action Plan of 2003,[15] one of its potential purposes is to serve as a 'toolbox' to enhance legal certainty of the present and future *acquis* by standardizing legal concepts at the EU level. In this sense, the CFR could also have the function of a dictionary with the aim of standardizing uniform definitions in all EU languages. Since dictionaries for standardization should be prescriptive in nature (Šarčević/Čikara 2009: 197), the effectiveness of the CFR as an instrument of standardization will depend largely on the degree of authority conferred on it by the European institutions. Although the future CFR is expected to be non-binding, various degrees of non-bindingness could come into play. For example, the CFR could provide that if the EU legislator were to use one or more of its model rules, then the concepts in those model rules must be interpreted in accordance with the definitions in the CFR. Alternatively, the CFR could provide that any of its concepts used in future EU legislation are to be interpreted in the light of its definitions,

15 See note 2 above.

model rules and principles. For example, if a new directive used "the terms *notice*, *loss*, *agreement*, *unfair exploitation* or *conclusion of the contract*, they would be interpreted as a reference to the definitions and rules governing these concepts in the CFR" (Whittaker 2008: 93). Such usage would lay the framework for establishing an autonomous conceptual system at EU level and consequently a common system of reference for all EU languages in the areas covered by the CFR.

In both situations, the instructions in the CFR would have to specify whether the interpretative value of the definitions is to be absolute or presumptive. In the latter case, the ECJ would have the power to revise or even reject the definition of a concept if it held another definition more suitable for the purpose of a particular directive. In any case, the ECJ would always be entitled to refer to the CFR whenever it deemed it appropriate.

Currently there is considerable resistance to the DCFR, especially on the part of common law lawyers who fear that "Europe is aiming to civilise the common law" (Mance 2007) and who oppose the idea of a European Law of Obligations (House of Lords Committee's Report 2009). Clinging to their national law, language and culture, numerous civil law lawyers are also not convinced that further convergence of private law is the right way forward (see articles in Wilhelmsson/Paunio/Pohjolainen 2007; also Prechal/van Roermund 2008). If such forces prevail, the CFR could perhaps serve as an 'optional instrument' representing an independent regime of contract law which the parties to a cross-border contract could opt into if they so choose (von Bar 2008a: 37; 2008b: 2). For example, if contracting parties from Italy and Latvia do not want Italian, Latvian or another national law to govern their contract, they could choose to have the contract governed by the CFR. In this way, the CFR would function like an optional 28th legal system (see Smits 2007: 236; Lurger 2007: 181-184). However, it would have the advantage of having a common terminology with uniform definitions in all EU official languages and model rules to govern their usage in practice.

Regardless of the future role of the CFR, in my opinion, the first serious step towards creating a future pan-European legal language has already been taken in the DCFR. Even if the DCFR were to remain a purely academic endeavour of comparative law, it clearly shows that cooperation in European private law is feasible and that a dialogue to find common conceptual ground is desirable. Thus it seems to be a question of timing. Are European lawyers, politicians and EU citizens ready to embrace greater convergence in private law and the pan-European language and culture that comes with it? While some skeptics argue that creating a pan-European legal language is not in accordance with the Union's principle of preserving cultural and linguistic diversity, the intent is not to replace national languages and cultures, but to create a neutral meta-language which would serve as an inspiration to build a new European culture and a common European legal thinking (cf. Weigand 2008). In this sense, it is envisaged that the DCFR or the CFR will be used as teaching material at all law faculties throughout Europe and beyond (von Bar 2008b: 2). Over time a new European consciousness and culture is bound to develop among young lawyers who are taught common European values, transnational legal concepts and the multilingual terminology to express them.

As for lawyers who find trans-systemic neologisms such as *juridical act* artificial and awkward, I suggest they follow Professor Kasirer's advice[16] based on his own experience with the Trento Common Core Group (2002: 428), which can be adapted for our purpose as follows: Repeat the neologism 100 times before going to sleep at the Hotel San Lorenzo in Bergamo and upon waking, it may stick in your mind as part of a new meaningful terminology of a pan-European legal language.

References

Ajani, Gianmaria 2003. Legal Taxonomy and European Private Law. In Schulze, Reiner / Ajani, Gianmaria (eds) 2003. *Common*

16 Professor of law at the McGill School of Law in Montreal, Nicholas Kasirer is a perceptive legal linguist and advocate of Canada's legislative bilingualism.

Principles of European Private Law. Studies of a Research Network. Baden-Baden: Nomos Verlagsgesellschaft, 349-353.

Ajani, Gianmaria 2007. Coherence of European Private Law and Multilingualism: Two Opposing Principles? *Revue de droit des Affaires Internationales / International Business Law Journal* 4, 493-507.

Ajani, Gianmaria / Ebers, Martin (eds) 2005. *Uniform Terminology for European Contract Law (europäisches Privatrecht)*. Baden-Baden: Nomos Verlagsgesellschaft.

Bar, Christian von 2005. Working Together Toward a Common Frame of Reference. *Juridica International* 10, 17-26.

Bar, Christian von 2008a. Introduction to *Principles, Definitions and Model Rules of European Private Law. Draft Common Frame of Reference (DCFR)*. Münich: Sellier. European Law Publishers, 1-39.

Bar, Christian von 2008b. A Common Frame of Reference for European Private Law – Academic Efforts and Political Realities. *Electronic Journal of Comparative Law (EJCL)* 12/1, 1-10 at <www.ejcl.org/121/art121-27.pdf>.

Bar, Christian von / Clive, Eric / Schulte-Nölke, Hans *et al.* (eds) 2008. *Principles, Definitions and Model Rules of European Private Law, Draft Common Frame of Reference.* Münich: Sellier European Law Publishers.

Beale, Hugh 2006. The European Civil Code Movement and the European Union's Common Frame of Reference. *Legal Information Management* 6/1, 4-11.

Black's Law Dictionary 2000. Garner, Bryan (editor in chief). St. Paul, Minn.: West Group.

Campana, Marie-Jeanne 1999. Vers un langage juridique commun en Europe? In Sacco, Rodolfo / Castellani, Luca (eds) *Les multiples langues du droit européen uniforme*. Torino: L'Harmattan Italia, 7-34.

Denkinger, Fleur 2007. *Der Verbraucherbegriff*. Berlin: De Gruyter Recht.

European Contract Law: the Draft Common Frame of Reference. Report with Evidence. 2009. House of Lords. European Union

Committee. 12th Report of Session 2008-09. London: The Stationery Office Limited.

Groot, Gerard-René de 1999. Das Übersetzen juristischer Terminologie. In de Groot, Gerard-René / Schulze, Reiner (Hrsg.) *Recht und Übersetzen*. Baden-Baden: Nomos Verlagsgesellschaft, 11-46.

Hesselink, Martijn 2001. *The New European Legal Culture*. Alphen aan den Rijn: Kluwer Law International.

Hesselink, Martijn 2004. The Concept of Good Faith. In Hartkamp, Arthur / Hesselink, Martijn / Hondius, Ewoud *et al. Towards a European Civil Code*. Third fully revised and expanded edition. Nijmegen: Ars Aequi Libri / Alphen aan den Rijn: Kluwer Law International, 471-498.

Heutger, Viola 2003. Law and Language in the European Union. *Global Jurist Topics*. The Berkeley Electronic Press 3/1, 1-17 at <www.bepress.com/gj/topics/vol3/iss1/art3>.

Heutger, Viola 2004. A More Coherent European Wide Legal Language. *European Integration Online Papers* 7/2, 1-7 at <http://eiop.or.at/aeop/texte/2004-002.htm>.

Heutger, Viola, 2008. Legal Language and the Process of Drafting the Principles on a European Law of Sales. *Electronic Journal of Comparative Law* 12/2, 1-15 at <www.ejcl.org/122/ abs122-3.html>.

Joint Practical Guide of the European Parliament, the Council and the Commission (for persons involved in the drafting of legislation within the Community institutions) 2003. Available at <http://www.europa.eu.int/eur-lex/lex/lex/en/techleg/index.htm>.

Kasirer, Nicholas 2002. The Common Core of European Private Law in Boxes and Bundles. *European Review of Private Law* 10/3, 417-437.

Kjær, Anne Lise 2004. A Common Legal Language in Europe? In van Hoecke, Mark (ed.) *Epistemology and Methodology of Comparative Law*. Oxford / Portland, Oregon: Hart Publishing, 377-398.

Kjær, Anne Lise 2007. Legal Translation in the European Union: A Research Field in Need of a New Approach. In Krzysztof, Kredens / Goźdź-Roszkowski, Stanisław (eds) *Language and the Law: International Outlooks*. Frankfurt am Main: Peter Lang, 69-95.

Kjær, Anne Lise 2008. Introduction: Language as Barrier and Carrier of European Legal Integration. In Petersen, Hanne / Kjær, Anne Lise / Krunke, Helle / Rask Madsen, Mikael (eds) *Paradoxes of European Legal Integration*. Aldershot: Ashgate, 149-156.

Legrand, Pierre 1996. European Legal Systems are not Converging. *International and Comparative Law Quarterly* 45/1, 52-81.

Legrand, Pierre 2008. Word/World (of Primordial Issues for Comparative Legal Studies). In Petersen, Hanne / Kjær, Anne Lise / Krunke, Helle / Rask Madsen, Mikael (eds) *Paradoxes of European Legal Integration*. Aldershot: Ashgate, 185-233.

López-Rodríguez, Ana M. 2003-2004. Towards a European Civil Code without a Common European Legal Culture? The Link between Law, Language and Culture. *Brooklyn Journal of International Law* 29/3, 1195-1220.

Lurger, Brigitta 2007. The Common Frame of Reference / Optional Code and the Various Understandings of Social Justice in Europe. In Wilhelmsson, Thomas / Paunio, Elina / Pohjolainen, Annika (eds) *Private Law and the Many Cultures of Europe*. Alphen aan den Rijn: Kluwer Law International, 177-199.

Mance, Lord Jonathan 2007. Is Europe Aiming to Civilise the Common Law? *European Business Law Review* 18, 77-99.

Pasa, Barbara 2007. Old Terms for New Concepts in Consumer Contracts? Jean Monnet Working Paper No. 9, 1-29 at <www.jeanmonnetprogram.org/papers/papers07.html>.

Pozzo, Barbara 2003. Harmonisation of European Contract Law and the Need of Creating a Common Terminology. In *European Review of Private Law* 6, 754-767.

Pozzo, Barbara 2006. Multilingualism, Legal Terminology and Problems of Harmonizing European Private Law. In Pozzo, Barbara / Jacometti, Valentina (eds) *Multilingualism and the Harmonisation of European Law*. Alphen aan den Rijn: Kluwer Law International, 11, 3-19.

Prechal, Sacha / van Roermund, Bert (eds) 2008. *The Coherence of EU Law*. Oxford: Oxford University Press.

Sacco, Rodolfo 1996. Molte lingue per un diritto che si va uniformando. *Rivista di diritto civile* 42/1, 57-65.

Schulze, Reiner / Ajani, Gianmaria (eds) 2003. *Common Principles of European Private Law. Studies of a Research Network*. Baden-Baden: Nomos Verlagsgesellschaft.

Smits, Jan M. 2007. Convergence of Private Law in Europe: Towards a New *Ius Commune*? In Örücü, Esin / Nelken, David (eds) *Comparative Law: A Handbook*. Oxford: Hart Publishing, 219-240.

Šarčević, Susan ^{2}2000. *New Approach to Legal Translation*. The Hague: Kluwer Law International.

Šarčević, Susan 2006. Die Übersetzung von mehrsprachigen EU-Rechtsvorschriften: Der Kampf gegen Sprachdivergenzen. In Gotti, Maurizio / Šarčević, Susan (eds) *Insights into Specialized Translation*. Bern: Peter Lang, 121-152.

Šarčević, Susan 2007. Making Multilingualism Work in the Enlarged European Union. In Krzysztof, Kredens / Goźdź-Roszkowski, Stanisław (eds) *Language and the Law: International Outlooks*. Frankfurt am Main: Peter Lang, 35-54.

Šarčević, Susan / Čikara, Emilia 2009. European vs. National Terminology in Croatian Legislation Transposing EU Directives. In Šarčević, Susan (ed.) *Legal Language in Action: Translation, Terminology, Drafting and Procedural Issues*. Zagreb: Globus, 193-214.

Takoff, Christian 2009. The Draft Common Frame of Reference – Chance or Charge for European Private Law? Part II. Interview of 8.10.2009 available at Sellier's database <www.law-net.eu>.

Teubner, Gunther 1998. Legal Irritants: Good Faith in British Law or How Unifying Law Ends Up in New Divergences. *Modern Law Review* 61/1, 11-32.

Van Hoecke, Mark / Warrington, Mark 1998. Legal Cultures, Legal Paradigms and Legal Doctrine. *International and Comparative Law Quarterly*, 47, 495-536.

Wagner, Gerhard 2009. The Law of Torts in the Draft Common Frame of Reference. Online Working Paper Series, 1-41 at <http://ssrn.com/abstract=1394343>.

Weigand, Edda 2008. Towards a Common European Legal Thinking: A Dialogic Challenge. In Petersen, Hanne / Kjær, Anne Lise / Krunke, Helle / Rask Madsen, Mikael (eds) *Paradoxes of European Legal Integration*. Aldershot: Ashgate, 235-252.

Whittaker, Simon 2008. The 'Draft Common Frame of Reference'. An Assessment at <www.justice.gov.uk/publications/docs/Draft_Common_Frame_of_Reference_an_assessment.pdf>.

Wilhelmsson, Thomas 2007. The Average European Consumer: a Legal Fiction? In Wilhelmsson, Thomas / Paunio, Elina / Pohjolainen, Annika (eds) 2007. *Private Law and the Many Cultures of Europe*. Alphen aan den Rijn: Kluwer Law International, 243-268.

Wilhelmsson, Thomas / Paunio, Elina / Pohjolainen, Annika (eds) 2007. *Private Law and the Many Cultures of Europe*. Alphen aan den Rijn: Kluwer Law International.

COLIN ROBERTSON

Legal-linguistic Revision of EU Legislative Texts

1. Introduction

This chapter takes a look at the work of legal-linguistic revision of legislative texts of the Council of the European Union.[1] It is convenient to present this activity within a series of contexts:

(a) the human context: who does the work and what are the qualifications required to undertake it;

(b) the legal-linguistic and cultural context within which legal-linguistic revision takes place, with particular reference to the EU linguistic regime and its implications;

(c) the operational context, limited by time, space and everyday political, administrative and negotiating realities which act on the process.

Following on from the contextual reality, a method for approaching the work of legal-linguistic revision of individual texts is suggested. It makes use of the notion of 'viewpoints' and argues that an approach based on adopting different viewpoints is useful for the practical work of legal-linguistic revision. The chapter next makes some brief remarks on restrictions and limitations, before concluding by making reference to the broader linguistic and semiotic context.

The chapter was prepared before the entry into force on 1 December 2009 of the Treaty of Lisbon amending the Treaty on European Union (TEU) and the Treaty on the functioning of the European Union (TFEU) and has been adapted to take account of it. The Treaty has been in force for a very short period and its full implications have

---

1 The opinions expressed are personal to the author.

not yet emerged. Consequently the context is primarily that of the pre-Lisbon practice, adjusted to take account of the new arrangements.[2]

2. Lawyer-linguists

Lawyer-linguists, also known as *juristes-linguistes* or *JLs*, are a relatively new type of professional who came into existence following the creation of the EEC, EC and EU and they typically work for the European institutions in Brussels responsible for making legislation in a multiplicity of languages. Originally there were *lawyers* and there were *linguists*. The lawyers prepared the texts with the negotiators, administrators and politicians. The linguists interpreted orally at meetings and translated the texts into the other languages needed for publication in the Official Journal of the European Union (originally the EEC published in six languages). With time it was discovered that there was a 'gap' between the lawyers and the linguists and a concern arose about quality of the texts and equivalence between the language versions. Lawyers with language skills were recruited with the specific task of examining all language versions to ensure legal and linguistic equivalence between them. There were originally two colleagues per language in the Council and over the years the numbers increased to three per language (1993) and more recently to four or five per language. Over the same period, the number of languages has increased from six to 23 and is expected to increase further. Lawyer-linguists are employed by several EU institutions. For example, the European Commission employs lawyer-linguists (*juristes-réviseurs*) as does the European Parliament since the advent of the codecision procedure of joint legislation with the Council. The European Central Bank employs lawyer-linguists for the languages of countries that adopted the euro. In the European Court of Justice lawyer-linguists are employed primarily as legal translators, and the translation tasks are

2 See <http://europa.eu/lisbon_treaty/full_text/index_en.htm> for the text of the Lisbon Treaty and the consolidated TEU and TFEU texts.

linked to court-based texts. There is some literature relating to the practical work of lawyer-linguists, notably the description by Morgan (1982: 109) that gives a picture of JL work as it was a few years ago; there have been structural changes since then, notably the introduction of the codecision procedure, more languages and computer technology for document handling, but the core description of method nonetheless remains valid. The most recent development is the coming into force on 1 December 2009 of the Treaty of Lisbon amending the TEU and the TFEU. This has changed many reference points since the EC Treaty has been replaced by the TFEU and the European Community, under that name, has ceased to exist and been replaced solely by the European Union.

Lawyer-linguists are recruited to the Council by open competitions organized by EPSO.[3] The eligibility criteria are laid down in each competition notice, but broadly the requirement is to possess a law degree and at least two foreign languages in addition to mother tongue. The language skills are tested by stiff and exacting competition papers that involve the translation of legal texts, revision of a poor quality legal text and an oral examination. In general JLs work on revising texts in their mother tongue and compare their text with a base text as model; this is usually English or French but can in theory, and sometimes in practice, be any other language.

3. EU linguistic regime

The background to the work of legal-linguistic revision of EU legislative texts in the Council lies, naturally, in the EU legal environment. EU law is derived law and represents delegated powers passed down by the Member States as expressed in the primary treaties and other acts. The EU is not autonomous; every act must be justified in terms of the powers conferred. The foundation is in the primary treaties creating the EU. Pursuant to the Lisbon Treaty, these are principally the

3 For EU websites and information generally see <http://europa.eu>.

Treaty on European Union (TEU) and the Treaty on the functioning of the European Union (TFEU), as well as the Treaty establishing the European Atomic Energy Community. The pre-existing secondary legislation was constructed in a context of the 'European Community' (previously 'European Economic Community') and continues in force subject to changes resulting from the Lisbon Treaty which operate on it. Thus, for example, a regulation that refers to the 'EC' is now deemed to refer to the 'EU'.

The primary treaties set out the linguistic regime. There are different ways of looking at this aspect of language: for example, one can look at the languages in which the text is physically written, but also look and see which languages are declared to be authentic – that is to say can be used directly for interpretation by the courts without other evidence necessarily being brought as regards the meaning or interpretation. The EU Treaty is drawn up in 23 languages and each is declared to be authentic (Article 55 TEU). This provision is routinely amended by each new accession treaty when a new Member State with a new language joins. (The equivalent provision in the TFEU is Article 358 which incorporates Article 55 by reference). Article 55 TEU, however, tells us only about the languages of the text and nothing about the linguistic regime itself. For that information we must look to Article 342 TFEU which provides for the Council to determine the language rules of the institutions of the Union except for the European Court of Justice which has separate arrangements, which are not under consideration here. The Council implemented its task in Regulation No. 1 determining the languages to be used by the EEC (now EU). Regulation No. 1 has also been routinely amended by each accession treaty and now provides for 23 languages: Bulgarian, Czech, Danish, Dutch, English, Estonian, Finnish, French, German, Greek, Hungarian, Irish, Italian, Latvian, Lithuanian, Maltese, Polish, Portuguese, Romanian, Slovak, Slovenian, Spanish and Swedish. It is anticipated that more languages will soon be added. The broad implication is therefore that the EU treaties and EU law generally are drawn up in 23 language versions, but there have been temporary derogations for Irish and Maltese for practical operational reasons linked to the size of the speaker populations. The Council, however, is also involved with making international agreements with third states since the EU is very active on the international level. The texts of EU agreements also pass through the legal-linguistic stage as part of the finalization process before signature. Normally the texts are negotiated by the Commission in coordination with the Member States and 'initialled' so as to 'fix' their contents. Then comes the process of preparing the texts for formal signature on special paper. The lawyer-linguists check all the language versions on the basis of the initialled text, together with any minor technical adjustments to it which have been agreed with the negotiating parties. There are usually 22 EU language versions (Irish is generally excluded) as well as the language of the non-EU contracting state, if that is different. These are all listed at the end of the agreement as can be seen from the concluding article of any EU/third party agreement.

4. Implications of the EU linguistic regime

The natural implication of the linguistic regime is that in principle all EU legislation must be drafted in all language versions (except where derogations are authorized). That is the case with the primary treaties, but most of the work is undertaken on secondary level texts drawn up under powers conferred by primary treaty. Each new text sets out its aims and objectives and detailed contents in particular ways which are highly structured and based on internal guidance manuals and an inter-institutional agreement, as mentioned below. In the texts, the same information, or 'message', has to be reproduced faithfully in all the language versions. The citizen is entitled to take any language version and to use it for the purpose of knowing and enforcing his or her rights, and undertaking obligations. Citizens are equal and therefore the aim must be that the 'message' carried by each version is the same. This is where the skill comes in of all the participants in preparing the texts collectively, and of the lawyer-linguists when checking and revising, to spot inconsistencies. This is also the point of departure for thinking about the structure and content of each text in each language version – and how the languages interact – as well as the whole topic of transposition of EU-created obligations into national law through transposition. In effect EU legal texts are written in EU legislative 'dialect', for each language version, and then transposed, or translated, into the national legislative 'dialect'. How this transposition is done is a specialized topic for national drafters, under the close scrutiny of the European Commission. There is not space to mention it here, but the topic is discussed in an extended paper (Robertson 2009), to be published online.

Conceptually, EU law aims at being a self-coherent system of legal rules where there is only one instruction as to how to act in any given situation. This is inherent in the concept of a single legal system, as conflicts in the message create problems and require resolution (often through the courts) in order for the appropriate course of conduct to be clear and known to the persons concerned; for example, what customs duty to pay on a particular product where the categorization of the product is uncertain; or what Value Added Tax, etc. The role of the lawyer-linguist is to be sensitive to these points. Legal knowledge is essential in that respect because the texts in question are legal. But they often deal with non-legal matters, such as agricultural products, customs, antidumping, environment, chemicals, industry, and more recently justice and foreign policy. The lawyer-linguist does not have specialist knowledge in these areas, but comparing terms and concepts leads to asking questions and checking on meaning and intention. But here we have moved into the realm of terminology, which lies at the very heart of legal-linguistic work, and in a context of multilingualism it raises the issue of comparison of terms across languages. We have also moved into the realm of legislative drafting, which is a highly skilled art: how to use language so that there is only one meaning and one course of action in every situation. Lawyer-linguists are primarily legal-linguistic revisers, but they are drawn into questions that involve legislative drafting; for example standard formulae for parts of acts in all languages, and whether a particular wording is clear and precise or obscure and ambiguous.

The EU linguistic framework imposes multilingualism and the nature of EU law and the wording of the treaties impose equality of treatment. Thus languages become placed in parallel and have to convey recognizably similar information, so as not to mislead. That places a pressure on each language. First, each language must have words for the EU concepts. If they do not exist they must be created, so there is important work for terminologists and lexicologists. Second, each language has its own structure in terms of grammar, syntax, etc. These must be respected, yet also adapted to a standardized EU product, where all texts appear in parallel in the Official Journal. So each language becomes adapted to the EU context. Languages which serve as negotiating languages are regularly drafted and negotiated by non-native speakers who incorporate ideas from mother-tongue into the text. French and more recently English have been subject to this process and it creates a tendency towards becoming a form of dialect. The other languages have to follow the base language, and this can affect them too, with a similar result. Another aspect is that language versions become interchangeable in the negotiating process and translations can become the base text for negotiation at a later stage should, for example, the Council Presidency prefer to work in another language. Different presidencies can have different preferences; in practice this is mainly a question between using French or English as the base language, since the other languages are not so widely known by all the participants in the legislative process. The system nonetheless works pretty well on the whole, provided that an extremely high level of linguistic and terminological vigilance is maintained.

To give a flavour of a multilingual text, here is a short example from Article 7 of Regulation No. 1. The information conveyed is intended to be the same, but one can note that the way in which each language structures that information is by no means uniform; for example the subject of the sentence varies (language regime, languages to be used, linguistic regime, the use of languages…). In every case the question is whether the same meaning, and message, is conveyed.

(1) *(Bulgarian)* Езиковият режим на процедурата на Съда на Европейските общности се определя в неговия процедурен правилник.
(Czech) Užívání jazyků v řízení před Soudním dvorem stanoví jeho jednací řád.
(Danish) Den sproglige ordning for sagerne ved Domstolen fastlaegges i dennes procesreglement.

(Dutch) Het taalgebruik bij de procesvoering van het Hof van Justitie wordt geregeld in het Reglement voor de procesvoering van het Hof.
(English) The languages to be used in the proceedings of the Court of Justice shall be laid down in its rules of procedure.
(Estonian) Euroopa Kohtu menetlustes kasutatavad keeled määratakse kindlaks Euroopa Kohtu töökorraga.
(Finnish) Yhteisön tuomioistuimen oikeudenkäyntimenettelyssä käytettäviä kieliä koskevat järjestelyt vahvistetaan tuomioistuimen työjärjestyksessä.
(French) Le régime linguistique de la procédure de la Cour de Justice est déterminé dans le règlement de procédure.
(German) Die Sprachenfrage für das Verfahren des Gerichtshofes wird in dessen Verfahrensordnung geregelt.
(Greek) Το γλωσσικό καθεστώς της διαδικασίας του Δικαστηρίου καθορίζεται στον κανονισμό διαδικασίας του.
(Hungarian) A Bíróság saját eljárási szabályzatában állapítja meg, hogy eljárásai során mely nyelveket alkalmazza.
(Irish) [No version currently available as secondary legislation was not produced in this language]
(Italian) Il regime linguistico della procedura della Corte di Giustizia è determinato nel Regolamento di procedura della medesima.
(Latvian) Tiesas tiesvedībā izmantojamās valodas nosaka Tiesas reglamentā.
(Lithuanian) Kalbos, vartojamos Teisingumo Teismo nagrinėjamose bylose, nurodomos Teismo darbo tvarkos taisyklėse.
(Maltese) Il-lingwi li għandhom jintużaw fil-proċeduri tal-Qorti tal-Ġustizzja għandhom ikunu stabbiliti fir-regoli ta' proċedura tagħha.
(Polish): System językowy postępowania przed Trybunałem Sprawiedliwości jest określony w jego regulaminie.
(Portuguese) O regime linguístico dos processos no Tribunal de Justiça será fixado no regulamento processual deste Tribunal.
(Romanian) Regimul lingvistic al procedurii Curţii de Justiţie se stabileşte prin regulamentul de procedură al acesteia.
(Slovak) Používanie jazykov v konaní pred Súdnym dvorom sa upraví v rokovacom poriadku Súdneho dvora.
(Slovenian) Jeziki, ki se uporabljajo v postopkih Sodišča, so določeni v njegovem poslovniku.
(Spanish) El régimen lingüístico del procedimiento del Tribunal de Justicia se determinará en el reglamento de procedimiento de éste.
(Swedish) I fråga om förfaranden vid domstolen skall språkanvändningen regleras i domstolens rättegångsregler.

5. Legislative text production line

Like all activities, legal-linguistic revision in the Council takes place in a concrete physical and temporal context. The workings of the Council machine are complex (but also efficient). Essentially, there are three operational contexts.

5.1. Classic procedure

The classic procedure involves the European Commission services being responsible for drafting legislative proposals which are then transmitted to other institutions for their opinion and amending suggestions. The text is discussed in the Council at the official and political levels and this leads in a long or a short time to political agreement on its contents in at least one language version. Thereafter the text moves to the final stages of preparation for adoption by the Council, signature and publication in the Official Journal of the European Union. These final stages include the checking, revising, correcting and linguistic alignment of all language versions of the text. In general there is limited scope for major change at this stage and the objective is to work within the limits that the policy intention has been established and there are no changes of substance. The lawyer-linguists work on the texts in their offices, but if the text is more important or lengthy, or involves 'codecision', then the finalization work takes place in a meeting with national experts during which the text of the base-language version is settled, and subsequently the other language versions are aligned by the lawyer-linguist for the language, working with (or without) a national expert. The Council lawyer-linguists receive comments and suggestions from national delegations on wording but as EU officials for an EU text they have to decide what terminology is appropriate. This first context applies also to primary law texts, notably amending treaties and accession treaties, except that these are more complex and more demanding and there is always a meeting with the negotiators to settle the text. Time pressures also tend to be at their most intense.

Under the Lisbon Treaty some examples of what was the 'classic' procedure appear to be subsumed within the broad classification of "special legislative procedure" (Article 289(2) TFEU) within the context of "specific cases provided for by the treaties". This covers the situation of an act by the Council alone, or the European Parliament alone, but with the 'participation' of the other institution. The case of the Council acting alone and without the involvement of another institution would seem to remain unchanged. At the time of writing it is still early days for the new arrangements.

5.2. Codecision procedure

Codecision procedure entails the Commission preparing its legislative proposal and the European Parliament and Council jointly adopting and signing it. Under Article 289(1) TFEU this is renamed "ordinary legislative procedure" and it becomes the normal, or standard, method for enacting EU legislation. Article 294 TFEU lays down the procedural steps.

The European Parliament and Council are equal partners; each follows its own internal methods and procedures; the final stages are supervised linguistically by the European Parliament and Council lawyer-linguists working together. On the Council side, there is a meeting with experts to settle Council Positions (stages in the procedure) at which lawyer-linguists are able to present legal-linguistic points for consideration by the national, and Commission, experts. The legislative proposal also goes through the European Parliament's legislative process, where its own lawyer-linguists are involved and undertake a similar role to those of the Council. There may subsequently be *conciliation* between Parliament and Council on political and drafting issues. The final stage of the text before adoption, the Lex stage, is again subject to linguistic collaboration between the lawyer-linguists of the two institutions.[4]

5.3. International agreements

The Commission typically negotiates an international agreement, under instructions, and submits an initialled text for approval by the Council. All language versions come to the lawyer-linguists for checking, editorial adjustments and linguistic alignment. Suggested changes to the initialled text are subject to approval by the negotiating parties. The structure, style and wording do not necessarily conform to EU models. Other issues arise, such as differences between South American Spanish and Spanish Spanish, American English and UK English, and so on. Each text has to be examined separately and looked at in terms of consistency internally, as well as with what has been done before, and also as regards the possible effects of particular terms for each party.

There are other variants to these basic scenarios, but they are less frequent. There is in any case broad similarity: the Commission drafts; other institutions are involved to give an opinion, amend, approve, and then the text is considered satisfactory and ready for finalization. Drafting takes place on one language version, but that does not mean that that language remains the basis for negotiation and drafting throughout. An important feature of EU procedures is that the language versions can to some extent become interchangeable. Thus the Commission might draft in French and the Council Presidency select the English translation for negotiation and amendment in the Council. In that case the French text becomes like a translation and is aligned on the revised English model. Or it may be the other way round. Or maybe there is a German original text, translated, worked on in French, then in English. Sometimes there is an agreement where the Spanish, or Portuguese, or German, or other language is the authentic language version and then it becomes the basis. This inter-

---

4 See <http://ec.europa.eu/codecision/index_en.htm> for more details on codecision.

changeability has linguistic implications and it is the task of translators and revisers to be aware – and here it is appropriate to emphasize that the translators and linguistic revisers play a fundamental role in the quality of the EU legislative texts since their texts are those which are being seen by the negotiators and form the basis on which legal-linguistic revision later takes place.

It must also be added that the drafting of legislative texts typically involves many partners and through them many cultural and linguistic viewpoints, if one considers the EU institutions involved, the number of delegations and their different interests. These can have impacts on the individual texts and their wording; for example, as regards terminology and establishing whether concepts are the same in all languages, and whether terms in different languages have the same meaning. Very complex issues frequently arise and in a context in which something new is being undertaken where no one is entirely sure how things will work. Preparing draft laws and trying to identify all possible relevant factors that might affect the situation are an exercise in futurity. This is the case for legislation in general but it is more complex in the EU context because of multiculturalism and multilingualism.

6. Legal-linguistic revision

The process of legal-linguistic revision in the Council serves several aims and purposes:

(a) it is the means by which, with the close cooperation of the secretarial assistants for each language, whose knowledge, experience and skills are vital, each language version of each draft legislative text is prepared in final form for signature and transmission for publication in the Official Journal;

(b) it provides a context in which all the language versions of a text can be reviewed at the same time, differences between them minimized and the language versions aligned, to ensure as far as possible that all language versions express the same message so as to implement the policy and lead to the intended actions. This implies mediation between the language versions, and this action is referred to as *co-drafting* (Gallas 1999: 135);

(c) linked to the idea of 'same message', each language version of a text is formatted and laid out, in terms of presentation, in the same way, so that there is the same number of pages, the same information on each page, the same number of articles and paragraphs, each in the same place on each page, so that a reader can take any language version, examine any page and find the same information in the same place. Thus the language versions become interchangeable between each other. The same principle is applied to publication in the Official Journal;

(d) the task of revision involves checking the accuracy of the information and details set out in the texts. That means checking titles, article and paragraph numbers, footnotes, internal cross-references and references to other texts and documents to ensure they are correct and that readers of the text will find the correct information when they follow the references;

(e) as a result of doing all these individual actions on a text, an impression is gained concerning its quality and whether it seems to be doing what it claims to be doing in a manner which is consistent with the treaties. This is a legal role and the specialized policy lawyers deal with it, but since texts can be subject to heavy negotiation right up until the last minute, there is a place for a final overview check which provides an opportunity for last-minute linguistic adjustments in the interests of legal precision and clarity.

Through constant revising and checking, legal-linguistic revisers develop a feeling for EU legal language. They follow guidance in the internal *Council Manual of Precedents*, the *Interinstitutional Agreement on common guidelines for the quality of drafting of Community legislation* and the *Joint Practical Guide for the drafting of Community legislation*. The latter two are public documents aimed at enhancing the quality of drafting of EU legislative texts by everyone involved in the process.[5]

The practical context in which revision work is carried out can be summarized as involving two stages and two phases. The two 'stages' involve:

(a) settling the contents of the language version which is being treated as the *source* or *base* text (it being understood that the text may not originally have been drafted in that language). This becomes the reference text for all the other languages. The base text is revised, checked, corrected, discussed with experts and generally made ready;

(b) the base version, or model, is made available electronically to all other language colleagues who check it and align their language versions on it. In so doing, they can request explanations, clarifications and sometimes minor stylistic redrafting if necessary to assist their language versions being clear.

The two 'phases' consist of first the preparation of a corrected draft and second a rereading of each text after formatting by the secretarial assistants. The base language version serves as the model. All versions undergo specialized technical secretarial work on layout, presentation and formatting. The time-interval between the first draft and the rereading can be used to resolve problems and pick up details – useful when time is short. Typical examples would be about terminology, the meaning of particular concepts and their equivalence, or ambiguous phrases and their intended meaning. Lawyer-linguists generally work with mother-tongue texts, but for the base versions it is frequently the case that the work is done by a non-native speaker, backed up by a native speaker. The most frequent base language is now English, followed by French. In the past French was the main language and one has to be aware of repercussions on texts where a former translation into English becomes a base, because the English terminology can occasionally be variable across texts over time for the same concept in French as a result of translation variations. This is where it is necessary to check several language versions if in doubt.

5 For a view from the EU Commission context on drafting see Robinson (2008).

7. Viewpoints

In real life activities are intertwined, but by adopting various viewpoints (see Perrin-Taillat 2009) it is possible to inject some structure. Many viewpoints are possible, for example that of a lawyer, linguist, policy-administrator, politician, financial controller, budget manager, accountant, member of the public, industrialist, farmer… . Each viewpoint generates a particular reading of any given text according to expertise, culture, experience and needs. With that in mind, it is proposed to adopt four viewpoints that are useful for the work of legal-linguistic revision: *legal, linguistic, policy* and *action*. Each of these viewpoints can be seen as reflecting deeper realities; for example, the *legal viewpoint* reflects the need for order, stability, structure, foreseeability and regularity – order imposed on a chaotic and messy world; the *linguistic viewpoint* can be connected to the idea of communication, of converting thoughts, ideas, feelings into language in the form of speech or written texts; the *policy viewpoint* reflects the field in which the text is operating and requires using terms and concepts relevant to that field and consistency with the rest of the policy field and other interconnecting policy areas; the *action viewpoint* is an extension of the foregoing viewpoints and places a focus on the doing and expected behaviour from the text. It can be seen as an 'acid test' for the language versions, because if there is a single intention and a single message then each language version should aim to achieve it. If the resulting action from each language version is different, then there is some element that requires attention. Furthermore, the viewpoint of action leads to interpretation and ultimately, in the event of uncertainty or dispute, to the courts and the European Court of Justice to make a definitive ruling. We will explore the viewpoints a little further and see how they can be used for the day-to-day revision work, while bearing in mind that any legal text merges them all into a composite single product.

One obvious way to check any text is to read it through, starting at the beginning and to note and correct any errors detected. However, legislative texts have a characteristic: they appear as a linear narrative from start to finish but the information contained in them is not linear. There are links and connections between parts of the text which jump forwards or backwards (for example, internal references to other articles or paragraphs); there are also definitions which determine the meaning of words throughout the text. A legislative text also frequently makes references to other legislative texts, some from the past, others in the present and yet others being future texts not yet written. The meaning of words is governed by definitions given in higher-ranking texts, in particular in treaty texts, and also by interpretations made by the courts through judicial rulings (case law) of particular terms and expressions. The reading and interpretation of legislative texts therefore becomes a specialized activity that has to be learned; it follows that their preparation requires a mastery of the techniques. This aspect becomes clearer by using different viewpoints.

7.1. Legal viewpoint: requirements as to form, structure, layout and linkage of the parts of the text, linkage to other legal texts, standardized wording

When a new text arrives for revision, the base language is established by the administrator. The legal viewpoint, for the purposes of revision, implies looking at the overall structure of the document as a whole: type of act (regulation, directive, etc); governing treaty, enacting body, subject matter as revealed by title, and so on. This information fixes the legal and linguistic (including terminological) context. Then the main parts of the structure can be identified: title, enacting body, citations, recitals, enacting provisions, annexes. From there, by working through each part from the highest level to the lowest, the structure and numbering of each part can be checked and fixed as necessary. Guidance is obtained from the internal *Council Manual of Precedents*, the *Interinstitutional Agreement* and the *Joint Practical Guide* previously mentioned, as well as any particular instructions or information that has been furnished. The initial structural frame thus becomes fixed. Next one can check the formal aspects such as titles of documents, correct articles referred to, legal powers referred to, consultations required, procedures, such as codecision procedure, referred to, and so on. By now first impressions have been obtained of the draft text – which is seen as a whole product, or 'sign'. Its place within the EU context, the policy context, the linguistic context and what it is seeking to achieve start to become clearer. The legal point of view also covers other matters which are internal to the text, for example, the sequence of contents in accordance with the Joint Practical Guide (subject-matter, scope, definitions, general provisions, committee procedure (comitology), transitional provisions, implementation, etc.).

The legal viewpoint can be thought of as also covering such matters as the case law relating to the domain, but from a drafting and revision point of view case law does not play a primary role, since a new act is being created. The case law reflects rather the way the pre-existing law has been interpreted and thus forms part of the background policy environment being adjusted.

7.2. Linguistic viewpoint: layout, presentation, spelling, grammar, syntax, terminology, intertextuality, semantic aspects, polysemy, words and expressions which create ambiguity or uncertainty

The text is read as it stands for its message. If it is clear, that is fine. If the text 'stumbles' or becomes unclear or ambiguous, that is a sign that intervention may be required. The text is read for spelling – usually not an issue nowadays with good spell-checkers, but there are varieties of English and attention may be needed as to whether the spelling is standard British English or American.

The text is checked for grammar and syntax; since English does not generally distinguish by gender markings or declension endings and other inflections, these are less of a problem, but this can generate uncertainties for other languages which do have them. Issues may cover questions of singularity or plurality, use of definite or indefinite articles, and what nouns particular adjectives are qualifying. This can be a problem for translation from English; for example *black cats and dogs*. Does this mean black cats and black dogs, or black cats and all dogs? How is that to be translated? This touches on ellipsis which is frequent in legislative drafting and can be a source of interpretation and translation problems. Sometimes it is better to spell out in full what is intended, even if it seems pedantic.

The text is checked for consistent use of concepts and terminology. Is the same term used for the same idea throughout or are synonyms introduced? If the latter, then there is doubt whether the concept is the same. How should the two words be translated? By the same or different words? Where words are defined, those words must be used afterwards in the text. Also, the terminology in higher level texts can be binding on lower level texts.

The various elements are checked for accuracy, for example footnotes, titles and citations are checked against the sources where possible (overlap with the legal viewpoint here). Standard phrases and clauses are checked against the guidance models, such as for committee procedures (comitology). As this process of reading and checking takes place, the message is being checked and this brings us to what the text is seeking to do and achieve, which touches on questions of message, communication and the policy viewpoint.

7.3. Policy viewpoint: clarity and efficiency of policy message reviewed, discussed, clarified from viewpoint of 'first innocent reader', quality controller, final editor, working with authors and experts

The legal-linguistic reviser is not a policy expert and in general has no background knowledge of the field or text in question. However, each text purports to do something, and from training and experience the reviser reads and integrates the information into a general picture or structure which becomes familiar. The text may be self-contradictory, or repetitious or have gaps in the logic, etc. These can be noticed and raised with the experts and authors for advice and to consider whether rewording is needed. There is often a 'finalization' meeting with the experts when they and the legal-linguistic revisers jointly review a text and seek to identify and repair any defects and imperfections in it. However, the policy is fixed and so it is basically a question of making the message clearer and more precise linguistically. This is done through asking questions and working with the experts — and with codecision texts under the 'ordinary legislative procedure' with the lawyer linguists of the European Parliament who are conducting a similar review in parallel from the Parliament's point of view.

7.4. Action viewpoint: what would happen from the wording proposed?

We come now to the fourth viewpoint which concerns the action or actual behaviour which is expected to result from the text. What will be done in practice? What is the reality? This is the acid test by which all the language versions can be judged. The problem is that the text is a draft and the future is always unknown. The drafters try to anticipate and foresee and make provision accordingly, but there is always uncertainty. This is especially so when something new is being attempted and where there are many variables and 'unknown unknowns'. That is frequently the case with EU legislation. However, proceeding by small steps, reviewing constantly (Commission role) and the possibility to come back with new amending proposals, or to supervise implementation through committee procedures (comitology), all help to give reassurance. One can think of EU legislation as an exercise through time, as well as space. The texts are constantly being revisited and re-examined to see how they can be developed further. This thought is useful for reducing anxiety levels when a text is about to be launched, but it also means that the same topics tend to recur at intervals, there are models and precedents available for comparison, and experience is built up over time.

While the text is drafted for the future, once it is signed and published in the Official Journal it is part of the legal order and has effects which exist in the present. Actions flow from the text, but what is done depends on the reading made of the text, the interpretation and understanding of the multilingual message. Different readings may lead to different behaviour. The action viewpoint can be thought of as an 'acid test' for the clarity and precision of the message, across all languages. If each language version produces the same behaviour then in principle the message conveyed is the same in each text. This can be tested by asking questions such as: *What does this mean in prac-*

tice? What happens if...? What is the reality? throughout the preparation phase and comparing the answers for the various language versions. The roles of translator and reviser imply constantly asking these questions, even if only subconsciously, for every word and sentence of a text being translated.

The viewpoint of action is of interest because it is closely linked to the concept of 'message' and interpretation of the (multilingual) message. What rights are conveyed? What obligations are imposed? By whom? On whom? When? For what purpose? And so on. Individual readers may read a text in one way, and others using the same or different language versions may read it in a different way. This leads on to questions of the transposition of EU legislation (notably EU directives) into national law and the interpretation of EU legislative texts by the courts, in particular by the European Court of Justice. The courts have the final say on what texts mean. That is their role. Thus the drafters are also anticipating how the courts will interpret the legislative texts to try and ensure they will achieve what they want. One of the roles of the legal adviser is to give specialist advice on these matters, since they must defend the client institution before the courts. However, from a linguistic point of view, the action viewpoint places a focus on the effects of the act, and more specifically, on the effect of particular words and sentences. This touches on issues of ambiguity and complex drafting emerging from compromise negotiated solutions where a clear message may be difficult to identify. In the end the European Court of Justice will decide on the meaning, if called on to do so, and will do so in accordance with its methods and techniques. For these, reference should be made to the Court's case law and the relevant literature.

8. Restrictions and limitations

The context in which the legal-linguistic revisers work is highly constrained. The text worked on has been agreed by the negotiators as reflecting what they want and is *politically agreed*. This must be respected. The texts arise from often complex negotiations which can result in texts which are not the clearest. Often the political balance is very delicate. This also must be respected. The base language serves as the model and this must be interpreted and followed by other languages for the negotiators' intentions. However, once published every version is equally authentic. There are other temporal and contextual limitations, but these are perhaps the main ones that operate on the text.

9. Conclusion

This chapter has set out some personal thoughts on the role and work of legal linguistic revision of EU legislative texts by Council lawyer-linguists. The observations are drawn from experience over the years and have been structured to give a broad picture of the role. The approach of viewpoints has been used for the purpose of introducing structure into the method of work and because it leads one to examine the text from different angles in a way which can reveal different information, and different points that need to be clarified, and thus enhance the quality of the final product and its serviceability as a legal tool. There is, of course, much more that could be said, in particular on the structure of EU legislative texts, as well as on their interpretation and transposition into national law.

Legal linguistics is receiving growing academic attention and perhaps this can be seen as part of a trend towards research into areas of applied linguistics. From that point of view, lawyer-linguists can be seen as practitioners working in the field of legal linguistics. They have a lot of practical experience and it is hoped that this can be brought into contact with the knowledge, methods and insights of linguistic researchers to help us understand better what is going on and being done every time an EU legislative text is being drafted, translated, revised, published, transposed and acted on. To that end some further sources of information have been added.

References

Gallas, Tito 1999. Coredazione e traduzione giuridica nella legislazione multilingue, in particolare quella comunitaria. *Quaderni di libri e riviste d'Italia: la traduzione*, s*aggi e documenti* 43/4, 135-147.

Interinstitutional Agreement of 22 December 1998 on Common Guidelines for the Quality of Drafting of Community Legislation. *Official Journal* C 73, 17.3.1999, 1.

Joint Practical Guide for the Drafting of Community legislation 2003. *Office for Official Publications of the European Communities.* Luxembourg.

Morgan, James F. 1982. Multilingual Legal Drafting in the EEC and the Work of Jurist/Linguists. *Multilingua* 1/2, 109-117.

Perrin-Taillat, Michèle 2009. Computer Technologies and Legal Language. Paper presented at the 4th CERLIS Conference *Researching Language and the Law* (Bergamo, 18-20 June 2009).

Robertson, Colin 2009. LSP and EU Legal Language. XVII European Symposium on LSP, 17-21 August 2009. Aarhus. Denmark. extended paper to be published on-line at the Symposium website: <http://www.asb.dk/article.aspx?pid=20015>.

Robinson, William. 2008. Drafting of EU Legislation: A View from the European Commission. *Rivista di Diritto Pubblico Italiano, Comunitario e Comparat*o. At <http://www.federalismi.it> (accessed 15 October 2009).

Further sources

Brussels: lawyer-linguist positions. At <http://www.theposselist.com/2009/03/06/brussels-lawyer-linguist-positions> (Accessed 20.11.2009).

Creech, Richard 2005. Law and Language in the European Union; The Paradox of a Babel 'United in Diversity'. Europa Law Publishing.

Galdia, Marcus 2009. *Legal Linguistics*. Frankfurt am Mein: Peter Lang.

Glanert, Simone 2008. Speaking Language to Law: The Case of Europe. *Legal Studies* 28/2, 161.

Goldsmith, Oliver 2009. Is the EU Speaking the Right Language? *Law Society Gazette*. 26 October. At <http://www.lawgazette.co.uk/blogs/euro-blog/is-eu-speaking-right-language> (Accessed 20.11.2009).

Mattila, Heikki 2006. *Comparative Legal Linguistics*. Aldershot: Ashgate.

Pozzo, Barbara / Jacometti,Valentina (eds) 2006. *Multilingualism and the Harmonisation of European Law*. Alphen aan den Rijn: Kluwer.

Robertson, Colin Forthcoming. Multilingual Law: What is It? How is it Made? How is it Used and Applied? (With Reference to EU Practice). Paper presented at the International Conference 'Curriculum, Language and the Law' (Dubrovnik, 18-21/9/2008).

Salmi-Tolonen, Tarja 2004. Legal Linguistic Knowledge and Creating and Interpreting Law in Multilingual Environments. <http://www.brooklaw.edu/students/journals/bjil/bjil29iii_salmi-tolonen.pdf> (accessed 14.11.09).

Wikipedia. Languages of the European Union <http://en.wikipedia.org/wiki/Languages_of_the_European_Union> (Accessed 20.11.2009).

MARTINA BAJČIĆ

Challenges of Translating EU Terminology

1. Introduction

Translating EU legislation into Croatian can be difficult not only because of the absence of appropriate Croatian terminology for new EU terms, but also because the concepts to be transposed into the national law are new as well. Attempts are made to identify gaps in Croatian legal terminology to designate new EU legal concepts and to provide the most adequate equivalents, as will be illustrated by examples drawn from the Posted Workers Directive and from the Protocol on the application of the Charter of Fundamental Rights of the European Union to Poland and to the United Kingdom, that is yet to be enforced. Databases used for this purpose include Eur-Lex, the multilingual online database, *Eurovoc*, *Euroterm*, *Black's Law Dictionary* and Croatian dictionaries: *Hrvatski enciklopedijski rječnik* (Croatian Encyclopaedic Dictionary), *Englesko-hrvatski rječnik prava* (English-Croatian Dictionary of Law), *Četverojezični rječnik prava Europske unije* (EU Law Glossary), *Rečnik pravnih termina srpsko-englesko-francuski* (English-French-Serbian Legal Dictionary) and *Wirtschaftswörterbuch Deutsch Kroatisch* (German-Croatian Dictionary of Economics). As part of the scientific project 'Strategies for translating the EU *acquis*',[1] the aim of this chapter is to emphasize the need for a multidisciplinary approach including cooperation between linguists and lawyers, and the use of expert terminology know-how when translating EU legislation.

---

1 The project is conducted at the Faculty of Law of the University of Rijeka, principal researcher: Susan Šarčević.

In light of the EU enlargement, the free movement of workers constitutes an important foundation of the EU internal market. As such, this pivotal area of Community law encompasses the right of EU citizens to travel or settle anywhere in the European Union. European Union nationals are entitled to work or search for a job in another EU country. However, some restrictions apply to the free movement of workers from countries which joined the EU more recently. It should be noted that these restrictions are being implemented only in certain transitional periods by a few Member States and for specific worker categories. Special provisions apply to nationals of countries outside the EU. Agreements reached at the EU level also help to protect the social security rights of EU citizens who move or travel to other European countries (e.g. health care, pensions, unemployment, family benefits).

In this respect it is worthwhile mentioning that the European Personnel Selection Office (EPSO) published its first call for expression of interest for Croatian citizens at the end of 2008. Although Croatia is still a candidate country, 342 job openings at EU institutions currently await Croats: of these, 116 are designated for translators, 15 for lawyer-linguists, 10 for administrators, and 9 for lawyers. Of the 7,559 Croats who applied for the EPSO/CAST/CRO/09, 1,980 actually underwent the testing and 1,390 passed. Above-average salaries (by Croatian standards), varying from €1,700 to €4,800, account for such great interest on behalf of Croatian citizens.[2]

2. Posted Workers Directive (PWD)

In terms of protection of workers within the EU, the Directive 96/71/EC of the European Parliament and of the Council of 16 December 1996 concerning the posting of workers plays a significant role in the framework of the provision of services by regulating the protection of workers from one Member State employed by a company to carry out

2 Available at <http//www.vecernji.list> (visited on 30 November 2008).

work in another Member State. In addition, this Directive protects domestic undertakings from any kind of competition distortion caused by the posting of 'less expensive' workers from other Member States. Companies can thus employ their own staff on projects in other EU states, as long as this is for a limited time and the company abides by local working conditions. The Posted Workers Directive (PWD) guarantees the application of the host country's statutory and regulatory provisions relating to:

- maximum work periods and minimum rest periods;
- minimum paid annual holidays;
- the minimum rates of pay, including overtime rates etc.[3]

The Directive came to prominence during the 2009 Lindsey Oil Refinery strikes after British workers at the Lindsey Oil Refinery in North Killingholme, North Lincolnshire, claimed that they were being undercut by skilled foreign labour when the Italian construction contractor IREM appointed several hundred European (mainly Italian and Portuguese) contractors on the site at a time of high unemployment in the local and global economy. The action attracted considerable media attention. As a background note it is necessary to mention *Dirk Rueffert v. Niedersachsen* (Case C-346/06 of 3 April 2008),[4] a landmark case in terms of posting of workers. The facts of the case are as follows. The company Objekt und Bauregie GmbH & Co secured a public contract for construction work in Niedersachen, which it subcontracted to a Polish firm. It was agreed to ensure compliance with wage rates already in force on the site on the basis of a collective agreement. Upon discovering that the 53 posted workers were in fact earning 46.57% of the applicable minimum wage for the construction sector, the Niedersachsen authority withdrew the contract and demanded payment of contractual penalties. The law of Land Niedersachsen, Germany, on the award of public contracts obliges tenderers to public contracts to undertake in writing to pay their employees at least the remuneration prescribed by the collective agreement at the

3 Available at <http//www.eurofond.europa.eu> (visited on 20 May 2009).

4 Available at <http://eur-lex.europa.eu/LexUriServ/LexUriServ.do?uri=CELEX: 62006J0346:EN:HTML> (visited on 20 May 2009).

place where services are performed. The German Court of Appeal referred the case to the European Court of Justice (ECJ) on 18 July 2006 in order to determine whether public procurement rules in Niedersachsen are incompatible with the freedom to provide services in the EU.

The ECJ noted in particular that the PWD is to be read in the light of Art. 49 EC and seeks to bring about the freedom to provide services. In this regard, the Court states that applying the minimum wage laid down by the collective agreement in question may impose on foreign service providers an additional economic burden and is therefore capable of constituting a restriction to the free movement of services. Such restriction cannot be justified by the objective of ensuring the protection of workers since it applies only to workers employed in the context of public works contracts but not in the context of private contracts. In short, the ECJ concluded that the law of Niedersachsen is incompatible with the PWD, interpreted in the sense of Art. 49 EC.

In light of the free movement of workers, posting is bound to increase in the near future. Therefore, it is important to ensure its proper and timely transposition into Croatian domestic law. In order for this to be realized, a correct Croatian translation of the Directive with adequate and consistent terminology is essential.

3. Transposing new concepts of Community law into the national legal system: the need for new terminology

3.1. Example of Posted Workers Directive

Transposing the Posted Workers Directive into Croatian law requires the creation of new terminology. Translators are challenged, to say the least, when first confronted with a term such as *posting* or *posted workers*, which designates a new concept of Community law that has to be transposed into national law. The latter is easier said than done.

It should be noted here that the Independent Service for Translation in the Field of European Integration of the Ministry of Foreign Affairs and European Integration is in charge of translating EU legislation into Croatian for the purpose of transposition. The Department for Translation of *Acquis Communautaire* employs 15 translators and one lawyer. However, numerous free-lance translators and translation agencies participate in the translation process which impedes the cooperation among translators and makes the usage of consistent Croatian terminology in the translations more difficult. It should also be emphasized that it is the legislator who ultimately decides what Croatian term will be used. There are three ways in which translators (and lawyers) can proceed:

- First, to use national terms that already exist within the domestic law, in this case in the Croatian legal system, which, however, are only partially equivalent to the source concepts. Šarčević (2000: 255; 2007: 47) recommends using neutral terms whenever possible. The use of national terms can imply different concepts and thus be misleading.
- Second, to create new terms to denote new concepts of Community law. However, linguistic equivalents, i.e. neologisms, can cause interpretation problems since lawyers are unfamiliar with the underlying concepts (Šarčevič 2007: 47).
- Finally, to borrow the term already used in the Community law, such as *posting*. This is often the case in academic circles. In particular, professors of law frequently use the original term in their scholarly writing. While this solution achieves precision and accuracy, it still means taking the easier path. It goes without saying that adequate equivalents for such terms need to be provided in Croatian.

As mentioned above, the PWD has not yet been transposed into Croatian law. The title of the PWD has been officially translated into Croatian by the above Ministry as *Direktiva ... o raspoređivanju radnika u okviru pružanja usluga.*[5] In addition, in the Croatian text of

5 Available at <http://www.mvpei.hr/pre/default.aspx?p=05.20.20> (visited on 20 May 2009).

the Directive 2004/18 the title of the Directive has been translated as: *Direktiva ... koja se odnosi na slanje radnika na rad u inozemstvo u okviru pružanja usluga.*[6] Due to the evolution of terminology in different phases of Croatian history (in 1918 the creation of Croatian legal terminology stopped and it was not further developed until the 1990s and the establishing of the independent Republic of Croatia, Sikirić 2007: 135), legal terminology is used inconsistently as illustrated here, thus making the translator's task all the more challenging.

Apart from the lack of terminological consistency in different translations, in both versions the term *posted workers* has been translated with a paraphrase; in the first text as *slanje radnika na rad u inozemstvo* (sending workers abroad to work – which in fact is incorrect) and in the second one as *raspoređivanje radnika* (distribution of workers; cf. Table 1).

PWD	CROATIAN TRANSLATION
Art. 2 Definition 1. For the purposes of this Directive, 'posted worker` means a worker who, for a limitedperiod, carries out his work in the territory of a Member State other than the State in which he normally works. 2. For the purposes of this Directive, the definition of a worker is that which applies in the law of the Member State to whose territory the worker is posted	Članak 2. Definicija 1. U smislu ove Direktive '*raspoređeni radnik'* označava radnika koji u ograničenom vremenskom razdoblju obavlja svoj posao na području države članice koja nije država u kojoj uobičajeno radi. 2. U smislu ove Direktive definicija radnika je definicija koja vrijedi u zakonu države članice na čije je područje radnik raspoređen.

Table 1. Article 2 (1) of the Directive 96/71,[7] Croatian translation.[8]

As for the second example, the Croatian translation is too vague, thus failing to convey the precise concept denoted by the English and German terms (see Table 4). Translators should not completely refrain

6 Available at <http://www.dkom.hr/direktive/32004L0018hrv.pdf> (visited on 20 May 2009).

7 Available at: http.www.eur-lex.europa.eu (visited on 10 May 2009).

8 Available at: http/www.mvpei.hr (visited on 10 May 2009).

from using paraphrases in legal texts; however, as Šarčević points out, knowledge of the law is essential in the formation of descriptive paraphrases (Šarčević 2007: 252).

As will be shown later, the concept conveyed by *raspoređeni radnik* is not narrow enough. Moreover, instead of being precise, it is descriptive and requires further specification. Translating *posting* with the noun *raspoređivanje* is even more confusing, as the term in question has not yet been used in Croatian legal language, but is a term in ordinary language usage. That said, using this equivalent would bring about the same effect as neologisms or coins, i.e. the underlying concepts would be unfamiliar to lawyers.

3.2. Terminology used in national legislation

Generally speaking, EU legal experts discourage using the legal terminology of a Member State's national legal system since EU legal terms are not to be interpreted in the sense of national legal terms (Mazor 2005).[9] Describing the working methods of lawyer-linguists at the ECJ, Gallo (2006: 191) says:

> In order to avoid errors or inadequate results the search for a term in the source language that most closely corresponds to a specific term in another language must be conducted through a close comparison of the legal systems to which the two terms belong. […] In this respect the author considers the combined use of monolingual and bilingual dictionaries particularly useful. The definition of a concept in a monolingual dictionary can often provide a clue that helps expose an imperfect correspondence of meaning between terms in a bilingual dictionary.

While it is true that a close comparison of the two legal systems (to which the source and the target language belong) is a *sine qua non* of legal translation, monolingual dictionaries will not always provide the legal translator with the desired answers. *Black's Law Dictionary* for example, provides six different meanings for *posting*, none of which

---

9 Available at <http://www.drustvoprevoditelja.htnet.hr/prevoditelj_2005/mazor .htm> (visited on 10 August 2009).

corresponds to the EU concept of *posting of workers* (*Black's Law Dictionary* 2004: 1205). The reason for this is that the EU terms denoting new concepts of Community law are often new themselves. Therefore, rather than relying on monolingual dictionaries, translators (of the candidate countries) should look for definitions of the relevant terms in the EU legislative texts drafted in one of the official EU languages. Definitions can, in turn, contain the explanation needed to limit the meaning of the term in question, thus facilitating the translator's search for equivalents in the respective target language.

Likewise, it is unlikely that bilingual dictionaries will provide the translator with a solution to his or her search for adequate equivalents for an EU term. For example, the Croatian equivalent for *posted workers* in the *Englesko-hrvatski rječnik prava* (*English-Croatian Dictionary of Law*, Gačić 2004: 1006), is *premještanje radnika*, whereas under *posting* we find: *raspored na radno mjesto, premještaj; raspoređivanje. Premještaj* in the Croatian standard language means *ex officio transfer from one place of work to another with a change of residence* in *Veliki rječnik hrvatskoga jezika* (Croatian Dictionary, Anić 2006: 1163). The *Wirtschaftswörterbuch Deutsch Kroatisch*, (German-Croatian Dictionary of Economics 2004: 221) also cites several equivalents for *entsenden*: *poslati, delegirati, imenovati*; whereas *Entsendung von Arbeitnehmern* is translated as *upućivanje zaposlenika na rad u stranu zemlju. Delegirani radnik* was considered by the author as a potential equivalent for *posted worker* but rejected because *delegirati* has different meanings: *delegirati: odrediti / određivati, ovlastiti / ovlašćivatui, (po)slati kao delegata* (*Hrvatski enciklopedijski rječnik*, Croatian Encyclopaedic Dictionary 2003: 225). Moreover, there is a shortage of bilingual legal dictionaries for EU languages. For example, legal Cypriot, Irish, Maltese, Lithuanian, and Luxembourgian are not found in any dictionary (see van Laer/van Laer 2004: 88).

3.3. Conceptual analysis

As Wüster (1985: 1) points out, every terminological research should start from the concept. On the basis of conceptual analysis (Chroma

2004: 82), i.e. by comparing the legal languages of the target and source legal systems, one can investigate whether a given concept exists in the target legal system, here Croatian law, and if so, what terminology is used. A study of the relevant Croatian legislation showed that the following terminology is used to denote the concept of *posted workers*: *radnik upućen na rad u inozemstvo* [worker sent abroad to work] is cited in the Croatian Labour Act (Official Gazette, No. 30/04),[10] but does not convey the meaning of posted workers without further clarification (see Table 2). The term *izaslani radnici* is defined in para. 9 of Art. 3 of the Croatian Act on Obligatory Insurance Contributions (Official Gazette No 84/08)[11] as follows:

> Izaslani radnik je fizička osoba koja za poslodavca sa sjedištem u Republici Hrvatskoj obavlja posao u drugoj državi te osoba na radu u diplomatskoj misiji ili konzularnom uredu Republike Hrvatske u inozemstvu; [A posted worker is a natural person who works in another state for an employer, whose seat is in the Republic of Croatia, or a person engaged in a diplomatic mission or at a consulate office of the Republic of Croatia situated abroad.] (Translation by the author).

On the basis of the definitions in the Croatian Labour Act and those in the PWD, the term *upućeni radnik* could be considered as an equivalent for *posted worker*. *Upućeni radnik* denotes a worker sent abroad to work for a limited period (not less than one month) and the employment terms and conditions are governed by 'foreign' regulations (Art. 37). *Posted workers* are also employed for a limited period of time and their employment contracts are subject to the regulations of the MS to which they are posted. Exemptions from the PWD are possible if the period of posting does not exceed one month or if the work performed is insignificant.

---

10 Available at <http://narodne-novine.hr/clanci/sluzbeni/313055.html> (visited on 10 May 2009).

11 Available at <http://www.hzz.hr/DocSlike/ZAKON_DOPRINOSI_ZA_OB VEZ NO_OSIGURANJA.doc> (visited on 10 May 2009).

HR	EN
Obvezni sadržaj pisanog ugovora o radu, odnosno pisane potvrde o sklopljenom ugovoru o radu u slučaju ***upućivanja radnika u inozemstvo*** Članak 20. (1) Ako se radnik **upućuje na rad u inozemstvo** za razdoblje duže od mjesec dana, a za vrijeme rada u inozemstvu na ugovor o radu će se primjenjivati inozemni propisi, pisani ugovor o radu mora se sklopiti ili se radniku mora uručiti pisana potvrda o sklopljenom ugovoru o radu prije odlaska u inozemstvo te mora sadržavati, osim uglavaka iz članka 17. ovoga Zakona i dodatne uglavke o: 1. trajanju rada u inozemstvu, 2. novcu u kojem će se isplaćivati plaća, 3. drugim primanjima u novcu i naravi na koja će radnik imati pravo za vrijeme rada u inozemstvu te 4. uvjetima vraćanja (repatrijacije) u zemlju.	*Mandatory contents of a written labour contract or a written certificateon the conclusion of a labour contract for workers sent abroad* Article 20 (1) If a worker is **sent to work abroad** for a period exceeding one month, and during the work abroad the labour contract is subject to foreign regulations, either the labour contract must be concluded in written form or the worker must be given a written certificate on the conclusion of a labour contract before he or she goes abroad which, in addition to the provisions under Article 17, shall also contain provisions on: 1. the duration of the work abroad; 2. the currency in which the salaries shall be paid; 3. other payments received in money and in kind to which the worker will be entitled during the work abroad; and 4. the conditions for repatriation.

Table 2. Croatian Labour Act (Official Gazette, No 30/04), English translation available at <http//www.vsrh.hr>.

As seen above, under the Croatian Act on Obligatory Insurance Contributions *izaslani radnik* denotes any natural person hired to perform work for an employer situated in the Republic of Croatia, and persons working for a diplomatic mission or at a consular office of the Republic of Croatia. However, the monthly wages of these persons are 20% higher than the average amount they would receive for the same work in Croatia. Furthermore, the employer lays down the amounts of workers' contributions. Nonetheless, further research showed that the term *izaslani radnik* is used more frequently than *upućeni radnik*. In addition, the Croatian Pension Insurance Act (Official Gazette No 35/

08)[12] uses the term *izaslani radnik* as well as official categories of types of worker insurance posted on official websites in Croatia[13] (cf. Table 3).

ZAKON O DOPRINOSIMA ZA OBVEZNA OSIGURANJA (NN 84/08) : Članak 3. U smislu ovoga Zakona, pojedini pojmovi imaju sljedeća značenja: ... 9. izaslani radnik je fizička osoba koja za poslodavca sa sjedištem u Republici Hrvatskoj obavlja posao u drugoj državi te osoba na radu u diplomatskoj misiji ili konzularnom uredu Republike Hrvatske u inozemstvu; Članak37. (1) Mjesečna osnovica za obračun doprinosa iznos je što ga utvrđuje poslodavac polazeći od najviše mjesečne plaće koju bi izaslani radnik ostvario za iste, odnosno za slične poslove u Republici Hrvatskoj prema ugovoru o radu, pravilniku o radu, kolektivnom ugovoru ili posebnom propisu, uvećana za 20%. (2) Mjesečna osnovica prema stavku 1. ovoga članka ne može za rad s punim radnim vremenom biti niža od najniže mjesečne osnovice uvećane za 20% niti viša od najviše mjesečne osnovice. (3) O iznosima mjesečnih osnovica za obračun doprinosa za izaslane radnike i za pojedina radna mjesta odnosno poslove i zadaće koje obavlja izaslani radnik poslodavac donosi opći akt sukladno odredbama propisa o radu

Table 3. Croatian Act on Obligatory Insurance Contributions (Official Gazette, No 84/08).

In this case the national legal term can be used, as long as the reader is aware that the substance of the national term differs from that of the source concept but fulfils the same function. This is an example of a functional equivalent:

> Wenn die Rechtsvergleichung ergibt, dass ein Rechtsinstitut mehreren Rechtsordnungen gemeinsam ist, weil es jeweils dieselbe Funktion erfüllt, so sind die terminologischen Schwierigkeiten nur noch von zweitrangiger Bedeutung. Man kann durchaus den Begriff einer nationalen Rechtsordnung beibehalten, vorausgesetzt man ist sich darüber im Klaren, dass dieser Terminus sich auf einen in der Funktion gleichartigen, aber inhaltlich nicht identischen Begriffsge-

12 Available at <http://narodne-novine.nn.hr/clanci/sluzbeni/269150.html> (visited on 10 May 2009).

13 Available at <http://www.mirovinsko.hr> (visited on 10 May 2009).

genstand bezieht, weil Entstehungsgründe und Anwendung, Rechtstruktur und Rechtsfolgen im einzelnen abweichen können. (Constantinesco II 1983: 168).

Consulting other EU language versions can be very helpful when searching for Croatian equivalents for EU terms, especially the German and Slovene versions. In particular, it is helpful for the translator to note whether the German version cites a national term or whether the Slovene drafter opted for a neologism or kept a localism, as can be seen in Table 4.

EN	DE	FR	IT	SL	HR
posting	Entsendung	détachement	distaccato	napotitev	*Slanje* (radnika)
posted worker	entsandter Arbeitnehmer	travailleur détaché	lavoratore distaccato	napoteni delavec	*Izaslani* radnik*

Table 4. Article 2 (1) of the Directive 96/71[14]; * author's proposal.

The German equivalent *Entsenden* which is cited in the Arbeitnehmer-Entsendegesetz (Law on the Posting of Workers)[15] is also used for slightly different concepts, for example, the use of *Entsenderecht* (right of representation) in § 101 Absatz 1 Aktiengesetz (AktG).[16] The Slovene term *napoteni delavec* is also used in other national Acts. Therefore, in my opinion, the term *izaslani radnik* seems more appropriate than *raspoređeni* or *upućeni radnik.* However, at present, it is too early to predict what the legislator will decide.

14 Available at <http//www.eur-lex.europa.eu> (visited on 21 May 2009).

15 Available at <http://www.gesetze-im-internet.de/aentg_2009/index.html> (visited on 10 June 2009).

16 Available at <http://www.gesetze-im-internet.de/aktg/index.html> (visited on 10 June 2009).

4. Justiciability

The second example from Protocol (No. 30) to the Treaty of Lisbon on the Application of the Charter of Fundamental Rights of the European Union to Poland and to the United Kingdom is another interesting term mentioned in the context of workers' social rights, namely *justiciability.* A legal matter is *justiciable* when it serves as the basis for a claim or complaint before a court. For example, there has been considerable debate on whether 'subsidiarity' is *justiciable.* In other words, can courts, including the ECJ, adjudicate complaints claiming that laws adopted by the EU institutions violate the principle of subsidiarity? It appears to be generally agreed that the subsidiarity principle is not justiciable.

Justiciability is an aspect of the enforcement of EC law, which relates to the judicial system. For example, the doctrine of vertical direct effect means that the provisions of directives may be *justiciable* against the State. Most of the rules which are laid down in directives include a provision on *justiciability*. Other EU legal measures, such as recommendations, do not provide for *justiciability*. Soft law measures, such as the open method of coordination used in the European Employment Strategy in the employment title of the EC Treaty, are also not *justiciable.* A major question of *justiciability* arises concerning certain provisions in the Charter of Fundamental Rights of the European Union. According to its present legal status it is not *justiciable.* However, if the Charter is incorporated into the EC Treaty, it is possible that the ECJ could attribute binding 'direct effect' to its provisions, thus enabling individuals to bring claims before national courts based on Charter provisions. This could have important consequences for the numerous provisions in the Charter on employment and industrial relations. Great Britain and Poland have been granted a special protection status in regard to the enforcement of Charter rights before their national courts by way of a Protocol to the Treaty of Lisbon (which entered into force on 1 December 2009).[17] Unlike the

---

17 Available at <http.www.eurofound.europa.eu> (visited on 10 May 2009).

first *posted workers* example, *justiciability* is cited in *Black's Law Dictionary* with the following clarification:

Justiciablity	the quality or state of being appropriate or suitable for adjudication by a court. See MOOTNESS DOCTRINE; RIPENESS. "Concepts of justiciability have been developed to identify appropriate occasions for judicial action (…) – feigned and collusive cases, standing, ripeness, mootness, political questions, and administrative questions." Charles Allen Wricht et al., *Federal Practice and Procedure* § 3529, at 278-79 (2d ed. 1984).
Justiciable	(of a case or dispute) properly brought before a court of justice; capable of being disposed of judicially (a justiciable controversy).

Table 5. Definition of *justiciability* and *justiciable* in Black's Law Dictionary (2004: 882).

Englesko-hrvatski rječnik prava (The English-Croatian Dictionary of Law, 2004: 724) lists a handful of potential equivalents for *justiciability* and *justiciable*: *sudsko rješavanje, podložnost sudu, primjenjivost u sudu, raspravljivost pred sudom; kojem se može suditi, podčinjen sudu, prihvatljiv sudu, na kojeg se može podnijeti žalba*. None of the equivalents is acceptable except for the vague paraphrase *kojem se može suditi*. In addition, the above Dictionary explains *justiciable controversy* as *spor koji zahtijeva sudsko rješenje* which, though vague, is on the right track. Instead of *zahtijeva*, which means *requires* or *needs*, *suitable for, podoban za* would be more appropriate in Croatian.

Rečnik pravnih termina srpsko-englesko-francuski (Serbian-English-French Legal Dictionary, 2004: 602) contains only the adjective *justicable* with the following explanation: *koji spada u sudsku nadležnost* [belonging to judicial jurisdiction] which is not precise, although correct in the area of social rights. This paraphrase could imply that *justiciability* can be translated as *sudbenost*, which is misleading. *Sudbenost* denotes a wider concept and its usage in Croatian refers to jurisdiction. However, *sudbenost* could be used in the context of social rights although Croatian legislation does not provide for such an option. Moreover, it is back-translated into English as *jurisdiction*

(Act on the Application of the Rome Statute of the International Criminal Court).[18]

4.1. Utuživost or *justiciabilnost*?

The above-mentioned equivalents are imprecise and incorrect, making it difficult for the translator to make a choice among them. After careful consideration *utuživost* appears to be the best equivalent for *justiciability* and *utuživa prava* for *justiciable rights* (see Table 6). The Croatian terms *utuživost* and *utuživa prava* would be the exact equivalents of the German, Italian and Slovene version. Furthermore, they correspond in meaning denoting judicial enforcement of subjective rights. This is supported by the entry in the *Hrvatski enciklopedijski rječnik* (Croatian Encyclopaedic Dictionary, 2003: 1398) for *utužiti: obratiti se sudu ili mjerodavnom tijelu radi primjene zakona ili propisa u obliku tužbe; tražiti sudskim putem;* and *utuživ: 1. onaj protiv kojega se može pokrenuti sudska parnica; koga se može zakonski procesuirati. 2. koji ima razloga za sudsku tužbu.*

Another option would be to use a descriptive paraphrase: *prava ostvariva sudskim putem* (rights enforced by a court). In my opinion, one should follow George Orwell's advice here: "Never use a long word where a short one will do" (Orwell 1946: 170). According to De Groot (2006: 427), "the desirability and the usefulness of paraphrasing as a subsidiary solution is contingent on the length and complexity of the paraphrase, and the purpose of the translation.". The purpose of the translation of terminology here lies in making terminology as transparent as possible in order to make it easier to understand the underlying concepts as emphasized in connection to the example of *raspoređivanje* (see Section 3.1).

The last option is to borrow the term *justiciability*, which is of Latin origin, and form a new term (a loan word): *justiciabilnost* and *justiciabilna prava.* For example, the Croatian Arbitration Act (Of-

---

18 Available at <http://www.infolex.hr/htm/26723.htm> (visited on 10 June 2009).

ficial Gazette, No 88/01)[19] uses the term *arbitrabilnost* (for English *arbitrability*) which is also a loan word adapted to Croatian. *Arbitrabilan predmet* would be suitable for arbitration; *justiciabilan*, on the other hand, would be suitable for court adjudication. While this last option would be plausible and transparent, Croatian lawyers are reluctant to accept new terms created in this way. Furthermore, *utuživost* is more appropriate in light of the fact that the German and Slovene translators also use national terms: *Einklagbarkeit* and *utužljivost* (see Table 5), although the internationalism *Justiziabilität* is also used in German. Finally, *utuživo* will be easily recognizable for Croatian judges, public prosecutors and attorneys as well as for the wider public. After all, consistent use of correct terminology constitutes a precondition for achieving and safeguarding legal certainty.

EN	DE	FR
justiciability	Einklagbarkeit	justiciabilité
justiciable	Einklagbar	justiciable
justiciable rights	Einklagbare Rechte	droits justiciables
IT	SL	HR
azionabilità	iztožljivost	utuživost
azionabile	iztožljivo	utuživo
diriti azionabili	iztožljivih pravic	utuživa prava

Table 6. Overview of multilingual terms from Protocol No. 30 to the Treaty of Lisbon on the Application of the Charter of Fundamental Rights of the European Union to Poland and to the United Kingdom[20] (Croatian equivalents are the author's proposals).

5. Concluding remarks

Standardization of terminology facilitates the translator's task as it speeds up the translation process and improves the quality of a transla-

19 Available at <http://narodne-novine.nn.hr/clanci/sluzbeni/233069.html> (visited on 15 May 2009).

20 Available at <http//www.eur-lex.europa.eu> (visited on 21 May 2009).

tion. As Katičić (1992: 344) put it, standardization is "a creative quest for an adequate expression". Naturally, the standardization of legal terminology calls for a strict approach. Firstly, it requires clear differentiation of terms which have to be standardized. Terms having more than one meaning are especially problematic, as are terms whose meaning in ordinary language differs from their meaning in specific fields (Wright 1997: 20), which is often the case in legal language (e.g. *consideration* in contract law or *challenge* in administrative law). Unlike terms in ordinary language usage, field-specific terms are unambiguous: "Terms, i.e., words that are assigned to concepts used in the special languages that occur in subject-field or domain-related texts" (Wright 1997: 13). Similarly, dictionary entries for words of ordinary language may include more than one equivalent, whereas only one equivalent can be correct for field-specific terms. Once the above quest is brought to an end, i.e., the appropriate equivalent is found, its consistent usage in future translations must be ensured. As illustrated by the example of two different Croatian versions of the title of the PWD, the use of inconsistent terminology or 'parallel terminology' (Gallo 2006: 192), undermines legal certainty. Cases of 'parallel terminology' could be avoided by establishing a reliable centralized terminological database. The Croatian *Euroterm* represents a step in the right direction; however, it needs considerable improvement (see Bratanić/Ilijevski/Ostroški Anić 2009: 233-260). Suffice it to say that the Croatian *Euroterm* and *Eurovoc*, as well as the *Četverojezični rječnik prava Europske unije* (EU Law Glossary with basic terminology in four languages) do not contain the above-mentioned terms *posting* and *justiciability*.

Nevertheless, the search for adequate equivalents is by all means creative. The translator's task is thus twofold: being inventive while respecting the limits of legal translation (Šarčević 2007: 50). The examples above show just how difficult the search for appropriate equivalents can be. It calls for an interdisciplinary approach, as neither linguistic nor legal knowledge alone will bring about the desired results. In addition to close cooperation between the target groups, i.e. lawyers and linguists, consulting several language versions of EU legislation is essential so as to ensure correct terminological choices and consequently reliable legal translations in Croatian.

Unfortunately, candidate countries are often under tremendous pressure to meet the benchmarks set by the European Commission. This is especially true in regard to the harmonization of the national legislation with the EU *acquis*, and Croatia is no exception. EU Directives are transposed into national law at tremendous speed. Limited resources and the lack of time result in poor-quality translations of EU legislation, which is reflected in terminological inconsistency and even inaccuracy. Linguistic mistakes are not nearly as harmful as legal mistakes in legal translation. At the end of the day, it is not linguists but lawyers who are (or at least should be) liable for them. Therefore, legal revision of the Croatian translations is a must. The legislator will have his final say in determining the terminology in a given legislative act. Sooner or later the Posted Workers Directive will be transposed into Croatian law as an obligation of the Republic of Croatia resulting from the ratification of the Stabilisation and Association Agreement (Šarčević/Čikara 2009: 194). It is our duty to ensure that the process of transposition of laws is approached with as much legal and linguistic preparation as possible. As illustrated by the example of the Posted Workers Directive, this cannot be done without joint efforts and cooperation among the relevant authorities, i.e. the Independent Translation Service in the Field of European Integration, Ministries, State Agencies and others. By attempting to offer concrete solutions to the above-mentioned terminological questions, this chapter is intended to provide an impetus to deal with terminological questions and uncertainties in due time, i.e. prior to accession. Otherwise, the translations of the *acquis* will not be reliable legal texts that can be applied by national judges.

Finally, let us not forget the possible repercussions of the failure to implement a directive. Once Croatia becomes a Member State, it could even be held liable for damages for the non-implementation of a directive. In its famous Francovich ruling the ECJ (Cases C-6/90 and C-9/90, *Francovich and Bonifaci v. Republic of Italy*, Craig/de Burca 1998: 210) declared that the State can be held liable to an individual for damages caused by its failure to implement a directive. Accordingly, an individual can choose to initiate proceedings for damages against the State for failing to transpose a directive as well as for inadequate transposition. The latter could be a result of terminological mistakes made in the translations of relevant EU legislation. Hopefully, this worst-case scenario will not become a reality in Croatia.

References

Anić, Vladimir 2006. *Veliki rječnik hrvatskoga jezika* (Croatian Dictionary). Zagreb: Novi Liber.

Black's Law Dictionary. [8]2004. St. Paul, Minnesota: West.

Bratanić, Maja / Ilijevski, Vedrana / Ostoški Anić Ana 2009. Croatian Euroterm – the Case for National and EU Harmonization in the Field of Law. In Šarčević (ed.), 233-260.

Četverojezični rječnik prava Europske unije (EU Law Glossary with basic terminology in four languages) 2003. Zagreb: Hrvatska informaijsko-dokumentacijsko referalna agencija i Ministarstvo za europske integracije.

Constantinesco, Léontin.-Jean 1983. *Rechtsvergleichung: Band II: Die rechtsvergleichende Methode,* Köln: Carl Heymanns.

Chroma, Martha 2004. *Legal Translation and the Dictionary*. Tübingen: Max Niemeyer.

Craig, Paul / de Búrca, Gráinne 1998. *EU Law: Text, Cases and Materials*. Oxford: Oxford University Press.

De Groot, Gerard René 2006. Legal Translation. In Smiths, Jan M. (ed.) *Elgar Encyclopaedia of Comparative Law*. Cornwall, UK: Edward Elgar, 423-431.

Gačić, Milica 2004. *Englesko-hrvatski rječnik prava* (English Croatian Dictionary of Law). Zagreb: Ljevak.

Gallo, Giovanni 2006. Organisation and Features of Translation Activities at the Court of Justice of the European Communities. In Pozzo, Barbara (ed.) *Multilingualism and Harmonisation of European Law*, The Hague: Kluwer Law International, 179-197.

Hrvatski enciklopedijski rječnik (Croatian Encyclopaedic Dictionary). 2003. Zagreb: Novi Liber.

Jovanović, Jasminka / Todorović, Svetlana 2004. *Rečnik pravnih termina srpsko-englesko-francuski* (English-French-Serbian Legal Dictionary) Beograd: Savremena administracija.
Katičić, Radoslav 1992. *Jezikoslovni ogledi*. Zagreb: Školska knjiga.
Mazor, Ines 2005. *Prevođenje pravne stečevine EU-a i prevođenje hrvatskoga zakonodavstva*. Prevoditelj, 82-83.
Orwell, George 1946. Politics and the English Language. In Orwell, George 1981. *A Collection of Essays*. Harvest Books, 156-171.
Rodek, Snježana / Kosanović, Jasenka 2004. *Njemačko-hrvatski poslovni rječnik* (Deutsch-Kroatisches Wirtschaftswörterbuch) Zagreb: Masmedia.
Sikirić, Hrvoje 2007. Jezik u pravu. In Barbić, Jakša (ed.). *Godišnjak Tribine*. Zagreb: Faculty of Law, University of Zagreb, 135-159.
Šarčević, Susan 2000. *New Approach to Legal Translation*. The Hague: Kluwer Law International.
Šarčević, Susan. 2001. *Legal Translation: Preparation for Accession to the European Union*. Rijeka: Faculty of Law.
Šarčević, Susan 2007. Making Multilingualism Work in the Enlarged European Union. In Kredens, Krzysztof / Gozdz-Roszkowski, Stanislaw (eds) *Language and the Law: International Outlooks*. Frankfurt am Main: Peter Lang, 35-57.
Šarčević, Susan / Čikara, Emilia 2009. European vs, National Terminology in Croatian Legislation. In Šarčević (ed.), 193-214.
Šarčević, Susan (ed.) 2009. *Legal Language in Action: Translation, Terminology, Drafting and Procedural Issues*. Zagreb: Globus.
Van Laer, Conrad / van Laer, Tom 2007. The Shortage of Legal Dictionaries Translating European Languages. *Terminology* 13/1, 85-92.
Wright, Sue Ellen / Budin, Gerhard 1997. *Handbook of Terminology Management*. Vol. I. Amsterdam: John Benjamins.
Wüster, Eugen 1985. *Einführung in die allgemeine Terminologielehre und terminologische Lexikographie*. Copenhagen: HEPU-tryk.

JAN ROALD / SUNNIVA WHITTAKER

Verbalization in French and Norwegian Legislative Texts: A Contrastive Case Study

1. Introduction

Contrastive studies of legislative texts can be a means to many ends. Texts can be compared not only with regard to their legal intent, but also with a view to identifying terminological equivalences or describing variation in textual features across languages and cultures. This study falls into the latter category. Our aim is to compare how concepts are verbalized in French and Norwegian legislative texts and to explore various factors that come into play. The investigation of this type of research question is greatly aided by the fact that EU member states, and in many cases also EEA countries such as Norway, are obliged to transpose EU directives into national legislation. The fact that texts are based on the same directives makes it easier to identify concepts across texts and languages than is the case of 'home grown' legislative texts. It is thereby possible to build a corpus of comparable texts that deal with the same subject matters, but are at the same time subject to national genre norms.[1] The concepts we find in these texts may be verbalized in a variety of ways. Lawmakers may choose to coin new terms, use already existing terminology, re-

---

1 The term 'comparable texts' must not be confused with the term 'parallel texts'. The latter term is used by Šarčevič to describe texts of the same instrument existing in two or more languages (Šarčević 2000: 21). Comparable texts are authentic texts of the same text type that have the same subject matter and the same communicative function. Even though the transposed texts are based on the same directives, they are not texts of the same instrument. It is also worth noting that the Member states are free to choose both the form and the means of meeting the goals laid down in the directive.

sort to paraphrases or leave concepts implicit. In this chapter we will present the results of a case study where we have investigated the strategies employed in French and Norwegian legislative texts for the verbalization of concepts relating to legal persons.

Concepts pertaining to legal persons lend themselves particularly well to the type of study we wish to undertake. Law regulates social activities and the persons performing these activities are at the core of any legal text. As the rights and obligations of legal persons change according to the type of activity they are engaged in or which step in a given process they are in, there are often a host of concepts, and potentially also terms, relating to these legal persons.[2]

The subject field we have chosen to investigate is public procurement. This field merits attention for both theoretical and practical reasons. Legislative texts on public procurement describe a competitive process involving two main parties: public bodies interested in purchasing goods, services or works and economic operators interested in providing these goods, services or works. These two parties are at the fore in the entire process and concepts relating to them are verbalized in a number of ways in the legislative texts. This makes them excellent candidates for a contrastive study on verbalization. From a more practical point of view, this subject field is particularly relevant because it is not only a highly important sector of the global economy, but also one of the cornerstones of the EEA agreement.[3] Within the EU, public procurement accounts for 16.3% of the GDP[4] at the present time and is likely to increase as a result of the financial crisis. As companies from different countries often compete for contracts, there is a great demand for translations of texts pertaining to this activity, and thereby a need for knowledge on relevant terminology as well as on the underlying concept system. Comprehending the

---

2 Pilke (2000) calls this type of dynamic relation between concepts a 'conceptual role-changing relationship'.

3 The European Economic Area was established in 1994 following an agreement between the European Community, the EU member states and Norway, Iceland and Lichtenstein. As a result Norway must enact legislation similar to the legislation passed in the EU countries in the areas covered by the agreement, e.g. company law, consumer protection and social policy.

4 <http://europa.eu/publicprocurement/index_en.htm>.

role(s) played by the legal persons within this subject field is therefore crucial to understanding the entire concept system of public procurement.

2. Empirical basis and methodology

Both France and Norway have amended their legislation on public procurement to meet the goals laid down by the European directive 2006/066/EC. Our corpus consists of the French *Code des marchés publics* (consolidated version 2009) and the Norwegian Law 1999 amended 2007 and regulations 2006 called *Offentlige anskaffelser*. The French *Code des marchés publics* is divided into four parts and a total of 179 sections. The total number of words is 35,025. The Norwegian law text, on the other hand, comprises only twelve sections (1,695 words) and the regulations 26 sections (22,954 words). There is thus a substantial discrepancy with regard to length and form of presentation (one French text versus two Norwegian texts, covering the same subject matter). These differences are an important aspect of the genre norms in the two legal cultures under investigation. We will discuss these genre norms in more detail further on.

Our methodology has consisted in close reading of the legislative texts with a view to identifying the status of the legal persons in the different steps of the competitive process. All verbalizations of legal persons have been extracted and systematized in both languages.[5] In the following, we will present the results for each party in the competitive process separately.

---

5 In recent years automatic term extraction has become increasingly popular due to advances in computational linguistics and the existence of large digitalized corpora (cf. Auger/Barrière 2008). Automatic term extraction is possible when terms have formal characteristics or occur in identifiable knowledge patterns, i.e. indicators of conceptual relations or attributes. In our case this has not been a viable solution as the mentions in question do not always correspond to terms or occur in specific knowledge patterns.

3. The public bodies

The legislation on public procurement applies when the procuring body matches the definition of 'contracting authority'.[6] The terms used in the French and the Norwegian texts are only provided with extensional definitions, i.e. a list of the type of public bodies and utility sector bodies that have the authority to award contracts. The terms corresponding to *contracting authority* in the French text – *pouvoir adjudicateur* (for public bodies, i.e. government, regional and local authorities) and *entités adjudicatrices* (for certain utility sector bodies) – were coined in connection with the drafting of the EU directive.[7] These polylexical units contain a highly frequent head noun (*pouvoir, entité*) and a modifying adjective derived from the verb *adjuger* (to award) and their meaning is thereby readily understood. These compound nouns are exclusively used in the context of public procurement.

Norwegian lawmakers, on the other hand, have chosen to use an already existing term – *oppdragsgiver* – covering both types of contracting authorities. The term is an agentive derivation of the verb *gi* (to give) meaning someone who gives a commission. It is used in a wide range of contexts other than public procurement concerning all types of commissions. In this particular context, however, the term acquires the additional feature of 'public body'. This narrow meaning of the term is not registered in dictionaries. The French equivalents offered in bilingual dictionaries are *employeur, mandant, commettant* and *donneur d'ordre*, none of which would be a correct rendering in the context of public procurement.

Both the French and the Norwegian texts are consistent in their use of these terms to designate this party in the process. In both cases the concept underlying these terms is specifically related to the public bodies' function in the competitive process.

---

6 An additional requirement is that the estimated value of the contract exceeds the threshold determined by the EU.

7 In texts prior to the directive the term *personne responsable du marché* with the acronym PRM was used.

To conclude regarding this party in the process, French lawmakers have chosen to coin new terms to designate public bodies in their role as contracting authorities, whereas their Norwegian counterparts have chosen to use a well-established term, giving it a narrower meaning.

4. The economic operators

The other party in the competitive process, i.e. the economic operators interested in providing goods, services or works, gives rise to many concepts. Economic operators can be classified according to the type of activity they engage in: *constructors, service providers* and *suppliers.*[8] This classification is based on the economic operators' permanent features, i.e. the designation is valid also outside the competitive process. They can, however, also be classified according to their status in the competitive process. At the outset, when the invitation to tender is issued, the relevant economic operators are *interested parties*. When they submit their tenders, they become *tenderers*. In the selection process, they are *candidates* and once the selection has been made, they can be divided into *successful* and *unsuccessful candidates*. When the contract has been awarded, the selected candidate is the *awardee*, and upon signature of the contract, the awardee becomes a *contracting party*. These latter designations are referentially non-autonomous, i.e. the referents can only be identified with reference to the competitive process. The concepts relating to this party can in other words be systematized both in a hierarchical structure and according to the outcome of the competitive process.

In the French legislative text, concepts relating to this party are lexicalized in a number of manners. The term *opérateur économique*,

8 These concepts are a part of a hierarchical system and each of them has various hyponyms. However, the hyponyms are not activated in the texts in question.

as well as the three hyponyms *fournisseur, prestataire de service* and *entrepreneur* are all used. In addition, the text contains the following terms relating to the various steps of the process: *soumissionnaire, candidat retenu / non retenu, participant au dialogue, lauréat, attributaire, titulaire, partie contractante.*[9]

The latter terms are found in the parts of the text that deal with the specific steps in the process. The terms are either agentive deverbal nominalizations or high frequency words that acquire a narrower contextual sense. Their meaning is transparent and the context generally provides information making it possible to establish coreference, as in the following example where the terms *opérateur économique* and *titulaire* are coreferential:

(1) Lorsqu'un accord-cadre est attribué à un seul opérateur économique, le pouvoir adjudicateur peut, préalablement à la conclusion des marchés fondés sur l'accord-cadre, demander au titulaire de l'accord-cadre de compléter, par écrit, son offre.

As we can see, the discourse referent is designated in two different ways in the same sentence. The term *titulaire de l'accord-cadre* is used as an unfaithful anaphor with *un seul opérateur économique* as its antecedent. In the first part of the sentence, a given step in the process (the awarding of a framework contract) is explained and this explanation paves the way for the recategorization of the discourse referent, *titulaire* (awardee). In this particular case, the move is from a designation based on the referent's permanent features to a designation referring to the referent's status in the process. The same device can also be used to move from a designation relating to one step in the process to a designation relating to the next step:[10]

(2) La procédure de dialogue compétitif est une procédure dans laquelle le pouvoir adjudicateur conduit un dialogue avec les candidats admis à y participer en vue de définir ou de développer une ou plusieurs solutions de nature à

9 There are three different types of competitive process: open, restricted and negotiated. The term *participant au dialogue* is only relevant in the context of processes with negotiations.

10 Lundquist (2007a) calls this type of anaphor 'evolving anaphors'.

répondre à ses besoins et sur la base de laquelle ou desquelles les participants au dialogue seront invités à remettre une offre.

The use of unfaithful anaphors is an efficient way of recategorizing an already known discourse referent, providing the context yields enough information to establish coreference (Kleiber 1993; Lundquist 2007b).

The Norwegian text, on the other hand, makes very little use of this device. One term is used almost consistently throughout the text, namely *leverandør*. This term is an agentive derivation of the verb *levere* 'to deliver'. The terms *anbyder* (tenderer) and *vinner* (winner) are used on very rare occasions, but never in the same section as *leverandør*. The latter term can take on a number of context-dependent meanings. It is most commonly used to describe an actor in a situation that is anchored to a specific occurrence in the referent world, i.e. to designate an entity that delivers something specific at a given point in time. It is also used in hypothetical mental spaces as the reciprocal term to customer and presupposes that a commercial transaction, generally involving goods, has taken place. In the context of a competitive process, however, it is employed in the sense of economic operator, i.e. a legal person who can potentially deliver goods, services or works. However, depending on the context, the extension of the term can be narrowed down to tenderer, i.e. a legal person interested in delivering goods, services or works, or even more to contracting party, i.e. the economic operator who will de facto be delivering goods, services or works. The different meanings of the term are illustrated in the examples below:

(3) Oppdragsgiver skal for anskaffelser som overstiger 100.000 kroner kreve at samtlige norske leverandører som leverer tilbud fremlegger skatteattest for merverdiavgift og skatteattest for skatt.
[For procurements exceeding 100,000 kroner the contracting authority shall request that all Norwegian economic operators who submit tenders present VAT declarations and tax declarations. (Our translation)]

(4) Oppdragsgiver kan innhente nærmere opplysninger hos leverandørene for å få klarlagt uklarheter og ufullstendigheter i tilbudene.
[The contracting authority may ask for additional information from the tenderers in order to clarify ambiguities and omissions in the tenders. (Our translation)]

(5) Oppdragsgivers beslutning om hvem som skal tildeles kontrakt eller som er valgt til leverandør til rammeavtalen skal meddeles til alle deltakerne innen rimelig tid før kontrakt eller rammeavtale inngås.
[The contracting authority shall inform all participants of its decision regarding who will be awarded the contract or who is selected as party to the framework agreement in due time before the contract or the framework agreement is signed. (Our translation)]

The use of the term *leverandør* in the legislative text is a good illustration of the fact that the nature of terms in a specialized text can be as chameleonic as words in non-specialized discourse (cf. Antia 2001).

Interestingly, the Norwegian text does not distinguish explicitly between suppliers of goods, service providers and constructors. Instead of this classification, which we find in the French text, the Norwegian text distinguishes between three types of contracts (pertaining to works, services or goods). The existence of three types of economic operators can be inferred from the classification of contracts but is explicitated only in sections dealing specifically with works where the term *entreprenør* (constructor) is used. The term *leverandør* thereby covers all three types of economic operators in the context of public procurement, whereas its most common meaning in Norwegian is 'supplier of goods'. The broader meaning of the term in the context of public procurement is not registered in bilingual Norwegian–French dictionaries, where the only equivalent provided is *fournisseur* (supplier of goods). The Norwegian Ministry of Foreign Affairs terminology bank, which specifically deals with EU terminology, also lists *fournisseur* as the only equivalent. The term therefore represents a considerable pitfall for translators. In contrast to the French text which makes use of a wide range of lexicalizations specifying the discourse referent's status at a given step in the process, the Norwegian text tends to use the term *leverandør* at all steps of the process. When necessary, the change of status is specified using a relative clause or a pronominal paraphrase: *leverandør som er utvalgt* (the economic operator who is selected), *den som får tildelt kontrakten* (the one who is awarded the contract). The change of status of the discourse referent is simply inferred from the context. There is, in other words, a striking difference in how this party in the process is verbalized in the two texts. The Norwegian text uses almost exclusively one term, the meaning of which is context-dependent. This term is used with or without a modifying clause, and pronominal paraphrases specifying the meaning. The French text, on the other hand, makes use of a plethora of lexicalizations relating either to the discourse referent's permanent features or to its function in the competitive process and switches between the various designations.

5. Discussion

Several factors can contribute to explain why these concepts are verbalized differently in the French and the Norwegian text. One important factor is the difference in length and amount of detail. As mentioned earlier, the Norwegian legislative text (law and regulations) is more succinct than the French *Code des marchés publics*. It is reasonable to assume that there is a correlation between the degree of elaboration and the degree of lexicalization of concepts. The Norwegian law contains only 1,695 words. There is, in other words, scant context for the introduction of new terms. The regulations are much longer and provide more detail, but adhere to the same terminology as the law text. The French Code has much longer sections and each provision is therefore dealt with in more detail in one coherent text. Access to a larger context makes it easier to establish coreference between different designations used in the text.

Stylistic differences between the languages the texts are written in also affect the genre norms. One very important aspect, which has already been touched upon, is the use of unfaithful anaphors in the French text. Korzen and Lundquist (2005) have observed that this type of anaphor is much more frequently used in Romance languages than in Germanic languages.[11] As we have seen, this is a very convenient

11 Korzen and Lundquist (2005) also claim that the use of unfaithful anaphors can be explained by systemic differences between Germanic and Romance languages. Romance languages are exocentric i.e. convey more precise infor-

device for recategorizing already-known discourse referents. Coreference is inferred from the information provided in the context. According to Korzen and Lundquist, the abundant use of unfaithful anaphors in Romance languages is a cultural phenomenon. It is a part of a rhetorical tradition where stylistic variation is favoured. Using different designations for the same discourse referent is one way of ensuring variation. In the Germanic rhetoric tradition, on the other hand, avoiding ambiguity is of paramount importance and lexical repetition is preferred at the expense of variation. These rhetorical preferences seem highly relevant for the results of our study. In contrast to the French text, the Norwegian text contains many examples where the discourse referent is mentioned twice in the same sentence, using the same designation:

(6) Anskaffelsens anslåtte verdi beregnes på grunnlag av oppdragsgivers anslag av det samlede beløp oppdragsgiver kan komme til å betale, eksl. mva. for de kontrakter som utgjør anskaffelsen.
[The estimated value of the procurement is calculated on the basis of the contracting authority's estimate of the total amount the contracting authority will have to pay (excl. VAT) for the procurement contracts. (our translation)]

Higher tolerance for lexical repetition in Norwegian than in French may be part of the explanation of why the same terms are used throughout the Norwegian text. Another stylistic factor that comes into play is a lower propensity for nominalizations in Norwegian than in French. The term 'noun disease' is often employed to characterize texts with a high ratio of nominalizations to verbs (Inselset *et al.* 2008).

The frequent use of nominalizations in a text is explicitly associated with stilted language and language users are advised to use verbal phrases instead. This rule applies first and foremost for general language, but it does seem to have an effect on legal language. Research in LSP has shown that nominalizations are an important feature of specialized texts due to the fact that they make it possible to

---

mation through nouns whereas Germanic languages choose to package more information in verbs. For a more detailed presentation of this theory see Lundquist (2005)

classify abstract notions such as properties, actions and states (Andersen 1998; Arbogast 2008; Lerat 1995). Norwegian for special purposes is no exception (cf. Andersen 1989). It is, however, reasonable to assume that when the receivers of specialized texts are non-specialists, the text producers will strive to keep their writing style more in line with general language use. As pointed out by Šarčević (2000: 58), legislative texts have collective addressees, including the general public. This has led to campaigns advocating plain legal language in many countries (c.f. Stern 2008; Wagner/Cacciaguidi-Fahy 2006).

In Norway, a campaign called *Klarspråk* (clear language) has been launched, calling for the use of plain language in all texts produced for the general public by the public authorities (cf. Klarspråk-regjeringen.no). The fact that a high frequency of nominalizations is considered to render a text more opaque may explain why the Norwegian text resorts to expressions such as *den som får tildelt kontrakten* (the one who is awarded the contract) instead of the corresponding nominalization *anbudsvinneren* (the awardee). As we have seen, the rhetorical tradition in France is no hindrance to the use of different lexicalizations of the same discourse referent.

6. Conclusion

The various factors discussed above all seem to have a bearing on the paucity of terms for the concepts under investigation in the Norwegian text. As mentioned earlier, the verbalization of legal persons is particularly interesting since the same discourse referent can give rise to a host of concepts. Further research is required to establish whether some of the differences observed in French and Norwegian legislative texts can be generalized to other types of concepts. Regardless of whether this proves to be the case, the results of this study are relevant for translators and other professionals working with texts on public procurement in both languages. Existing lexical resources are far from sophisticated enough and, as we have seen, the differences in the way concepts relating to legal persons are verbalized can lead to many pitfalls in translation. Our study also illustrates the hurdles automatic term extraction programs are faced with when it comes to legal terminology. Many of the verbalizations of concepts we have identified would have escaped attention in a term extraction program and could therefore not replace an onomasiological approach, which seems to remain the only viable solution to mapping legal terminology across languages.

References

Andersen, Øivin 1989. Fagspråk som forskningsdisiplin. *Hermes, Journal of Linguistics* 3, 73-98.

Andersen, Øivin 1998. *Lingvistikk og dokumentasjonsbasert thesaurus-konstruksjoner*, HIT-senterets publikasjonsserie 1/98, Bergen.

Arbogast Gerzymisch, Heidrun 2008. Fundamentals of LSP Translation. In Heidrun Gerzymisch Arbogast (ed.) *LSP Translation Scenarios*. Thematic Volumes on Multidimensional Translation 2. ATRC Group.

Antia, Bassey Edem 2001. Terminological Investigations into Specialized Knowledge and Texts. *Terminology* 7/1, 5-29.

Auger Alain / Barrière Caroline 2008. Pattern-based Approaches to Semantic Relation Extraction. *Terminology* 14/1, 1-19.

Innselset, Kai / Kristiansen, Marita / Øvsthus, Kari 2008. Looking back to Move Forward. Challenges Related to Deceitful Parallel Texts and Slippery Terms. *Synaps, Festskrift for Magnar Brekke.* Norges Handelshøyskole.

Klarspråk – regjeringen.no, St.meld 35 (2007 – 2008), <www.regjeringen.no/nn/dep/kkd/dokument>.

Kleiber, G. 1993. Anaphore associative, pontage et stéréotypie. *Linguisticae Investigationes* 17/1, 35-82.

Korzen, Iørn / Lundquist, Lita (eds) 2005. *Sprogtypologi og oversættelse.* Copenhagen: Samfundslitteratur.

Lerat, Pierre 1995. *Les langues spécialisées.* Paris: PUF.

Lundquist, Lita 2005. Noms, verbes et anaphores (in)fidèles: Pourquoi les Danois sont plus fidèles que les Français. *Langue française* 1/145, 75-92.

Lundquist, Lita 2007a. Comparing Evolving Anaphors in Danish and French. In Korzen, Iørn / Lundquist, Lita (eds) *Comparing Anaphors.* Copenhagen: Samfundslitteratur Press.

Lundquist, Lita. 2007b. Lexical Anaphors in Danish and French. In Schwarz-Friesel, Monika / Consten, Manfred / Knees, Mareile (eds) *Anaphors in Text.* Amsterdam: John Benjamins, 37-48.

Pilke, Nina 2000. *Dynamiska fackbegrep*, Acta Wasaensia 81, University of Wasa.

Šarčević, Susan 2000. *New Approach to Legal Translation.* The Hague: Kluwer Law International.

Stern, George 2008. *From Officialese to Plain English.* Centre for Continuing Education, Law and Justice Foundation, The Australian National University, <www.lawfoundation.net.au/ljf/>.

Wagner, Anne / Cacciaguidi-Fahy, Sophie 2006. *Legal Language and the Search for Clarity.* Bern: Peter Lang.

LELIJA SOČANAC

Linguistic Transference in Croatian Law Articles

1. Introduction

Influences of different legal cultures can be shown to change over a certain period of time. Foreign influences on national legal science can be shown by analysing loanwords and citations in foreign languages using statistical methods (Mattila 2006). This chapter will present results of research based on a corpus of Croatian law articles. The diachronic perspective offers an overview of different political and legal systems in Croatia in the past sixty years, from the Yugoslav Communist period, the war of independence in the 1990s, to recent trends of globalization and internationalization of law. By dividing citations and loanwords into groups according to donor languages, we shall try to identify which foreign legal cultures have influenced national legal thinking and, indirectly, the legal system of Croatia in the periods under consideration.

The corpus[1] used for this study consists of articles from *Zbornik Pravnog fakulteta u Zagrebu*, the journal of the Faculty of Law, University of Zagreb. Since this is only the beginning of a more extensive research on the topic, the corpus is not comprehensive but comprises individual samples: articles on various areas of law published in 1955, 1972, 1991 and 2008, exemplifying the periods marking certain historical transition points: 1955 exemplifying a decade marked by Yugoslavia's growing orientation towards the West, 1972 following student demonstrations and the suppressed 'Croatian spring' movement characterized by strong demands for political liberalization, market eco-

1 I would like to thank Ivana Težak-Bogović for her valuable assistance in collecting the corpus on which this chapter is based.

nomy and greater autonomy of the republics, 1991 marking the break-up of Yugoslavia and Croatian independence, and 2008 as the most recent period marked by Croatia's efforts to join the EU.

A quantitative method has first been applied to establish major sources of lexical transfers in the periods under consideration. The next step was to classify the data according to types of linguistic influence and areas of law where major legal languages left their impact. Finally, we have tried to establish motivation for transference.

2. Historical overview

In order to be able to correlate the socio-political framework with issues of language policies and planning, I will try to give a brief outline of Croatian history, focusing on more recent periods.

As a civil law country, Croatia's legal system is based on Roman law. Since continental Croatia was part of the Habsburg Monarchy for four centuries (1527-1918), the dominant influence was that of Austrian law. The French Civil Code was briefly introduced in Istria and Dalmatia during the short Napoleonic rule in the area (1797-1814), but it did not leave a significant impact (Steindorff 2006: 98). In 1816 it was replaced by *The Allgemeines bürgerliches Gesetzbuch (ABGB)*, the Austrian Civil Code, which was a major influence in all successor states of Austria-Hungary (Margetić *et al.* 2005).

After the disintegration of Austria-Hungary following World War I, Croatia became part of the Kingdom of Yugoslavia. The beginnings of a new republic, replacing the former monarchy, can be traced back to 1943. The Federal People's Republic of Yugoslavia was established in 1945 based on the principle of people's rule and the new state as a federal republic, with a bicameral federal assembly and centralized state administration. Significant changes took place between 1946 and 1953, such as Tito's breakup with Stalin (1948) followed by a growing orientation towards the West, the beginnings of the non-alignment movement and workers' self-management. The period after 1955 was marked by growing economic development, industrialization, and urbanization (Karaman 1980; Margetić *et al.* 2005).

The Constitution of the Federal People's Republic of Yugoslavia of 1946 was based on the Soviet Constitution of 1936, with federalism, collective ownership and state regulated economy as the main underlying principles. The constituent Yugoslav republics were entitled to have their own constitutions based on the federal Constitution; as a result, the Constitution of the People's Republic of Croatia was passed in 1947 (Margetić *et al.* 2005).

With the Yugoslav Constitution of 1963 the name of the state changed to the Socialist Federal Republic of Yugoslavia. Extensive economic reforms were initiated in 1964, granting more autonomy to economic subjects, with the aim of increasing productivity and promoting greater integration into the international economy. In 1966, radical reforms of state security started, opening the process of democratization. Borders became increasingly open, with large numbers of guest workers finding jobs in Western Europe, especially Germany (Goldstein 1996; Steindorff 2006).

Aspirations towards greater democratization increased during the 1970s demanding greater political, economic and national freedoms. The Constitution of 1974 affirmed the statehood/ sovereignty of the six constituent Yugoslav republics as well as the provinces of Kosovo and Vojvodina, thus creating new federal-confederal relations (Margetić *et al.* 2005).

The 1980s were marked by a precipitating economic crisis, the rise of formerly suppressed nationalisms, and clashes between authoritarian centralization efforts on the one hand, and the concept of political pluralism, sovereignty of the republics and market economy, on the other. The tensions erupted in the war which started in 1991 and lasted for four years. Croatia gained international recognition as an independent state in 1991 (Goldstein 1996; Steindorff 2006).

3. Language policies

This brief historical overview has been given as a framework determining to a large extent language policies. During the Austro-Hungarian rule, Latin remained the official language of the Croatian parliament until 1847 as an instrument of resistance to growing Germanization and Hungarization. In 1847 Croatian was introduced as the language of the Croatian parliament (Pavletić *et al.* 1997). The second half of the 19th century was marked by Pan-Slavic ideas, resistance to German dominance and purist efforts which resulted in replacing a large number of German and Hungarian loanwords by Croatian calques (Sočanac 2005).

Prior to the 19th century, the three Croatian dialects – Kajkavian, Čakavian and Štokavian – had the status of literary languages, with their own grammars and dictionaries and a corpus of literary works. With the language reforms of 1835 Štokavian was taken as the basis which could bring Croatian and Serbian together to form a common standard. Eventually, Serbo-Croatian became the official language of the Yugoslav state. In 1953 Serbo-Croatian was proclaimed the official language of the Federal People's Republic of Yugoslavia, with two varieties: Ijekavian and Ekavian, and two scripts (Latin and Cyrillic) (Franolić 1980; Moguš 1995).

In 1966, the *Declaration on the name and status of the Croatian language* was signed, proposing to introduce Slovene, Croatian, Serbian and Macedonian as equal official languages in the Yugoslav Federal Assembly, stressing the equality of Croatian with respect to Serbian, and pointing to the fact that the two languages had not been equal in practice in spite of official proclamations. The *Declaration* was publicly condemned and its authors were banned from public life (Moguš 1995; Goldstein 1996; Steindorff 2006).

With the Constitution of 1991, Croatian was proclaimed the official language of the Republic of Croatia. The 1990s were marked by a radical divergence from Serbian and strong purist efforts targeted against foreign lexical elements, especially Anglicisms whose presence increased at the time due to the rising status of English as the global language. The purist efforts were highly successful in rejecting Serbian elements, but had very little success in preventing the influx of English in the forms which moved away from traditional lexical borrowing to code-switching, syntactical influences (heavy nominalizations) and the growing hybridization of language (Sočanac/Nikolić-Hoyt 2006).

4. Language contact phenomena

Early studies in the field of contact linguistics mainly focused on lexical borrowing (Filipović 1960). Since the early 1970s there has been a growing interest in code-switching (CS), as the alternation of different languages within the same speech event. In various theoretical approaches (e.g. Milroy/Muysken 1995; Myers-Scotton 1997), CS has gradually encompassed different kinds of language contact phenomena, making it difficult to differentiate between CS and borrowing – the main criteria for differentiation being bilingualism, frequency and integration. In addition, while CS is employed both for single and multi-word elements, borrowing is usually limited to single word items. Borrowings are part of the lexicon of the matrix language while code-switches belong to the embedded-language lexicon (Myers-Scotton 2002; Clyne 2003).

In our analysis we will apply Clyne's terminological framework based on transference, which can be divided into lexical, multiple, morphemic, semantic, syntactic, graphemic, prosodic and pragmatic. Transfer is an instance of transference, with transference being the process and a transfer the product (Clyne 2003: 76).

5. Donor languages

Legal languages that have had an impact on Croatian legal terminology were traditionally Latin and German. The French influence was present due to its status as the international language of diplomacy, while the English influence has been growing throughout the twentieth century and the beginning of the twenty-first century (Sočanac 2005).

The first aim in our corpus analysis has been to determine the main sources of borrowing, i.e. the main donor languages. The results are as follows:

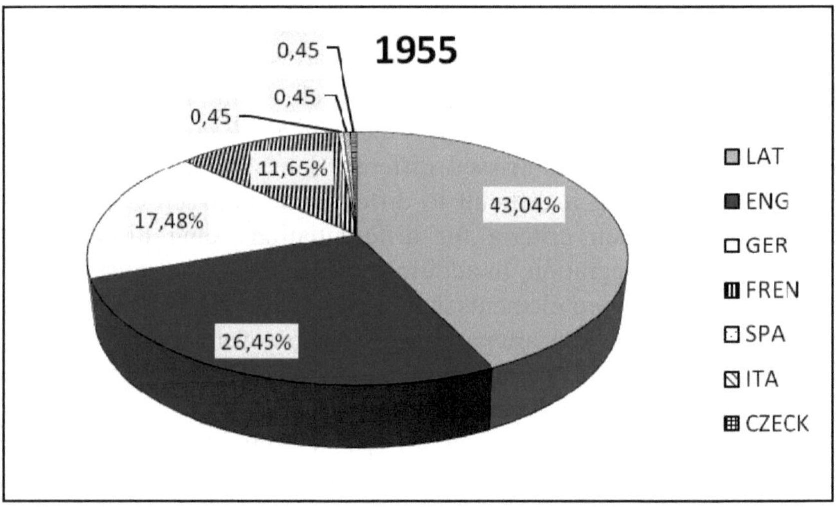

Figure 1: Main donor languages in 1955.

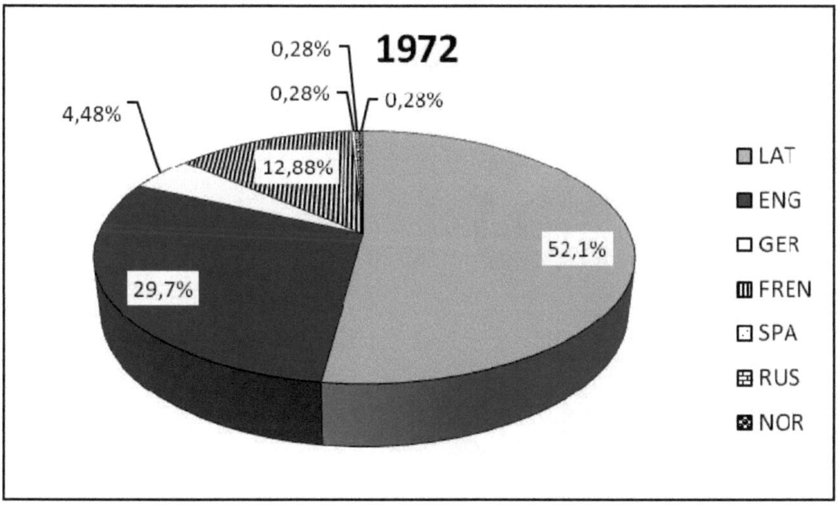

Figure 2: Main donor languages in 1972.

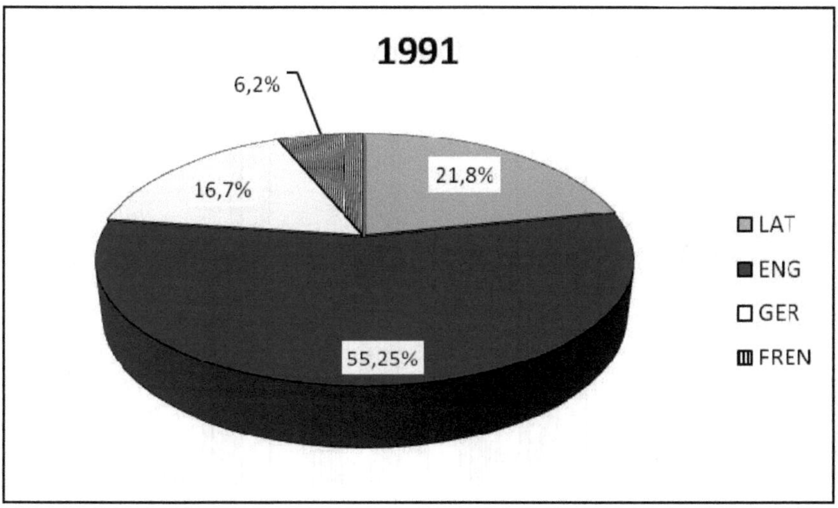

Figure 3: Main donor languages in 1991.

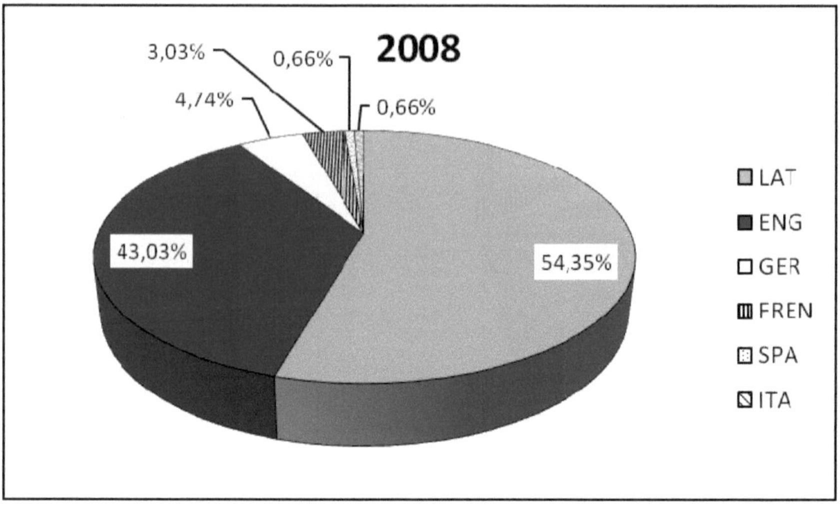

Figure 4: Main donor languages in 2008.

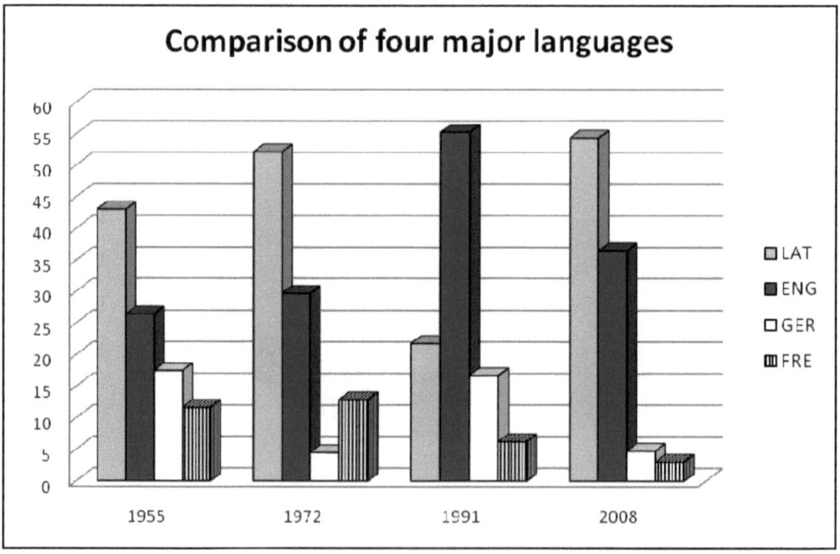

Figure 5: Comparison of the four main donor languages.

According to our data, Latin continued to be the main source of borrowing in most periods under consideration (1955: 43.04%; 1972: 52.1%, 2008: 54.35%,); the only exception was our 1991 corpus where English accounted for 55.25% of the borrowings, while Latin ranked second (21.8%), with English being the first most important donor language in 1991, and then reverting to second place in 2008. German mainly occupied the third, and French the fourth position. Given the fact that Croatia traditionally belonged to the German (more specifically, Austrian) legal culture, the percentage of German transfers is rather low. After World War II, this could be accounted for by negative language attitudes, whereas today it could be a result of insufficient language competence. The presence of other languages in our corpus is negligible.

6. Types of lexical transfers and areas of law

6.1. Latin transfers

Latin has left an important impact on all modern legal languages, in the form of a large number of words of Latin origin, loan translations, quotations and maxims, which are more often used in legal science than in legal practice (Mattila 2006). The influence of legal Latin is very strong in our corpus in all periods under consideration.

Excluding a huge number of Europeanisms coined from Latin and Greek elements, we have focused on Latin words and expressions in legal texts. What we could find is that multiple transfers in the form of expressions, maxims and quotations are far more frequent than single-word lexical transfers. The examples of single-word lexical transfers include the following:

1. Nouns: *animus, causa, civitas, commissium, corpus, denuntiatio, dicta, diffidatio, diminutio, dolus, fas, heres, interpellatio, ius, mora, nasciturus, novum, omissio, praeda, ratio, situs, successor;*

2. Verbs: *credo (>n.), facere;*
3. Adverbs: *tacite;*
4. Prepositions: *contra, pro;*
5. Cohesive devices: *infra, infra ad, supra, et seq.*

To be sure, Latin fixed expressions are very frequent, such as *ad acta, conditio sine qua non, de facto, de iure, de lege, de lege ferenda, de lege lata ex lege, in abstracto, ipso facto, ipso iure, lege artis, mutatis mutandis, nota bene, per se, pro futuro, status quo, sui generis.*

Regarding the prevalence of inserted Latin expressions, maxims, and quotations, the question is how to qualify them. They are obviously not simple lexical transfers; one is therefore tempted to describe them as instances of code-switching, which is rather unusual because in the vast majority of cases code-switching has been studied as an alternation between two spoken languages. Code-switching in written texts has been studied to a far lesser extent, while studies of code-switching between a living language and a 'dead' one are virtually non-existent. The main precondition for code-switching is bilingualism: in this case it would be learned bilingualism involving a good knowledge of legal Latin. If we take as our starting point the division into intersentential, intrasentential and tag switching, with Croatian as the matrix language and Latin as the embedded language, a number of examples would fall into the category of *tag switching*, involving insertion of fixed phrases:

(1) u zemlji u kojoj se, zahvaljujući zbiljskom funkcioniranju demokratskih ustanova, radi ostvarenja pravde *in concreto* može razmišljati i o odstupanju od principa koji je ipak tek instrumentalnog karatkera. (*Zbornik FFZ* 1991) [in a country where, thanks to the actual functioning of democratic institutions, we can speak of the realization of justice *in concreto,* we can also speak about giving up the principle which is of a merely institutional character after all.]

(2) Uostalom, isto vrijedi, *mutatis mutandis*, za komparativna istraživanja i historijske usporedbe (*Zbornik PFZ* 1991) [The same is true, *mutatis mutandis*, for comparative research and historical parallels.]

- Intrasentential switching:

(3) Uz *naturalis ratio*, koja je, smatra se, sadržana kako *in iure gentium* tako i *in iure naturale*, kao kriterij priziva se i *aequitas* (*Zbornik PFZ* 1971) [In addition to *naturalis ratio*, which is considered to be contained both *in iure gentium* and *in iure naturale*, what is often taken as a criterion is *aequitas*]

(4) Tako se, primjerice, *ius vendendi* od izričito ugovorenog uglavka transformira u *tacita condicio* fiducijarnog osiguranja (znači dolazi do prijelaza od *pactum de vendendo* k *pactum de non vendendo*). (*Zbornik PFZ* 2008) [Thus, for instance, *ius vendendi* is transformed from an explicitly agreed condition to *tacita condicio* of fiduciary insurance (with a transition from *pactum de vendendo* to *pactum de non vendendo*]

(5) U tom bi smislu stranci i drugom sudioniku trebalo, *argumento a maiori ad minus*, omogućiti da se, ako oni to traže ili ako na to pristanu, u postupku umjesto 'pravim' svojim jezikom, (*Zbornik PFZ* 2008) [In this respect the party and the other participant should *argumento a maiori ad minus* be enabled to use instead of their 'true' language]

- Intersential switching:

(6) U ovom posljednjem slučaju vrijedi načelo '*Dies interpellat pro homine*'. (*Zbornik PFZ* 1955) [In the latter case, the principle '*Dies interpellat pro homine*' is valid]

In some examples, however, there is evidence of a certain degree of flexibility, reflected in the appropriate use of Latin case, gender, and plural forms according to the requirements of the matrix language (Croatian) sentence structure.

- Case:

(7) primjena *legis loci delicti* (*Zbornik PFZ* 1971) [the application /of/ *legis loci delicti*]

(8) vraćanje primjene *legis fori* (*Zbornik PFZ* 1971) [re-introduction of the application /of/ *legis fori*]

(9) pogibelj *lacunarum legis* (*Zbornik PFZ* 1971) [the danger /of/ *lacunarum legis*]

(10) primjenu odredaba *legis rei sitae* (*Zbornik PFZ* 2008) [application of provisions *legis rei sitae*]

- Gender:

(11) mjerodavn**a** je *lex rei sitae* (*Zbornik PFZ* 1971) [*lex rei sitae* is applicable (f.)]

(12) tipičn**a** *lex imperfecta* (*Zbornik PFZ* 1991) [a typical *lex imperfecta* (f.)]

Generally, code-switching is a mode of communication existing only between bilinguals: in the case of alternation between Croatian and Latin, the communication is restricted to legal professionals sharing the same educational background. A law article displaying frequent alternation between Croatian and Latin is certainly not meant for the uninitiated. This alternation, therefore, contributes to the hermetic quality of scholarly articles and has a function of an in-group code that could be qualified as elite closure.

In some cases, Latin is used for the sake of greater precision, using a generally recognized Latin expression alongside the Croatian one, or providing a Croatian term, translation or paraphrase as an explanation.

(13) Ako netko umre bez nasljednika *(sine herede)*, može svojim dobrima slobodno raspoložiti (*Zbornik PFZ* 1972) [If someone dies without a heir (*sine herede*), there is freedom of disposition]

(14) Može se stoga reći da je normativna osnova odštetnog prava postizanje tzv. korektivne (ispravljačke) pravednosti (lat. *iustitia correctiva*), (*Zbornik PFZ* 2008) [It can therefore be said that the normative basis of the law of tort is corrective justice (Lat. *iustitia correctiva*]

(15) i obuhvaća stvarnu štetu *(damnum emergens)*, izmaklu korist (*lucrum cessans*), štetu samom morskom okolišu (*Zbornik PFZ* 2008) [and it includes actual damage (*damnum emergens*) and lost benefit (*lucrum cessans*), damage to the marine environment]

Sometimes we come across Latin expressions from common law systems denoting concepts which are less known or do not exist in civil law systems. In the following example, they are followed by Croatian explanation and English definition from *Black's Law Dictionary:*

(16) *Amicus curiae* jest osoba koja nije stranka u nekom postupku, ali koja sud ili od koje sud traži da u tom postupku dostavi podnesak jer ima snažan interest u predmetu [A person who is not a party of a lawsuit but who petitions the court or is requested by the court to file a brief in the action because that person has a strong interest in the subject matter.] (*Zbornik PFZ* 2008)

Certainly, examples of CS in legal texts can be found in other languages as well, where Croatian functions as the matrix language and English, German or French as embedded languages.

6.2. English transfers

With the rising status of global English today, legal English is not limited to common law countries any more. It is one of the official languages of a large number of international organizations, one of the working languages of the EU, and the most important language of international contracts (Crystal 2003; Mattila 2006: 250). In our corpus, English has been the second most important influence in most periods under consideration. Most examples belong to the category of morphologically unadapted multiple transfers, with the exception of a rather limited number of very frequent and completely integrated lexical transfers such as *budžet* and *trend,* and a few single-word transfers mainly denoting common law concepts.

Regarding the influence of all major legal languages, including English, the most obvious examples of transfers are those denoting elements of foreign legal systems. In the case of English, most such examples involve features of the common law system. Terms denoting common law concepts are borrowed to fill the lexical gaps in the recipient language.

(17) U srednjem vijeku postoji izraz *constitution*, ali je on bio smo jedan od imena (*assize*, *provision*, *statute*, *prohibition*, itd.) kojim se označava akt (*Zbornik PFZ* 1971) [In the Middle Ages there was a term *constitution*, but it was only one of the terms (*assize*, *provision*, *statute*, *prohibition*, itd.) to denote an act]

(18) nego koja empirističku pojedinačnost u čitavom njenom šarenilu podiže na nivo norme-općenitosti, na nivo *case-precedenta* .(*Zbornik PFZ* 1971) [that elevates a range of diverse individual facts to the general level of *case-precedent*]

As a rule, multiple transfers are more frequent than single word transfers:

(19) Single-word transfers: *barrister, court, impeachment, jury, negligence, whips*

(20) Multiple transfers: *arrestable offence, checks and balances, common law, case-precedent, case method, court order to pay damages, discovery stage, duty solicitor, House of Lords, law of tort, privity rule, writs of summons*

English legal terms related to procedural law are often closely related to the English legal system:

(21) pravo petcije i pravo podnošenja peticije: *right of petition – right to petition*) u materijalnopravnom (*substantive law*) i proceduralnom (*procedural law*) smislu (*Zbornik PFZ* 199 [right of petition and right to petition in substantive and procedural law in the sense of…]

(22) postupovna pravila, koja jamče *due process of law* (*Zbornik PFZ* 1991) [procedural rules safeguarding due process of law]

(23) tzv. privilegij na uskratu iskaza, odnosno 'privilegij od (obaveze) samookrivljenja' (*the privilege against self-incrimination*) (*Zbornik PFZ* 1991) [the so-called privilege against self-incrimination]

Among the first areas where the English influence came to be felt in Croatia was the law of the sea and regulations related to ships, navigation, sea transport, and marine insurance. This is illustrated by a number of examples in our corpus:

(24) *Bare boat charter, berth-to-berth, charter by demise, clean bill of lading, flag register, general average expenditure, general average sacrifices, hazard to navigation, maritime performing party, ocean bill of lading, pilot exemption certificate, port to port, real rights register, short sea shipping, Shipboard Emergency Plan, service operating ports, single ship companies, stowage, time charterer, voyage charterer, wreck*
Hybrid forms: *chartering odjel* [chartering department]

(25) Marine insurance: *Blue Card, captive insurance, indemnity insurance, liability insurance, traditional maritime liens, pay to be paid, wilful misconduct*
Hybrid forms: *common benefit* troškovi [common benefit expenses]

In our 1955 corpus, most English transfers come from the field of employment law and trade unions:

(26) *agency shop, augmentation of labour, check-off, class action, closed shop, company-security clauses, earned income, earnings capacity, hiring hall, maintenance of membership, modified union shop, no-strike clause, preferential hiring, sole bargaining, Trade Unions, union shop*

An area where the English influence is especially strong today is international commercial and company law. Multiple transfers and hybrid forms are much more frequent than single-word transfers:

(27) Multiple transfers: *bulk purchasing, debt-equity ratio, joint venture, loss of profit, managing director, profit sliding scale, selling price sliding scale, stock, utility goods, value in use, value in exchange*
Hybrid forms: centri *off-shore* poslovanja [centres of off-shore business], *input-prerada-output procesa* [input processing of output process], *management politika* [management policy], *negative pledge klauzula* [negative pledge clause]

Today English plays an increasingly important role in international relations, as evidenced by the following multiple transfers and hybrid forms:

(28) Multiple transfers: *'affected state', coastal state, Convention area, the crime of crimes, peace-keeping forces, peace-keeping missions, peace-keeping operations, State-to-State complaints, supervisory/observer missions, umbrella organizations*

(29) Hybrid forms: *soft-law instrumenti* [soft-law instruments], *summit-diplomacija* [summit diplomacy]

6.3. German transfers

The international importance of legal German can be explained by the spread of the laws of German-speaking countries to the Baltic countries, the Nordic countries, the eastern part of Central Europe and Eastern Europe. The great codifications of the 19th and 20th centuries were particularly important in this respect. A new wave of German legislative influence was felt following the transition of the European socialist countries to the market economy in the late 1980s and early 1990s (Mattila 2006: 180-181). In our corpus, German lexical transfers, mainly in the form of compounds, denote concepts related to the German, Austrian or Swiss legal systems:

(30) *Amtsgericht, Arbeitsgericht, Bundestag, Bundesrat*; *Bundesrepublik*, *Bundesverfassungsgericht*, *Bundesnotarordnung*, *Handelsgericht, Notariatsordnung*; *Obergericht, Reich*, *Reichstag*, *Schöffengerichte*, '*Sozialistiche Reichspartei*' *Verwaltungsgerichtshof; Zivilprozeßordnung*

The German influence is also present in the theory and philosophy of law, procedural law, administrative law, constitutional law, tax law, law of contract, law of succession, employment law, etc.

- Philosophy of law:

(31) Ustavni sud zastupa mišljenje, da postoji pravo, koje prethodi svakom ustavu, i koje obavezuje ustavotvorce (tzv. *Überpositives Recht*). (*Zbornik PFZ*, 1955) [The Constitutional Court holds that there is law which precedes any constitution, and which is binding for creators of a constitution (the so-called *Überpositives Recht*]

(32) Međutim spoznalo se da ni država, koja je na nekim područjima smatrana podobnijom od tržišta, ne može riješiti sve probleme koji se pojavljuju pri suvremenoj organizaciji društva (*Theorie des Staatsversagen*) (*Zbornik PFZ*, 1991) [It has become clear that the state, which was considered to be a more appropriate agent than the market, cannot resolve all problems of modern society (*Theorie des Staatsversagen*)]

- Procedural law:

(33) *Aussetzung, Berichtigungsverfahren, Moniturverfahren Rechtsgrund, Unmittelbarkeitsgrundsatz*

- Administrative law:

(34) Ustavna žalba (*Verfassungsbeschwerde*) je moguća protiv svakog akta javne vlasti, a upućuje se Ustavnom sudu. (*Zbornik PFZ* 1955) [Constitutional appeal is possible against any act of public authorities and it is submitted to the Constitutional Court]

- Constitutional law:

(35) Ustavni sud je u toj presudi zauzeo stanovište, da može vršiti kontrolu ustavnosti ratifikacionih zakona *(Vertragsgesetz)* o nekom međunarodnom ugovoru i prije nego što ovaj stupi na snagu (*Zbornik PFZ* 1955) [The Constitutional Court held that it can control the constitutionality of ratification laws *(Vertragsgesetz)* concerning an international treaty before it comes into force]

- Tax law:

(36) To su tzv. politički porezi, ili kako ih Gerloff naziva *ordnungssteuer* (*Zbornik PFZ* 1972) [These are so-called political taxes which are referred to as *ordnungssteuer* by Gerloff]

- Insolvency law:

(37) Tako određuje čl. 59 švicarskog zakona o izvršenju i stečaju *(Schuldbetreibung und Konkurs)* (*Zbornik PFZ* 1955) [This is stipulated by Article 59 of the Swiss insolvency law *(Schuldbetreibung und Konkurs*]

- Law of inheritance:

(38) imaju sunasljednici na ostavini dio diobe tzv. skupno vlasništvo *(Gesamteigentum)* (*Zbornik PFZ* 1955) [co-heirs are entitled to share the so-called joint inheritance *(Gesamteigentum)*]

6.4. French transfers

Since the 17th century French has been an important language of legal science, the language of diplomacy and a tool of international communication in legal circles. After the Second World War, its position as a global language of lawyers has weakened, as the position of English became stronger. Today it is one of the two main working languages of Community institutions and it is still use in the frame of international organizations (Mattila 2006: 211-219). The French lexical influence can obviously be found in terms related to the French legal and political system.

(39) U starom poretku (*Ancien Régime*) sistem patrimonijalizma i privilegija dolaska na upravne položaje (*Zbornik PFZ* 1991) [During the *Ancien Régime*, the system of patrimonialism and privileges in acquiring administrative positions]

(40) *Code civil* povremeno se mijenja različitim zakonima. (*Zbornik PFZ* 2008) [*Code civil* was changed from time to time by different laws]

Furthermore, the French impact is reflected in a large number of multiple transfers in the area of administrative law.

(41) U francuskoj se literaturi mnogo operira s pojmom tzv. nepostojećeg upravnog akta (*acte inexistant*) (*Zbornik PFZ* 1955) [In French literature one often comes across the concept of non-existent public act (*acte inexistant*)]

(42) susrećemo najprije grješku u svrsi akta – tzv. *détournement de pouvoir* (*Zbornik PFZ* 1955) [in the first place we come across the mistake in the purpose of an act – the so-called *détournement de pouvoir*]

Since French has traditionally been the language of diplomacy, its impact can be found in international law:

(43) ako su odredbe njegovog nacionalnog zakona u protivnosti s javnim poretkom (*ordre public*) naše države (*Zbornik PFZ* 1955) [if the provisions of its national law are contrary to public order (*public policy*) of our state]

(44) Neka običajna pravila iz odgovornosti država, položaju stranaca, sukcesije država, o naknadi štete u vezi sa restriktivnim merama, tzv. stečena prava (*les*

droits acquis) itd. su nepotpuna (*Zbornik PFZ* 1972) [Certain customary rules regarding state liability, the status of aliens, state succession, compensation regarding restrictive measures, the so-called acquired rights (*les droits acquis*) etc. are incomplete]

(45) pitanjima iz isključive nadležnosti država članica (*domaine réservé*) te mogućnostima 'ustavnog sudovanja' u krilu međunarodnih organizacija (*Zbornik PFZ* 2008) [to issues belonging to the exclusive competence of member states (*domaine réservé*) and possibilities of 'constitutional settlement' within international organizations]

Some French fixed expressions are quite common both in everyday language and legal texts: *raison d'etre, par excellence, en general, vis-a-vis, a propos.*

7. Motivation for transference

First of all, the most obvious function of transfers of legal terms is to fill lexical gaps in the recipient system. Examples are primarily, but not exclusively, terms related to a particular legal culture. Moreover, transfers in legal texts are often related to a comparative approach: terms for the same concept are given in different languages, involving comparison of legal terms, analysis of their adequacy, and search for precision or attempts to find translation equivalents:

(46) Upravo zato, kao što je poznato, ondašnje *jus gentium* – od koga terminološki vuče koren naziv međunarodno pravo (*droit des gens*, *law of nations*, *Völkrrecht*) (*Zbornik PFZ* 1971) [Since, as is well-known, *jus gentium* – the etymological source of the term international law (*droit des gens*, *law of nations*, *Völkrrecht*)]

(47) uz priuzdržaj propisa člana 59, sudske rješidbe (*les décisions judiciaires*, *judicial decisions*, *las decisiones judicales*, *sudbenye rešenija*) (*Zbornik PFZ* 1971) [adhering to the provision of Article 59, judicial decisions (*les décisions judiciaires*, *judicial decisions*, *las decisiones judicales*, *sudbenye rešenija*)]

(48) te obveze nazivaju se glavnim poslovima (*Hauptgeschäft*, *main contract*, *l'operation principal*) (*Zbornik PFZ* 1971) [these obligations are referred to as main contract (*Hauptgeschäft*, *main contract*, *l'operation principal*)]

Terms in different languages are often given in comparing different language versions of EU legislation:

(49) Izvorni termin *equality body* u drugim jezicima Europske unije preveden je na sličan način: *organismi per la promozione della paritá di trattamneto* (tal.), *organismos de promocíon de la igualdad de trato* (španj.), *organismes de promotion de l'egalité de traitment* (franc.), *organi za spodbujanje enakega obravnavanja* (slo.). (*Zbornik PFZ* 2008) [The original term *equality body* has not been translated in a similar way in other languages of the European Union: *organismi per la promozione della paritá di trattamento* (Italian), *organismos de promocíon de la igualdad de trato* (Spanish), *organismes de promotion de l'egalité de traitment* (French), *organi za spodbujanje enakega obravnavanja* (Slovenian)]

Transference is often a result of the consulted literature in foreign languages, so that original terms, sometimes even whole sentences or parts of sentences, are used alongside Croatian translation for the sake of precision, sometimes reflecting uncertainties regarding appropriate translation of certain terms and expressions.

(50) Zadatak tih komiteta bilo je održanje poretka (*to maintain law and order*), kontrola upravnih aktivnosti u regiji i informiranje o raspoloženju naroda. Sličan sistem uveden je i na razini okruga (*district*) (*Zbornik PFZ* 1991) [The task of these committees was *to maintain law and order*, to control administrative activities in the region and to inform about the public sentiment. A similar system was introduced at the *district* level]

8. Conclusion

Linguistic transference in law articles is an indicator of changing influences of other legal cultures. Latin is the most important source of borrowing in Croatian legal texts in all periods under consideration,

English ranks second, followed by German and French. The impact of other languages is negligible. In our corpus, multiple transfers are more frequent than single-word lexical transfers, and there is a strong tendency to use morphologically unadapted forms. The most common reason for transference of legal terms is to refer to foreign legal and political concepts and institutions. Latin is used as the traditional language of law in all areas, whereas transfers from other languages are more frequent in some specific areas: German in private and public civil law, French in administrative and international law, English in law of the sea and international commercial law. A comparative approach in scholarly articles, which is evident throughout the periods under consideration, is reflected in the parallel use of synonymous legal terms from other languages. In general terms, the study of transference in legal texts can provide insights into encounters of legal cultures and their linguistic consequences.

References

Clyne, Michael 2003. *Dynamics of Language Contact*. Cambridge: Cambridge University Press.

Crystal, David [2]2003. *English as a Global Language*. Cambridge: Cambridge University Press.

Filipović, Rudolf 1960. *The Phonemic Analysis of English Loan-Words in Croatian.* Zagreb: Institute of Phonetics, Faculty of Philosophy.

Franolić, Branko 1980. *A Short History of Literary Croatian*. Paris: Nouvelles Éditions Latines.

Goldstein, Ivo 1996. *Hrvatska. Europa. Svijet. Kronologija*. [Croatia. Europe.World. Chronology] Zagreb: Liber.

Karaman, Igor (ed.) 1980. *Enciklopedija hrvatske povijesti i kulture*. [Encyclopedia of Croatian history and culture] Zagreb: Školska knjiga.

Margetić, Lujo / Beuc, Ivan / Čepulo, Dalibor 2005. *Hrvatska pravna povijest u europskom kontekstu.* [Croatian legal history in the European context]. Zagreb: Pravni fakultet Sveučilišta u Zagrebu.

Mattila, Heikki 2006. *Comparative Legal Linguistics*. Hampshire/ Burlington: Ashgate.

Milroy, Lesley / Muysken, Pieter (eds) 1995. *One Speaker, Two Languages. Cross-disciplinary Perspectives on Code-Switching*. Cambridge: Cambridge University Press.

Moguš, Milan 1995. *A History of the Croatian Language: Towards a Common Standard*. Zagreb: Nakladni zavod Globus.

Myers-Scotton, Carol 2002. *Contact Linguistics. Bilingual Encounters and Grammatical Outcomes*. Oxford: Oxford University Press.

Pavletić, Vlatko / Stančić, Nikša / Moguš, Milan 1997. *Hrvatski jezik u hrvatskom saboru* [The Croatian Language in the Croatian Parliament]. Zagreb: Narodne novine; Dom i svijet.

Sočanac, Lelija (ed.) 2005. *Hrvatski jezik u dodiru s europskim jezicima. Prilagodba posuđenica*. [Croatian in contact with European languages. Adaptation of loanwords]. Zagreb: Nakladni zavod Globus.

Sočanac, Lelija / Anja Nikolić-Hoyt 2006. English in Croatia: Past and Present. In *Innovation und Kontinuität in Sprache und Kommunikation verschiedener Sprachkulturen* [Innovation and Continuity in Language and Communication of Different Language Cultures]. Frankfurt am Main: Peter Lang.

Steindorff, Ludwig 2006. *Povijest hrvatske od srednjeg vijeka do danas*. [History of Croatia from the Middle Ages to the present]. Zagreb : Naklada Jesenski i Turk; Institut društvenih znanosti Ivo Pilar.

Sources

Zbornik Pravnog fakulteta u Zagrebu (Zbornik PFZ). (vol.5, no. 1-4, 1955; vol. 22, no. 1-4, 1972; vol. 41, no. 1-6, 1991; vol. 58, no. 1-6, 2008.)

SILVIA CACCHIANI / CHIARA PREITE

Law Dictionaries across Languages: Different Structures, Different Relations between Communities of Practice?*

1. Introduction

This chapter concentrates on the representation of borrowings from French into English and from English into French within the latest editions of English and French desk law dictionaries in paper format: *Oxford Dictionary of Law*, 2006 [*ODL*] and *Longman Dictionary of Law*, 2007 [*LDL*] for English; *Vocabulaire juridique*, 2007 [*VJ*] for French. Following their prefaces, all three dictionaries seem to address the same or similar target user groups. Insofar as they must reflect to some extent the publisher's directions and the compiler's approach to the dictionary, if it is true that they share the same 'genuine purpose' (Wiegand 1985 ff.) and target user groups in the context(s) of use (Bergenholz/Tarp 1995, 2003; Bergenholz/Nielsen 2006), then we would expect similar products showing some degree of similarity across languages and cultures. All the more so with borrowings from international regulations which are used in national legal systems and languages. Recent work on *ODL* and *VJ* (Cacchiani/Preite in press), however, provides evidence to the contrary. Whereas the different treatment of borrowings from one national language and legal system into the other might be accounted for in terms of their highly culture-dependent nature, and, therefore, of the two different underlying legal

* Silvia Cacchiani is responsible for Sections 3, 4.4. and 5. Chiara Preite is responsible for Sections 1, 2 and 4. Sections 4.1, 4.2 and 4.3 are the result of cooperative work. Cacchiani worked on the entries from *ODL* and Preite on the entries from *VJ*.

systems, the same does not seem to hold good for recent borrowings from commercial law, international regulations (e.g. *Incoterms 2000*) or European law (e.g. *copyright* (*ODL*) vs. *copyright* (*VJ*), or *CE* (*ODL*) vs. *Communauté Européenne* (*VJ*)). This might result from differences in disciplinary culture and different relations between discourse communities (Swales 1990) and communities of practice (Wenger 1998), most notably professionals and lexicographers in specialist lexicographical practice.

If this is the case, then choices and solutions adopted in *LDL* must come closer to the dictionary practice of *ODL*, its direct competitor on the market, than to the dictionary practice of *VJ*. To test this assumption, we shall proceed as follows. Section 2 provides some introductory remarks on the functions and target users of the dictionaries. Section 3 gives a brief outline of Wiegand's (1977, 1985, 1992, 1998, 2001, 2003, 2005) theory of dictionary form, which we adapt in order to compare a restricted number of entries across the three dictionaries. Although we are aware of the need for a more systematic analysis of their macro-, medio- and microstructure, in the absence of dictionaries in electronic format we prefer to opt for a fine-grained, qualitative analysis which enables us to better highlight and motivate subtle differences in structure and in meaning description within dictionary entries in particular. Specifically, in Section 4 we contrast dictionary entries from *VJ* and *ODL* as a first step, and then discuss the findings against data from *LDL*. In Section 5 we return to our initial question, or the role of disciplinary culture and discourse communities of practice in shaping dictionary form.

2. Dictionary function and target users

In this section we deal with target users, functions and some macro-, medio- and microstructural features of *ODL*, *LDL* and *VJ*, as briefly outlined in the prefaces and back-cover blurbs. Following Bergenholz/Tarp (1995, 2003), by functions of the dictionary we mean knowledge-oriented and communication-oriented functions which amount to assisting reception and production of texts in the native or foreign language, translation and inverse translation (Bergenholtz/Nielsen 2006: knowledge-oriented and cognition-oriented functions). These are not to be equated with Wiegand's (1977 ff.) notion of *genuine purpose* [genuiner Zweck].[1] Every dictionary fulfils one single genuine purpose via a set of partial lexicographic texts with external reference structure [Teiltexten mit äußerer Zugriffstruktur]). This enables the user to access and infer information on the features given for the relevant designative expression and thus gain access to the underlying disciplinary knowledge.

Although prefaces and back-cover blurbs do not all provide the same kind of information, all dictionaries have among their target users legal practitioners and, second, law students who may also belong to identical or different legal systems. Target users of *ODL* and *VJ* are also professionals in other fields and laypeople (cf. Table 1). In principle, addressing the needs of multiple target groups within a utilitarian, commercial paper dictionary which adapts to size constraints has a bearing on word list, mediostructure and type and amount of information included in the entry. Specifically, we expect strict alphabetical order of lexical entries, both simple and compound words. Indeed, the semasiological structure of all three dictionaries allows students and non-practitioners to retrieve information. They would not be able to look for a word via the underlying concept or hyperonym.

---

1 See Bergenholtz/Tarp (2003) for extensive discussion of Wiegand's (1977 ff.) notion of *genuine purpose*, his theory of dictionary form and the relationship it establishes to the *modern theory of lexicographical functions* developed by researchers from the Center for Lexicography at the Aarhus School of Business since the early 1990s.

	Function/user	*1. Outside matter*	*2. Entry*	*1+2*
ODL	- quick reference for legal professionals			
	- clear explanations of concepts and terminology for law students at all levels	- introduction to online legal resources - writing and citation guides	- also legal reference to key cases (+ full citations)	- jargon avoided
	- reference material for professionals in other fields	- introduction to online legal resources		- jargon
	- reference material for laypeople to understand various aspects of life			- jargon avoided
LDL	- legal practitioners	- link to Companion Website update	- legal references	
	- students		- legal references	
	- those who wish to make an intensive study of the subject matter of the entries			
VJ	- specialist lexis, not terminology of words and morphemes, to assist reception	- law maxims (Maxims et adages du droit français)		
	- French and foreign legal practitioners, also professionals in other fields			

Table 1. *Dictionary functions, target users and structure* (cf. preface and/or back-cover blurb).

Modularity is also assumed to be a distinctive feature of user-friendly dictionary entries. As is only natural, different senses are listed within a nested structure. We take the following features as playing a crucial role in keeping entry size within reasonable limits:

a. at the mediostructural level, cross-referencing to related entries as a form of meaning description and further explanation via synonymy, hyperonymy, etc.;

b. at the microstructural level, condensation via standard dictionary conventions (cf. Section 3);
c. very little information, if any, on form and etymology;
d. a trade-off between the inclusion of semantic and encyclopaedic information. Specialist dictionaries do necessarily comprise encyclopaedic factual knowledge and encyclopaedic object-constituting meaning knowledge (both knowledge of stereotypes and knowledge of categories) (cf. Wiegand 2001).

3. Wiegand's (1992 ff.) actional-semantic theory of dictionary form

In this section we briefly outline the basic tenets of Wiegand's (1992 ff.) actional-semantic theory of dictionary form [aktional-semantische Theorie der Wörterbuchform]. The key-terms here are:

a. *Lexicographical definition*: a text made up of *definiendum* (*LZGA* [Lemmazeichengestaltangabe]), *definitor* (*definition copula* or absent relational expression) and *definiens* or *meaning paraphrase* (*BPA* [Bedeutungsparaphrasenangabe]).
b. *Functional text segment* [funktionales Textsegment] within the dictionary entry (Wiegand 1992) or *(basic) reference unit* [lexikographischer akzessiver Eintrag] (Wiegand 2005): it is possible to identify discrete segments within the reference unit on the basis of their function (and position). They are *items* (*A* [Angabe]) or *sentences* (*AnT* [Angabetext]). Next to a main genuine function, secondary functions may be identified. *Functional additions* (*ZuA* [funktionale Zusatzangabe]) are enlarging text segments that are not separable in a functional-positional way (e.g. usage glosses or specifications of the reference domain in the BPA). Elementary items only have one text segment and one function. Non-elementary items can be divided into homogeneous segments or heterogeneous segments. Text segments are organized hierarchically within the reference unit.

c. *Lexicographical meaning description*: helps solve communication problems via answering prospective users' questions (Wiegand 1985: *user prerequisite principle*). Different entries answer predictable questions on the part of the prospective user in order to solve specific problems in actual situations of use.

d. On this basis we can envisage and build a *frame-based entry structure*, answering questions about a number of basic descriptors for the *definiendum*, which we can mainly group into six broad categories: perception, membership within a superordinate class, role/function in a process or activity, role of the *definiendum*'s arguments, importance of *definiendum*, (dis)-similarities among category members (Konerding 1992 as adapted in Wiegand 1992: 259-261). In Wiegand's (1992) notation, they fit into the following categories in the BPA:
   i. *A-KatW* [Angabe zum Wissen der Kategorie]: knowledge of categories (structural indicator: *K(K)*);
   ii. *A-FunkW* [Angabe zum Wissen der Funktion]: knowledge of functions (structural indicator: *K(F)*);
   iii. *A-FBTW* [Angabe zum Wissen der Form und Bestandteile]: knowledge of forms and components (structural indicator: *K(FBT)*);
   iv. *A-MaW* [Angabe zum Wissen des Materiales]: knowledge of materials (structural indicator: *K(M)*).[2]

e. *Hierarchical microstructure* and *abstract representation/ structural graphs*: the hierarchical structure of the reference unit (*WA* [Wörterbuchartikel]) can be outlined in abstract representations, both strings and structural graphs, via comments on forms (*FK* [Formkommentar]), comprising word formation and grammatical items, on semantics (*SK* [Kommentar zur Semantik]), etc. One example for *SK*:
   - *SK* – [*PA1* (item giving polysemy [Polysemieangabe]) – *SSK* (subcomment on semantics [Subkommentar zur Semantik])]

---

2 Note, however, that while *K(M)* is peripheral to legal language, other categories and labels might be used, e.g. concerning participant relations in compliance with norms and regulations.

> [*PA2* (item giving polysemy [Polysemieangabe]) – *SSK* (subcomment on semantics [Subkommentar zur Semantik])];

- *SK* – [*SSK* (subcomment on semantics [Subkommentar zur Semantik]) – *PragsemA* (pragmatic-semantic item [pragmatisch-semantische Angabe]), e.g. *StilA* (item on style [Stilschichtenangabe]) – *BA* (item on meaning [Bedeutungsangabe]), e.g. *SynA* (item giving the synonym [Synonymenangabe]) – *BPA* (item giving the meaning paraphrase [Bedeutungsparaphrasenangabe])] – [*KBeiA* (item giving the competence example [Kompetenzbeispielangabe])].

Items giving meaning (*BA* [Bedeutungsangabe]) constitute the *integrate core*, which may be followed by an optional front integrate and an optional back integrate (e.g. notes on etymology, grammar or morphology). Items giving the meaning paraphrase play a crucial role in lexicographical meaning description. *PräK* (pre-comment [Präkommentar], expanding to the left) and *PostK* (postcomment [Postkommentar], expanding to the right) provide other types of information (chiefly *FK* [Formkommentar]).

f. (Non-natural) *condensation* (*v.*: condensed [verdichtete]) can be achieved via lexicographical conventions for summarizing, substituting, shifting, abbreviations and ellipses. Some examples for BPAs (Wiegand 1992: 199-214) are *o.* = *oder / or*, an abbreviation, and *grammar [...] (the study of) the rules used to form words and to combine words in sentences*, which illustrates the case of ellipsis in a condensed meaning paraphrase from which two meaning paraphrases can be inferred (*v.*BP^2A).

In the following we shall adapt Wiegand's (1977 ff.) theory of dictionary form in order to partially analyse dictionary entries taken from *VJ*, *ODL* and *LDL* and focus on some micro- and mediostructural features which mainly contribute to meaning description within the entries. When needed, further details on the notation adopted will be given while commenting on the entry under investigation. This will enable us to compare lexicographical practices across the three dictionaries and thus address the question whether and to what extent French and English law dictionaries reflect different relations between legal and lexicographic communities of practice.

4. Borrowings in *VJ*, *ODL* and *LDL*

ODL, VJ and *LDL* are products of specialized lexicography. Although we do not expect the systematic inclusion and representation of dictionary entries and underlying body of knowledge available to the products of applied terminology, we still expect ample coverage of what the compilers (most often, legal practitioners) find to better address the needs of their target users. Next to lemmas which illustrate the knowledge related to the national legal system, borrowings are also included. They are either part of the underlying body of knowledge, or belong to legal systems which are found to interact with the national legal system and body of knowledge in different ways and to different extents. As suggested above (Section 1), borrowings are represented differently across *ODL* and *VJ*. Our research question is whether this can be accounted for in terms of different practices within different disciplinary cultures (in other words, different lexicographical traditions). Thus, in this section we contrast entries from *VJ* and *ODL* as a first step, draw some initial generalizations (Sections 4.1, 4.2, and 4.3), and then move on to *LDL* for further evidence (Section 4.4).

Lemmas have been selected from a preliminary list based on etymological information from *VJ* for French and the *Oxford English Dictionary* online (*ODL*), 2nd edition and later updates, for English, in order to illustrate the case of: a) borrowings that are now part of one legal system, b) lemmas found in both *VJ* and *ODL* (also lemmas belonging to both legal systems), and c) borrowings from international regulations that are part of both legal systems (cf. Cacchiani/Preite in press). We took into considerations all 129 lemmas returned by *VJ*. As far as *ODL* is concerned, however, they run into the hundreds. We therefore concentrated on 130 lemmas which were selected from the A-Z list keeping to the ratio of borrowings to lemmas in *ODL*. After a cursory analysis of the entries by kind of information provided, a more detailed investigation was carried out into the micro- and (to a lesser extent) mediostructure of 21 entries across *VJ* and *ODL*, and the results tested against *LDL*. Sections 4.1 to 4.4 concentrate on the lemmas and entries which seem to better illustrate the lexicographical practices adopted in the three dictionaries.

4.1. Borrowings which are now part of one legal system

Our intention here is to provide a fine-grained representation of different types of borrowings in *VJ* and *ODL*, based on their partial abstract representations.[3] For each lemma we give the dictionary entry and a list of the main functional segments and conventions adopted.

The first lemma under investigation is (1) *sinécure*, a loanword integrated in French morphology and no longer part of the knowledge base of the English legal system:

(1) **sinécure**
Subst. fém. – Empr. à l'anglais *sinecure*, construit sur le lat. *sine cura*, sans soin, sans travail, sans souci.
- (vx) *Poste rétribué sans travail à fournir; *emploi rémunéré sans avoir rien à faire (ou pour ne rien faire). V. *fictif.* (*VJ*)

As far as (1) is concerned, we can observe the presence of information to the left of the integrate core (*PräK* [Präkommentar]), on a) form (*FK* [Kommentar zur Form]), and morphology in particular (*MorA* [Angabe der Morphologie]: *sine cura*), b) etymology (*EtyA* [Angabe der Etymologie]), source and direction of borrowing (*HerA* [Angabe der Herkunft] / *EntlRA* [Angabe der Entlehnungsrichtung]: *Empr. à l'anglais sinecure, construit sur le lat. sine cura*), c) synonyms/ equivalents (*SynA* [Synonymenangabe] / *ÄquA* [Angabe des Wortäquivalents]) which substitute the meaning paraphrase: *sans soin, sans travail, sans souci*. This seems to be a favourite choice in *VJ*. As regards the subsequent comment on semantics (*SK* [Kommentar zur Semantik]), meaning paraphrases (*BPA* [Bedeutungsparaphrasenangabe]) are given which also serve as dislocated cross-references (*i.VerwA* [integrierte / binnensituierte Verweisangabe]) to members of

3 See Cacchiani/Preite (in press) for a less detailed analysis of entries from *VJ* and *ODL* which outlines highly simplified abstract representations in the form of partial structural graphs.

the same set of synonyms (*V. *fictif*) and more basic superordinates (**poste*, **emploi*), which might be seen as part of the Natural Semantic Metalanguage (in the sense of Wierzbicka 1996) of the discipline (cf. Cacchiani 2009), but not to specialist explanations under the cross-referred entries.

Turning to *ODL*, let us focus on (2) *fème covert* and (3) *fème sole*, two borrowings which are no longer related to the knowledge base of the French legal system:

(2) **fème covert** [Anglo-French] A married woman, under the *coverture of her husband.

(3) **fème sole** [Anglo-French] An unmarried woman. The term includes a widow or divorcée or a woman whose marriage has been annulled. (*ODL*)

Both dictionary entries are very simple. They have been selected in order to illustrate choices and solutions which are regularly adopted in *ODL*. Items on etymology are highly infrequent. When present, the item on source language (*HerA* [Angabe der Herkunft]: *[Anglo-French]*) signals a specialist subfield (*FGA* [Angabe des Fachgebiets]: Common Law) and activates knowledge about it via inference. Another recurrent feature are BPAs enlarged via additions which a) introduce the classic definition *per genus et differentiam* (*a married woman under [...]*) and b) also cross-refer to specialist entries for further specialist information (*i.VerwA-FE* [integrierte/binnensituierte Verweisangabe zur fachlichen Erklärung]: **coverture*).

Fème sole illustrates other recurrent features of *ODL* entries: a) extended meaning paraphrases which replace or combine with (cross-references to) synonyms, and b) explicitation of the relator (*The term includes*) to introduce further specialist explanations in the form of non-condensed (encyclopaedic) information in a separate sentence or across subsequent sentences (*AnT-FE* [Angabetext zur fachlichen Erklärung]).

4.2. Lemmas found in VJ *and* ODL *(also part of the knowledge base of both legal systems)*

Borrowings that form part of the knowledge base of both legal systems are represented differently across *VJ* and *ODL*. Specifically, the dictionary entries below bring to the fore the same features highlighted for (1) as against (2) and (3). Example (4) *estoppel* (*VJ*) is a borrowing *aller-retour*, still perceived as a foreign word (*xénisme*) in French:

(4) **Estoppel**
Terme angl. signifiant 'fin de non-recevoir'.
- Notion empruntée au Droit anglo-saxon, souvent analysée comme une exception procédurale, destinée à sanctionner, au nom de la *bonne foi, les contradictions dans les comportements d'un État, celui-ci étant considéré comme lié par son comportement antérieur et, dès lors, *estopped* à faire valoir une prétention nouvelle. Ex. un Etat qui a expressément reconnu une ligne frontière est déchu de son droit de contester cette ligne auprès d'un autre Etat. V. *acquiescement, reconnaissance, irrecevabilité, fin de non-recevoir.* (*VJ*)

Meaning description proceeds through:

a) inclusion of etymological information (*EtyA* [Angabe der Etymologie]: *Terme anglais signifiant 'fin de recevoir'*), which cannot be taken to point to the relevant specialist domain unless we proceed to the immediately following segment on specialist domain (*FGA* [Angabe des Fachgebiets]: *Notion empruntée au Droit anglo-saxon*);

bi) systematic recurrence to relational expressions (*celui-ci étant considéré comme*, or *Ex.*, which introduces an item giving the competence example (*KBeiA* [Kompetenzbeispielangabe]));

bii) use of explicit relators in the initial meaning paraphrase of the integrate core (*Souvent analysée comme*), a practice which has no counterpart in *ODL*;

c) a meaning paraphrase which provides knowledge on category (*A-KatW* [Angabe zum Wissen der Kategorie]: *Souvent analysée comme une exception procédurale*), function (*A-FunW* [Angabe zum Wissen der Funktion]: *destinée à sanctionner*

[...]) and additional specialist information (*ZuA-FE* [Zusatzangabe zur fachlichen Erklärung]: *celui-ci étant considéré comme lié [...]*);

d) cross-references (*VerwA*) in the postcomment to related entries (*V. acquiescement, reconnaissance, irrecevabilité, fin de non-recevoir*).

ODL provides a more sophisticated meaning description for (5) *estoppel*:

(5) **Estoppel** n. [from Norman French *estouper*, to stop up] A rule of evidence or a rule of law that prevents a person from denying the truth of a statement he has made or from denying the existence of facts that he has alleged to exist. The denial must have been acted upon (probably to his disadvantage) by the person who wishes to take advantage of the estoppel or his position must have been altered as a result. There are several varieties of estoppel.
• **Estoppel by conduct** (or in pais) arises when the party estopped has made a statement or has led the other party to believe in a certain fact.
• **Estoppel by deed** prevents a person who has executed a deed from saying that the facts stated in the deed are not true.
• **Estoppel by record** (or *per rem judicatam*) prevents a person from reopening questions that are **res judicata* (i.e. that have been adjudicated upon by a court of competent jurisdiction). *See also* ISSUE ESTOPPEL.
There are two forms of equitable estoppel – promissory and proprietary. The doctrine of promissory estoppel applies when one party to a contract promises the other (by words or conduct) that he will not enforce his rights under the contract in whole or in part. Provided that the other party has acted in reliance on that promise, it will, though unsupported by consideration, bind the person making it: he will not be allowed subsequently to sue on the contract. When applicable, the doctrine thus modifies the common-law rules relating to *accord and satisfaction. Under the doctrine of proprietary estoppel, the courts can grant a discretionary remedy in circumstances where an owner of land has implicitly or explicitly led another to act detrimentally in the belief that rights in or over land would be acquired. The remedy may take the form of the grant of a *fee simple in the property (*Pascoe v Turner* [1979] 1 WLR 431), the grant of a short-term occupational *licence, or even a monetary sum equivalent to the value of the detriment suffered by the claimant in reliance upon the expectation (*Jennings* v *Rice* [2003] P & CR 8 (CA)). The court will always seek to do the minimum necessary to satisfy the equity.

As can be seen, *ODL* provides a more exhaustive treatment within an entry which lists different subsenses and comes close to a synopsis. An item on form (part of speech: *n*) is included on the assumption that the user might not be familiar with the semantico-linguistic knowledge (in the sense of Wiegand 2001) associated with the word and/or doubt between the noun or the verb reading of the lemma. Items on etymology (*EtyA* [Angabe der Etymologie]) are a marked option in *ODL*. Items on source language (*From Norman-French*) are only included to activate knowledge of a specific (sub-)domain via inference. Source word and translation equivalent help diminish processing effort. The BPA provides information on category (*A-KatW* [Angabe zum Wissen der Kategorie]: *a rule of evidence or a rule of law*) and function (*A-FunW* [Angabe zum Wissen der Funktion]: *that prevents a person from [...]*). Sentences and additions give specialist competence examples and explanations (*AnT-KBei* [Angabetext zum Kompetenzbeispiel] / *AnT-FE* [Angabetext zur fachlichen Erklärung]: *The denial must have been acted upon [...] as a result*; *ZuA-FE* [Zusatzangabe zur fachlichen Erklärung]: *(i.e. that have been adjudicated upon by a court of competent jurisdiction)*). Unlike *VJ*, which seems to favour specialist additions, specialist explanations in *ODL* provide further details for different types of *estoppel* across subsequent sentences, which are, in their turn, further expanded via legal references such as *Jennings* v *Rice* [2003] P & CR 8 (CA), an item on specialized references / literary titles (*LitA* [Angabe der Fachliteratur / Angabe eines Literaturtitels]). Cross-references are also made to sister-items (*See also* ISSUE ESTOPPEL) or to lemmas that point to key concepts in the relevant legal domain (**fee simple*).

Altogether, *ODL* shows a clear preference for the inclusion of encyclopaedic information in extended dictionary entries, which is a marked option in *VJ*. Evidence for this comes from numerous dictionary entries. Compare, in this respect, (6) *abattement* (*VJ*) and (7) *abatement* (*ODL*), a borrowing from French into English. Both words are currently used in the national legal systems. Only (7) *abatement* (*ODL*), however, receives a detailed meaning description across subsenses (*PA* [Polysemieangabe]) and matching specifications of the relevant referent (*BezSPA* [Angabe der Spezifizierung des Bezugsobjects]: e.g. *(of debts)*) or domain of application (*FGA* [Angabe des Fachgebiets] / *DiatechA* [diatechnische Angabe]: *(in land law)*).

(6) **Abattement**
Dér. du v. abattre. V. *abattage.*
• **1** *Réduction effectuée sur la matière imposable avant application de l'impôt. Ex. abattement à la base, abattement pour charges de famille, abattement sur la part des héritiers. Comp. *Exonération, dégrèvement, déduction, décharge.*
• **2** Diminution du salaire légal ou d'une prestation sociale, fondée sur les différences du coût de la vie (abattement de zone) ou des différences d'aptitude supposée (abattement d'âge). V. *discrimination.* (*VJ*)

(7) **Abatement** n. **1.** (of debts) The proportionate reduction in the payments that take place if a person's assets are insufficient to settle with his creditors in full. **2.** (of legacies) The reduction or cancellation of legacies when a solvent estate is insufficient to cover all the legacies provided for in the will or on intestacy after payment of the deceased's debt. The Administration of Estates Act 1925 (sch 1 pt II) provides that general legacies, unless given to satisfy a debt, abate in proportion to the amounts of those legacies; specific and demonstrative legacies then abate if the estate is still insufficient to pay all debts, and a demonstrative legacy also abates if the specified fund is insufficient to cover it. For example, A's estate may comprise a painting, £3000 in his savings account, and £7000 in other money; there are debts of £1000 but his will leaves the painting to B, £5000 from the savings account to C, £8000 to D, and £2000 to E. B will receive the painting, C's demonstrative legacy abates to £3000, and after the debts are paid from the remaining £7000, D's and E's general legacies abate proportionately, to £4800 and £1200 respectively. When annuities are given by the will, the general rule is that they are valued at the date of the testator's death, then abate proportionately in accordance with that valuation, and each annuitant receives the abated sum. All these rules are subject to any contrary intention being expressed in the will. **3.** (in land law) Any reduction or cancellation of money payable. For example a lease may provide for an abatement of rent in certain circumstances, e.g. if the building is destroyed by fire, and a purchaser of land may claim an abatement of the price if the seller can prove his ownership of only part of the land he contracted to sell. **4.** (of nuisances) The termination, removal, or destruction of a *nuisance. A person injured by a nuisance has a right to abate it. In doing so, he must not do more damage than is necessary and, if removal of the nuisance requires entry on to the property from which it emanates, he may have to give notice to the wrongdoer. A local authority can issue an abatement notice to control statutory nuisances. **5.** (of proceedings) The termination of civil proceedings by operation of law, caused by a change

> of interest or status (e.g. bankruptcy or death) of one of the parties after the start but before the completion of the proceedings. An abatement did not prevent either of the parties from bringing fresh proceedings in respect of the same cause of action. Pleas in abatement have been abolished; in modern practice any change of interest or status of the parties does not affect the validity of the proceedings, provided that the cause of action survives. (*ODL*)

4.3. Borrowings from international regulations that are part of both legal systems

The analysis suggests that *ODL* favours a comprehensive treatment of lemmas within encyclopaedic dictionary entries where the initial condensed meaning paraphrase is followed by meaning descriptions which stretch across sentences, and complemented with legal references and other types of references for further, specialist information. By contrast, the following features seem to characterize *VJ*: relational expressions replacing the absent definitor; synonyms also replacing meaning paraphrases proper; systematic inclusion of items on form and etymology; preference for non-condensed items and sentences (e.g. in comments on etymology, which are only found as condensed items in *ODL*); preference for specialist explanation in the form of additions to the meaning paraphrase (as against specialist explanations across sentences and paragraphs in *ODL*).

In this section we contrast *VJ* and *ODL* lemmas and borrowings from international regulations which have entered both national legal systems, working on the assumption that:

- similarity at the micro- and mediostructural levels depends on the shared underlying body of knowledge (international regulations vs. the national legal system). This would provide indirect evidence for the claim that the observed variability in the treatment of borrowings from one language / legal system into the other (Sections 4.1 and 4.2) depends on different underlying legal systems;
- variability at the micro- and mediostructural levels is not a function of different legal systems and the related underlying body of knowledge. Quite the contrary: if present, variability

suggests we add another point to our agenda, or the role and relations of different disciplinary cultures within discourse communities of practice, specifically, within the community of specialist lexicographers.

Let us start with (8) *CE* (*ODL*):

(8) **CE** [French *Communauté européenne*: European Community] A marking applied to certain products, such as toys and machinery, to indicate that they have complied with certain EU directives that apply to them, including *electromagnetic compatibility. A CE marking is not a quality mark, but it indicates that health and safety and other legislation has been complied with. The manufacturer or first importer into the EU must apply the CE marking; fines can be levied for breach of the rules. (*ODL*)

CE, an acronym for French *Communauté européenne*, is not included in *VJ*, possibly on the assumption that it is part of the non-specialist knowledge shared by the French target users. By contrast, the English speaker might not be familiar with this acronym (also used as short for *Civil Engineers* and other names). This motivates including the related dictionary entry, which provides information on etymology, form (specifically, *A.BaFAkr* [Angabe zur Basisform des Akronyms], or the basis of the acronym: *CE*) and the English equivalent (*ÄquA* [Angabe des Wortäquivalents]: *European Community*). Comment of semantics and postcomment follow the pattern already seen in *ODL* entries. Accordingly, an enlarged meaning paraphrase (minimally) specifies category and function of the lemma, also via sentences that provide meaning description, and a postcomment which provides specialist explanations.

A comparison of (9) *CIF* (*VJ*) and (10) *CIF contract* (*ODL*) points towards variability across dictionary meaning descriptions along the lines presented above:

(9) **CIF**
Expression anglaise correspondant à l'expression française *CAF, formée des initiales des trois mots: *cost, insurance, freight*. V. *vente*.

(10) **CIF contract**
(cost, insurance, freight contract) A type of contract for the international sale of goods by which the seller agrees not only to supply the goods but also to make a contract of carriage with a sea carrier, under which the goods will be delivered at the contract port of destination, and a contract of insurance with an insurer, to cover them while they are in transit. The seller performs his contract by delivering the relevant documents to the buyer: an invoice specifying the goods and their price, a *bill of lading evidencing the contract of carriage, a policy of insurance, and any other documents specified in the contract. The contract will normally provide for payment against documents. The risk of accidental loss or damage normally passes to the buyer on or as from shipment. CIF is a defined *incoterm under *Incoterms* 2000. (*ODL*)

It is easy to see that condensation is a feature of *ODL* as against *VJ* (e.g. *cost, insurance, freight* vs. **CAF formé de trois mots cost, insurance, freight*). *ODL* and *VJ* provide different types and amounts of information, with different degrees of condensation, not only in comments on semantics, but also in cross-references and literary references. Thus, in *CIF*, *VJ* cross-refers the user to **CAF* (coût, assurance, fret), its equivalent acronym in French (*i.VerwA.Äqu* [integrierte / binnensituierte Werweisangabe eines Akronymäquivalents]), and *V. vente*, a generic synopsis entry (*VerwA-synor* [synopseorientierte Verweisangabe]). By contrast, *ODL* signals cross-references to *incoterms* / *Incoterms 2000,* thereby selecting the knowledge domain underlying *CIF* (*i.VerwA-FG* [integrierte / binnensituierte Verweisangabe zum Fachgebiet]).

4.4. Evidence from LDL

So far we have considered dictionary entries across *ODL* and *VJ.* Clearly, the observed variation in type and amount of information brings us back to our initial question: do different structures mirror the interplay of different disciplinary cultures and communities of practice? Thus, we will now concentrate on *LDL* on the assumption that, if choices and solutions adopted in *LDL* come closer to the dictionary practice of *ODL* than to the practice of *VJ*, then this counts as a cue to the various interplay of legal and lexicographic communities of practice.[4]

For lack of space, we only focus on one entry, *copyright*, which epitomizes all the features variously present in *LDL* entries. Let us now have a closer look at (11) *copyright* (*VJ*), (12) *copyright* (*ODL*) and (13) *copyright* (*LDL*):

(11) **Copyright**
N. m. – Terme angl. signifiant: 'droit de reproduction' utilisé pour désigner:

- 1 la formalité de dépôt et d'enregistrement à laquelle certaines législations (Etats-Unis) subordonnent la jouissance des droits d'auteur.
- 2 Par extension (et improprement) les droits d'auteur, indépendamment de toute formalité exigée pour en jouir – ce qui est le cas en France. V. *dépôt légal.
- 3 Le sigle © qui doit être apposé en vertu de la convention universelle (V. *droits d'*auteur*) sur les exemplaires d'œuvres étrangères pour assurer la protection de celles-ci aux Etats-Unis. V. *réservé.* (*VJ*)

(12) **Copyright** n. The exclusive right to reproduce or authorize others to reproduce artistic, literary, or musical works. It is conferred by the Copyright, Designs and Patent Act 1988, which also extends to sound broadcasting, cinematograph films, and television broadcasts (including cable television).

---

4 A more comprehensive investigation would call for a comparison with at least another French dictionary which addresses the same target users and provides ample coverage of borrowings from English. Unfortunately, we are not aware of any such dictionary currently available on the market and thus for the moment we can broaden the analysis to only include *LDL*. More precisely, Lerat's (2007) *Vocabulaire du juriste débutant* [*VJD*], Bissardon's (2005) *Guide du langage juridique. Vocabulaire, pièges et difficultés* [*GLJ*], and Guillien/Vincents (2007) *Lexique des termes juridiques* [*VTJ*], all potential candidates for inclusion, turned out to be not fit for duty on the following grounds: *VJD* targets native and non-native law students and, in line with pedagogical specialized lexicography, only provides central (and most frequent) legal terms, which keeps borrowings to a minimum. *GLJ* claims to be a pedagogically-oriented law dictionary which concentrates on the reception and production needs of professionals from other fields and the general public. While giving a list of Anglicisms and French equivalents in the front matter, it only gives a handful of borrowings in the word list. Last, having law professionals and law students among its intended target user groups, *VTJ* seemed to be a good candidate for investigation. Unfortunately, only some 40 English borrowings are part of the word list, which forced us to do away with it.

Copyright lasts for the author's lifetime plus 70 years from the end of the year in which he died; it can be assigned or transmitted on death. EU directive 93/98 requires all EU states to ensure that the duration of copyright is the life of the author plus 70 years. Copyright protection for sound recordings lasts for 50 years from the date of their publication; for broadcasts it is 50 years from the end of the year in which the broadcast took place. Directive 91/250 requires all EU member states to protect computer *software by copyright law. The principal remedies for breach of copyright (known as **piracy**) are an action for *damages and *account of profits or an *injunction. It is a criminal offence knowingly to make or deal in articles that infringe a copyright. *See also BERNE CONVENTION. (ODL)*

(13) **copyright.** A property right (which is transmissible by assignment or will as a personal property), which subsists in original literal, dramatic, musical or artistic works, sounds recording, films, broadcasts or cable programmes, and the typographical arrangement of published editions: Copyright, Designs and Patents Act 1988, s 1(1). 'Original' means originating from the author, not copied: see *Interlego* v *Tyco Industries* [1989] 3 WLR 678. 'Author' means the person who creates the work: s 9(1); he is first owner of the copyright. For meaning of 'typographical arrangement', see *Newspaper Licencing Agency* v *Marks and Spencer plc* (2000) 150 NLJ 900. Usually endures for the holder's lifetime plus 70 years (EC Directive 93/98). An author has the right to be identified as such: s 77. Remedies for infringements include damages and injunctions: s. 96. See *Phonographic Performance Ltd* v *Maitra* [1998] 1 WLR 870 (grant of injunction with immediate effect and without express time limit); *Hyde Park Residence Ltd* v *Yelland* (2000) *The Times*, 16 February (inherent jurisdiction of court to refuse to enforce copyright where enforcement would offend against policy of the law); *Jones* v *Tower Hamlets LBC* (2000) *The Times*, 14 November (protection of architectural design by copyright). Given that title to property situated in England is to be determined by English law, title to English copyright may not be removed from England by any degree of a foreign government: *Peer International Corporation* v *Terminator Music Publishers* (2003) *The Times*, 2 January. *See* AUTHOR. (*LDL*)

We can observe here the gradual shift in interest from semantico-linguistic information (11) to semantico-encyclopaedic information in semantico-encyclopaedic comments (*sem-enzyK* [semantisch-enzyclopädischer Kommentar]) (12 and, more to the point, 13). Although *VJ* resorts here to two highly dispreferred options (condensation in the comment on form and inclusion of separate subsenses under separate sub-entries which do away with synonyms), no attempt is made at covering the underlying body of knowledge. Legal language is highly specialized, culture-dependent and most often polysemous (Lerat 1995, Cornu 2005). However, only *ODL* and *LDL* provide extensive and detailed coverage of multiple senses and encyclopaedic information under the relevant entry or via legal references and cross-references to entries which give specialist information on the underlying (sub-)domain or relevant legislation. The encyclopaedic concerns of *LDL* in particular are immediately apparent in (13), in which the initial BPA proceeds through specification of category (*A-KatW* [Angabe zum Wissen der Kategorie]: *A property right*), function (*A-FunW* [Angabe zum Wissen der Funktion]: *which subsists in original [...] editions*) and relevant legislation (*ZuA-Lit* [Zusatzangabe des Literaturtitels / Zusatzangabe der Fachliteratur]: *Copyright, Designs and Patterns Act 1988, s 1(1)*), and is then followed by the subsequent treatment of associated words (*original* and *author*, used in the BPA) and, most importantly, extensive reference to the specific legislation across sentences.

5. Conclusions: different structures, different relations between discourse communities of practice?

Our primary goal has been to detail meaning representation of borrowings across French and English law dictionaries on the assumption that variation across French and English dictionaries is a key to different lexicographic cultures as well as to different relationships between legal and lexicographic communities of practice. Although the hypothesis pursued here has necessarily been tested within a limited range of entries, there seems to be evidence for claiming that, unlike *VJ*, *ODL* and *LDL* focus on disciplinary knowledge and display a preference for the extensive inclusion of encyclopaedic information. More precisely, *ODL* and *LDL* favour a comprehensive treatment of lemmas within encyclopaedic dictionary entries characterized by an initial condensed enlarged meaning paraphrase. Second, the BPA is in turn followed by meaning descriptions which stretch across sentences, and are complemented with legal references and cross-references to the relevant discipline. By contrast, *VJ* shows a preference for non-condensed items and sentences (e.g. in comments on form and etymology, which are the exception in *ODL* and absent from *LDL*). When explanations and illustrations are present, they do not span across sentences, but take the form of additions to the meaning paraphrase.

The question that naturally arises from this concerns the factors that are likely to play a role in shaping the observed variation. Although it is true that different dictionary structures represent different ways of reconciling target users' profiles on the one hand and constraints on dictionary design, production and use on the other, *VJ*, *ODL* and *LDL* seem to address the same target users in similar contexts of use (cf. preface, back-cover blurb). In terms of Wenger (1998), they address the needs of relatively more engaged and active to relatively more peripheral and marginal participants in the legal discourse community.

Other things being equal, we would therefore argue that what contributes to dictionary variation relates to different assumptions on what enables to best fulfil the target users' needs. This is a fundamental aspect of the relation between legal professionals and lexicographers, of the compilers' approach to lexicography in French and English legal lexicography, and, specifically, of a different approach to lexicography within the latter. Whereas *ODL* and *LDL* were compiled by professionals who benefited from the expertise of lexicographers, *VJ* is the product of the joint efforts of linguists and law professionals within the framework of *legal linguistics* (Cornu 2005: *linguistique juridique*). Unlike *ODL* and *LDL*, *VJ* has a multiple focus on language, the law and the contribution of linguistic analysis to the legal system, which translates into an interest in form and language use and, consequently, results in a departure from the main emphasis on the encyclopaedia and disciplinary knowledge which, instead, is a distinctive feature of *ODL* and *LDL*.

References

Bergenholtz, Henning / Nielsen, Sandro 2006. Subject-field Components as Integrated Parts of LSP Dictionaries. *Terminology* 2, 281-303.

Bergenholz, Henning / Tarp, Sven 1995. *Manual of Specialized Lexicography*. Amsterdam: Benjamins.

Bergenholtz, Henning / Tarp, Sven 2003. Two Opposing Theories: On H.E. Wiegand's Recent Discovery of Lexicographic Functions, *Hermes, Journal of Linguistics* 31, 171-196.

Cacchiani, Silvia 2009. English Law Dictionaries from Native to Non-native Target Users. Is There Room for Improvement? Oral presentation, *XVII European Symposium on Languages for Specific Purposes,* 17-21 August 2009, Aarhus, Denmark.

Cacchiani, Silvia / Preite, Chiara in press, Procédés définitoires dans les vocabulaires juridiques français et anglais: le cas des emprunts. *Publif@rum*. <http://publifarum.it>.

Cornu, Gérard [3]2005. *Linguistique juridique*. Paris: Montchrestien.

Konerding, Klaus-Peter 1992. *Frames und lexikalisches Bedeutungswissen: Untersuchungen zur linguistischen Grundlegung einer Frametheorie und zu ihrer Anwendung in der Lexikographie.* PhD dissertation, Heidelberg. [Published 1993. Tübingen: Niemeyer].

Lerat, Pierre 1995. *Les langues spécialisées*. Paris: Presses Universitaires de France.

GLJ: Bissardon, Sébastien [2]2005. *Guide du langage juridique: vocabulaire, pièges et difficultés*. Paris: LexisNexis SA, Litec.

LDL: Curzon, Leslie B. / Richards, Paul H. [7]2007. *The Longman Dictionary of Law*. Harlow: Pearson Education.

LTJ: Guillien, Raymond / Vincent, Jean [15]2007. *Lexique des termes juridiques*. Paris: Dalloz.

ODL: Martin, Elizabeth A. / Law, Jonathan [6]2006. *Oxford Dictionary of Law*. Oxford: Oxford University Press.

OED: *Oxford English Dictionary* (2nd ed. and later additions). <http://www.oed.com>. [last accessed: 30 August 2009].

Swales, John 1990. *Genre Analysis: English in Academic and Research Settings*. Cambridge: Cambridge University Press.

VJ: Cornu, Gérard [8]2007. *Vocabulaire juridique*. Paris: Quadrige – PUF.

VJD: Lerat, Pierre 2007. *Vocabulaire du juriste débutant*. Paris: Ellipses.

Wenger, Etienne. 1998. *Communities of Practice: Learning, Meaning and Identity*. Cambridge: Cambridge University Press.

Wiegand, Herbert Ernst 1977. Einige grundlegende semantisch-pragmatische Aspekte von Wörterbucheinträgen. Ein Beitrag zur praktischen Lexicologie. *Kopenhagener Beiträge zur Germanistischen Linguistik* 12, 59-149.

Wiegand, Herbert Ernst 1985. Eine neue Aufassung der sog. Lexicographischen Definition. In *Symposium on Lexicography II. Proceedings of the Second International Symposium on Lexicography, May 16, 1984*. Tübingen: Niemeyer, 15-100.

Wiegand, Herbert Ernst 1992. Elements of a Theory towards a So-called Lexicographic Definition. *Lexicographica* 8, 175-285.

Wiegand, Herbert Ernst 1998. *Wörterbuchforschung. Unter-suchungen zur Wörterbuchbenutzung, zur Theorie, Geschichte, Kritik and Automatisierung der Lexicographie 1*. Berlin: de Gruyter.

Wiegand, Herbert Ernst 2001. Was eigentlich sind Wörterbuchfunktionen? Kritische Anmerkungen zur neueren und neusten Wörterbuchforschung. *Lexicographica* 17, 217-248.

Wiegand, Herbert Ernst 2003. Überlegungen zur Typologie von Wörterbuchartikeln in Printwörterbüchern. Ein Beitrag zur Theorie der Wörterbuchform. *Lexicographica* 19, 169-312.

Wiegand, Herbert Ernst 2005. Angaben, funktionale Angabezusätze, Angabetexte, Angabestrukturen, Strukturanzeiger, Kommentare und mehr. Ein Beitrag zur Theorie der Wörterbuchform. *Lexicographica* 21, 202-379.

Wierzbicka, Anna 1996. *Semantics: Primes and Universals*. Oxford: Oxford University Press.

Snježana Husinec

The Use of Comparative Legal Analysis in Teaching the Language of the Law

1. Introduction: legal language as a language for specific purposes

The language of law as a language for specific purposes has been developed by experts primarily for the purpose of professional communication. As such it uses technical terms and phrases and shows a number of structural peculiarities. Therefore, it differs considerably from ordinary speech and writing.

However, legal language differs also from other languages for special purposes in that it is closely linked to the culture of a particular society (Mattila 2006: 105). Legal languages are shaped by the legal system in which they are used. Since different legal systems have different legal rules, legal concepts differ as well. For this reason the semantic domains of legal terms do not always correspond with one another (Mattila 2006: 105). The extent of this disparity depends on the historical interaction between the two legal cultures concerned. For instance, Croatian legal concepts do not differ as much from German legal concepts as they do from English ones. Such intercultural differences between various legal systems are of central importance to legal language and cause frequent misunderstandings in international communication. At the same time they make legal language teaching different from teaching most other languages for specific purposes.

2. Teaching the language of law for cross-cultural communication

Citizens' increased mobility and the globalization of trade have intensified international communication in the area of law. In recent years many foreign companies have entered the Croatian market. Consequently, Croatian lawyers' international legal contacts have become more frequent as well. Moreover, a number of lawyers in Croatia are involved in the process of harmonization of Croatian law with EU law. In such circumstances legal practitioners are becoming aware of the importance of having a good command of foreign legal language and they show a growing interest in learning legal languages.

When teaching legal language for cross-cultural communication the teacher is confronted with an extremely difficult task. In order to appropriately equip the participants of legal language courses for successful international communication, the teacher needs to enable them to discuss different issues concerning foreign legal systems and their own legal system in a foreign language. To achieve this goal he/she first of all needs to teach foreign legal concepts and terminology, which are deeply culturally embedded and tied to the legal system rather than to the language (Pommer 2008: 18). The participants, on the other hand, mostly expect ready-made one-to-one linguistic equivalents where, because of different legal traditions, there is sometimes neither linguistic nor legal equivalence. For this reason, the teacher has to deal at the same time with the relevant grammatical and syntactic difficulties as well as terminological conventions, but also has to raise the student's awareness of the cultural differences between the legal systems concerned and potential dangers of misinterpretation arising from them.

3. A content-based approach to teaching legal language

The question is, how should one effectively teach legal concepts and terms that are specific for a particular legal system and differ from other systems? How does one avoid conceptual misunderstandings and terminological confusion that only to a minor extent arise from asymmetric languages and primarily are the consequence of the structural differences between legal systems (De Groot in Galdia 2003: 2)?

This approach calls for a model of teaching in which language cannot be separated from the content. In order for the participants of legal language courses to understand foreign legal concepts and exact meanings of legal terms it is essential that they learn them through the content and in their original form/legal context. In such circumstances the best teaching method is content-based instruction (CBI), an approach to foreign language teaching which postulates "the integration of content learning with language teaching aims" (Brinton *et al.* 1989: 2).

However, in order to avoid ambiguities it is not sufficient to study the language simply concerning a particular area of foreign law, but it is necessary to contrast it with one's own legal system. A knowledge of the similarities and differences between legal concepts of various countries helps avoid misunderstandings in international cooperation (David/Brierley in Mattila 2006: 106). Therefore, content-based teaching has to be supplemented by the comparative study of different legal systems in the particular areas taught in a legal language class.

4. Comparative legal analysis – an efficient tool for overcoming the cultural gap

The comparative analysis of particular areas of law can be a very useful and efficient tool for teaching legal languages for international communication. It facilitates teaching and learning by helping the participants overcome the cultural gap between their own legal language and a foreign one. Both the course participants and the language teacher who usually lacks any kind of formal legal training can profit from comparing and contrasting legal concepts, terms and areas of law in two legal traditions. Small comparative studies conducted in the classroom help us understand dissimilarities between legal systems, clarify the content of legal terms, recognize the closest functional equivalents and, finally, help the teacher raise the students' awareness of intercultural differences between legal systems and their consequences for the language.

4.1. Comparative legal analysis: methods

For the purpose of undertaking comparative legal analysis, two methods have proved to be very useful in the legal language classroom.

4.1.1. Juxtaposition of features of an area of law in two jurisdictions

The method of juxtaposition of features of some areas of law in two jurisdictions is used for the purpose of discovering possible inconsistent categorizations and terminological incongruity. It contrasts all relevant features of a particular aspect of law of one legal system with another by juxtaposing them in order for the participants to become aware and learn about the dissimilarities between legal systems and the potential dangers of misinterpretation they might cause. In this way the foundation for further language work in the particular area of law is laid.

4.1.2. Componential analysis of meaning of legal terms

In order to discover the conceptual information transmitted by certain terms, that is, to clarify the content of the terms and make it possible to recognize functional equivalents, componential analysis of meanings of legal terms can be conducted. By simply breaking down words into smaller parts (distinctive features or components of meaning) different features of terms are contrasted and the degree of similarity and equivalence is determined. The method is based on Nida's theory that "a meaning is not a thing in itself, but only a set of contrastive features" (Nida 1975: 51). Such an analysis reveals to what extent there is a semantic overlap between legal terms used in different legal traditions and helps avoid confusion in legal communication in a foreign language. For this purpose the usual procedure of denoting the existence of a certain feature with a plus (+) and the lack of it with a minus (–) is applied.

4.2. Comparative legal analysis: resources

The resources for conducting comparative analysis in the legal language classroom can be of different kinds. Wherever possible, it is recommendable to use legislative texts as the most trustworthy source of legal information. By analysing codes and their definitions of legal terms and regulations of a particular area we get the most accurate and reliable information about foreign and national law. Of course, other reliable sources such as good monolingual legal dictionaries (e.g. *Black's Law Dictionary*), legal textbooks and legal encyclopaedias, some reliable web pages dealing with law, as well as all other comparative law resources can be valuable sources of information.

5. The use of comparative legal analysis in teaching legal English in Croatia

The significance of different legal traditions underlying legal languages and their impact on the process of legal language instruction can most clearly be illustrated in the teaching of legal English in Croatia. The English legal system as a common law legal system differs considerably from Croatian law, which is part of Middle European continental law and is largely modelled on German law. Therefore, the participants of legal English classes are confronted with only a partial overlap of legal systems, which determines different classifications, divergent legal concepts and consequently a lack of linguistic and legal equivalence. In order to be able to fully understand the content of legal terms, to avoid misinterpretations and use the terminology properly as well as to develop an awareness of cultural differences, it is essential for the participants to learn about English law and to contrast it with Croatian law.

Owing to the considerable differences between continental and common law and the fact that business entities are defined in national legislations, company law is an area with significant terminological problems. Therefore, the use of comparative analysis in teaching legal languages can best be illustrated by using examples from UK and Croatian company law.

5.1. Example 1: Company law in the UK and Croatia – Fundamental regulations

The first step in the comparison of an area of law in two jurisdictions should be the identification of legislative acts governing the area as the basic source of reliable information. Legislative acts are necessary for more detailed analysis and help students discover the first similarities and differences in the structure of a particular area of law.

As shown in Table 1, company law in the UK is part of a common law legal system and is primarily governed by the UK Companies Act 2006 as the most extensive and important act in the field of company law regulating incorporated forms of business organization. There are three more acts referring to other types of business entities. On the other hand, company law in Croatia is governed mainly by the Croatian Companies Act (*Zakon o trgovačkim društvima*), a statute largely modelled on German legislation. The act regulates different types of business forms, incorporated ones as well as unincorporated ones.

UK	CROATIA
INCORPORATED ENTITIES 1)UK Companies Act 2006 *OTHER BUSINESS ENTITIES* 2) Limited Liability Partnership Act 3) Partnership Act 4) Limited Partnership Act	*ALL BUSINESS ENTITIES* 1) Croatian Companies Act 1993 (last amended in 2007) 2) Croatian Court Registry Act

Table 1. Company law : UK vs. Croatia – juxtaposition of principal legislative acts.

So, already at the beginning of our comparative study we come across a divergence. The term 'company' appears confusing here since, owing to the official English translation of the Croatian *Zakon o trgovačkim društvima* (Croatian Companies Act) we associate it with the British 'Companies Act'. The translation leaves the impression that the two acts are equivalent although in reality they do not regulate the same legal area. Incorporated business entities as well as partnerships are referred to as *trgovačko društvo* [trading society] in Croatia and are regulated by the same act, whereas the term *company* in its original meaning, as used under English company law, denotes exclusively 'incorporated entities'. However, since the literal translation of *trgovačko društvo* as 'trading society' may also cause false pairing (for instance with 'mutual society' mentioned in the EU legislation as a type of enterprise conducting activities with a social purpose and not for profit), the usage of the term 'company' as the most suitable translation is justified, especially if we take into consideration the influence of American English, where the term 'corporation' is used to denote an incorporated business and 'company' mostly stands for any form of business organization.

The analysis therefore reveals basic dissimilarities in the structure of company law of the two jurisdictions and clarifies the meaning of the crucial term in the area of company law which can easily cause confusion in real-life communication.

5.2. Example 2: Principal types of business entities

To be able to teach the terminology of company law and to discuss the area with the course participants it is necessary to identify and contrast the principal forms of business organization in the two jurisdictions. Since types of business entities vary across jurisdictions, the concepts are bound to differ and it is sometimes impossible to translate the terms into another language. As Table 2 shows, the UK Companies Act 2006 classifies business organizations differently from the Croatian Companies Act. UK law distinguishes between six principal business forms, two of them being incorporated (i.e. businesses with a separate legal identity from that of their owners) and four unincorporated (i.e. with no legal difference between the owners and the company). The Croatian Companies Act instead recognizes three principal types of business forms, which are then further subdivided.

UK	CROATIA
I . sole traders II. partnerships (or general partnerships) III. limited partnerships IV. limited liability partnerships V. limited companies - private limited companies LTD. - public limited companies p.l.c. VI. unlimited companies	I. *trgovac pojedinac* [sole trader] II. companies of persons - *javno trgovačko društvo* [general partnership] -*komanditno društvo* [limited partnership] III. companies of capital - *društvo s ograničenom odgovornošću – d.o.o.* [limited liability company] - *dioničko društvo - d.d.* [joint stock company]

Table 2. Principal types of business entities: UK vs. Croatia.

It is clear that due to different classification there is almost no linguistic equivalence between Croatian and UK business entities. This fact alone calls for caution when using foreign terms and trying to apply them to Croatian company law. Here, back-translation may be used as a useful method to solve the problem of inconsistency. The emphasis in back-translation, of course, should be on conceptual and cultural and not linguistic equivalence. For instance, if we decide to use 'limited partnership' as the functional equivalent of *komanditno društvo*, the accuracy of translation has to be confirmed by translating 'limited partnership' back to Croatian (for example by using the English-Croatian dictionary of law). If it can be back-translated as *komanditno društvo*, then the translation is acceptable. However, in order to be sure that particular business entities are really so similar that they can be used as functional equivalents (since bilingual dictionaries are very often not reliable enough and sometimes even offer more possible equivalents without clarifying the difference between them), a more detailed study of their characteristics must be carried out. The characteristics of the business forms in question have to be contrasted, that is, their semantic components have to be compared. Therefore, the next step in the comparative study of the field is the componential analysis of semantic features of particular business entities in the two legal systems based on the regulations from the UK Companies Act and the Croatian Companies Act as primary legislative texts in the field of company law.

5.3. Example 3: Public limited company vs. dioničko društvo

Let us illustrate the procedure by taking the Croatian *dioničko društvo* or *d.d.* and a public limited company, both being types of a joint stock company, and compare their features by means of componential analysis in order to see if they fulfil the same function and are thus comparable.[1] As the componential analysis shown in Table 3 reveals, both a public limited company in the UK and a *dioničko društvo* are owned by shareholders and are able to make shares available to the public. Neither of them, however, is necessarily a publicly quoted company (although p.l.c. bears the adjective *public* in its name). Further similarities are that *d.d.* as well as *p.l.c.* must have a minimum share capital in order to be registered and that their shareholders are limitedly liable depending on their contributions. Both companies are man-

---

1 As Pommer (2008: 19) points out, "Functionality is the basic principle of comparative law claiming that legal concepts are comparable only when they fulfil the same function".

aged by professional management: the UK public limited company by a board of directors, whereas the Croatian *dioničko društvo* can either have a two-tier board (consisting of the management board and the supervisory board) or a one-tier board (management board) (see §5.6). However, unlike the Croatian *dioničko društvo* the UK public limited company still cannot be owned by a single member/shareholder.

	UK – Public limited company p.l.c.	*CROATIA – Dioničko društvo d.d.*
Publicly traded shares	+	+
Minimum capital requirement	+	+
No personal liability/ liability limited to share-holder contributions	+ £ 50,000	+ 200,000 kuna (~ £ 25,000)
Managed by the board of directors	+	+/-
Can be a single member company	-	+

Table 3. Componential analysis of a public limited company and a *dioničko društvo* based on the UK Companies Act and the Croatian Companies Act.

On the basis of the comparative analysis of the basic features of the two companies we can conclude that although 'public limited company' and *dioničko društvo* are not linguistic equivalents and not 100% legal equivalents, the two companies are very similar forms of business organization which do not considerably differ in their characteristics and in the functions they fulfil, and can thus be used by Croatian lawyers as functional equivalents.

5.4. Example 4: Documents required for company formation

The same type of comparative analysis is beneficial when for one term there are two possible terms in another jurisdiction. This is the case with the documents needed for company registration in the UK and Croatia, the area which causes most confusion and misinterpretation and is of extraordinary importance for Croatian lawyers when advising their international clients about setting up a company in Croatia. Bilingual dictionaries are not helpful here, since they provide a range of terms which do not help the understanding of differences in the system, but only create additional confusion.

According to UK company law two documents are needed for registration with the Companies House (constitutional documents), whereas in Croatia there is one constitutional document which needs to be submitted to the Court Register. Only by contrasting the semantic components of the three documents extracted from the regulations of the two companies' acts, in other words, by contrasting the information that they must contain, can we decide what they have in common and to what extent the Croatian *društveni ugovor* overlaps functionally with the two UK documents. As shown in Table 4, *društveni ugovor* (Croatia) and the memorandum of association (UK) state that the subscribers wish to form a company and agree to become members, they set out the company's name, the registered office and address as well as the company's objects.

	Društveni ugovor	*Memorandum of association*	*Articles of association*
Main document for registration of the company	+	+	-
States that the subscribers wish to form a company	+	+	-
Sets out the company's name, registered office, address, the company's objects	+	+	-
States the authorized capital	+	+	+
Prescribes regulations for the company	+	-	+
Defines the inter-management, inter-member and inter-employee relationship	+	-	+

Table 4. Comparative analysis of Croatian and UK documents needed for company registration.

The authorized capital is stated in all three documents, whereas only *društveni ugovor* and the articles of association prescribe the regulations for the company and define the relations between the members, the members and the management and the employees. The analysis shows that the semantic domain and function of *društveni ugovor* is broader and that it encompasses the functions of both UK documents. Therefore, we can claim that the equivalence is only approximate. For the purpose of translation, the memorandum of association (being the main document for registration) could be taken as a closer equivalent, but for Croatian lawyers it is important to be aware of the fact that the documents contain different information, i.e. their meanings and functions correspond only partially due to cultural asymmetry. For this reason lawyers working for law firms which are typically engaged in organizing and conducting the company registration procedure must be extremely cautious in order to avoid confusion arising from a number of English and American terms used by experts and lay people in Croatia to refer to documents for company formation.

It should be noted here that the same technique can very effectively be applied to clearing up the confusion between different British and American terms in relation to Croatian terminology, since differences between British and US company law terminology may account for further ambiguities.

5.5. Changing of capital structure – merger

In the area of fundamental changes of a company, terminological confusion is partly influenced by parallel usage of legal and popular (widely used) terms. For merger, for instance, we come across nine different terms in the English-Croatian dictionary (*fuzija, integracija, preuzimanje, sjedinjenje, pripajanje, spajanje, udruživanje, konsolidacija, komasacija*). How do we know what the term *merger* actually stands for in UK law and what is its Croatian legal equivalent? All the ambiguities disappear once we have consulted the two companies' acts.

According to the definition found in the UK Companies Act (presented in Table 5), 'merger' refers to two different ways in which the company structure can be changed:

(a) the undertaking, property and liabilities of one or more public companies are to be transferred to another existing public company (a 'merger by absorption'); this in Croatia is referred to as *pripajanje* (i.e. a change in capital structure, where the acquired company ceases to exist, and is absorbed into the acquiring company);

(b) the undertaking, property and liabilities of two or more public companies are to be transferred to a new company, whether or not a public company, (a 'merger by formation of a new company'); this concept is covered in Croatian company law by the term *spajanje* (i.e. when both companies disappear and a new company is formed). Obviously, each type of structural change denoted by 'merger' is covered by a different term in the Croatian Companies Act.

	MERGER	PRIPAJANJE	SPAJANJE
the undertaking, property and liabilities of one or more public companies, are to be transferred to another existing public company	+ (merger by absorption)	+	-
the undertaking, property and liabilities of two or more public companies are to be transferred to a new company	+ (merger by formation of a new company)	-	+

Table 5. Componential analysis of meaning of the terms denoting change of capital structure.

The analysis discloses lexical asymmetry, that is, one English term is covered by two Croatian terms. Furthermore, it shows which of the dictionary terms are legal terms and appropriate translations of 'merger'. Such a comparative study clarifies the terms and their functions and clears away the ambiguity.

5.6. Example 6: Company management – public limited company vs. dioničko društvo

The terminological dilemmas concerning the management of publicly traded companies in the UK and Croatia can also be resolved by means of comparative analysis. The questions regularly asked by participants of legal English courses when discussing the management of UK companies are: Is the 'board of directors' the same as our *uprava* [management]? How would they call our *nadzorni odbor* [supervisory board] and who plays the role of supervisory board in the UK companies? In order to answer these questions, it is necessary to confront the students with the cultural differences between UK and Croatian company law regarding company management.

As can be seen in Table 6, by contrasting the management organs of the Croatian *d.d.* and the UK p.l.c., their structure and duties, the reasons for the confusion become obvious. In Anglo-Saxon countries there is a one-tier board in which all directors, executive as well as non-executive, are represented. They are all appointed by shareholders and elected at annual shareholder meetings. Their main duty is to manage the company and decide the company's general policy. Under Croatian law, on the other hand, until 1st April 2008, when the amendments to the Companies Act 1993 came into effect, only the dual structure of administration for *dioničko društvo* was possible. Therefore, the executive and supervisory responsibilities in Croatian companies were separated. In the so-called two-tier board (typical of countries where the German legal model prevails) these responsibilities were divided between the management board [*uprava*], sometimes also referred to as 'executive board', which manages the company and answers to the supervisory board, and the supervisory board [*nadzorni odbor*], which represents the shareholders' interests. Pursuant to the amendments to the Croatian Companies Act there is an alternative to the two-tier board for Croatian companies; namely, under the influence of Anglo-Saxon legal systems since 1st April 2008, Croatian *dioničko društvo* can decide to have only the 'board of directors' (whose structure and duties are almost the same as those of the UK board of directors) instead of both the 'management board' (*uprava* in the old two-tier system) and the 'supervisory board' [*nadzorni odbor*].

PUBLIC LIMITED COMPANY (p.l.c.)	DIONIČKO DRUŠTVO (d.d.)
ONE-TIER BORD The board of directors = executive and non-executive directors (two or more members) = appointed by controlling shareholders = elected at AGMs, answer to AGM = manage the company and decide its general policy	A) *TWO-TIER BOARD* The management [*uprava*] = one or more members, appointed by and answer to the supervisory board The supervisory board [*nadzorni odbor*] = outside experts and representatives of employees = appointed at and answer to AGM B) *ONE-TIER BOARD* (in force since 1 April 2008) The management board [*upravni odbor*] = executives and non-executives (+ representatives of employees if prescribed by the law) =elected at and answer to AGM =manage the company and decide general policy

Table 6. Company management of p.l.c. and d.d.

This comparative study leads us to the conclusion that the terminological ambiguities concerning the highest governing bodies in companies are due to different legal traditions. Additionally, it shows a tendency toward the international harmonization of company law in civil and common law jurisdiction. It seems that Croatian law, as a civil law legal system, has started adopting some elements of the Anglo-Saxon common law system, which evidently prevails in international business.

6. Classroom activities based on comparative legal analysis

There is a variety of classroom activities which can be based on comparative legal analysis and at the same time practise the four language skills. Let me describe a few very effective ones for the mentioned purposes which have proved very successful in the classroom.

6.1. What's the difference?

In the first activity the focus is on comparing two terms from the legal systems at issue. The students are supposed to find definitions of two given terms and in a componential analysis compare their content by extracting the components of their meaning from the definitions they have found. The teacher directs the students to particular sources of information (legislative texts, monolingual dictionaries, reliable Internet sites or law lexica). The students create a table, extract relevant features from definitions, fill in the table and present it to the class.

6.2. Expert chat

The second activity is a communicative activity in which pairs of students are given tables with features of different areas of law already filled in. Student A gets only the part of table containing the information on one legal system and student B gets the other part of the table. By asking questions about the other system and answering questions about their own legal system on the basis of the table the students collect the relevant information and complete the table. After the tables have been completed a class discussion follows.

6.3. Researching different legal systems

The third activity is a research task in which the students use the Internet to discover information about particular areas of law in their national and foreign law. By juxtaposing the relevant information in two parallel columns they contrast the two legal systems and present their findings to the class. As a follow-up activity the students write a report for a senior partner (in legal English) or an email to a client in which they present the newly acquired information (in plain English). The teacher prepares reliable Internet sites for the students to use.

6.4. Student presentations

In short 10 to 15 minute individual presentations on an aspect of law in their national and foreign legal systems the students practise their presentation skills in a foreign language along with the comparative study of a legal topic. After having researched about some area of law (by using the resources previously discussed with the teacher) the students prepare a contrastive analysis and present it in class.

All the above activities have a double purpose. On the one hand they can be well used to compare and clarify the differences between legal systems, concepts and terms and at the same time they lend themselves to the integrated teaching of the four traditional language skills.

7. Conclusion

To sum up, a course in legal language is primarily a language course and not a course in foreign law, and its main objective has to be to teach legal practitioners or future professional lawyers the language skills and legal terminology needed for cross-cultural communication in the area of law. However, due to cultural differences between legal systems and their linguistic implications, it is necessary to adopt a content-based approach to teaching the language of the law in which comparative legal analysis is a useful method to overcome the gap between legal cultures. The primary function of comparative legal analysis in teaching legal language is, firstly, to clear up possible conceptual and terminological misunderstandings and confusion arising from the asymmetry of legal systems by clarifying the content of legal terms and to establish functional equivalents, and secondly, to contrast whole areas of different legal systems in order to discover dissimilarities in the structure of the area and their consequences on the language. Only in this way will the participants of legal language courses be adequately prepared for accurate transmission of legal information in their international contacts.

References

Barbić, Jakša 2007. *Zakon o trgovačkim društvima.* Zagreb: Organizator.

Brinton, Donna M. / Snow, Marguerite Ann / Wesche, Marjorie Bingham 1989. *Content-Based Second Language Instruction*. New York: Newbury.

Dignam, Alan / Lowry, John 2009. *Company Law*. New York: Oxford University Press.

Galdia, Marcus 2003. Comparative Law and Legal Translation. *The European Legal Forum* 1/1-4 at <http://:www.european-legal-forum.com>.

Hutchinson, Tom / Waters, Alan 2005. *English for Specific Purposes.* Cambridge: Cambridge University Press.

Mattila, Heikki E. S. 2006. *Comparative Legal Linguistics.* Aldershot: Ashgate.

Nida, Eugene 1975. *Componential Analysis of Meaning – An Introduction to Semantic Structures*. The Hague: Mouton.

Pommer, Sieglinde 2006. *Rechtsübersetzung und Rechtsvergleich.* Frankfurt : Peter Lang.

Pommer, Sieglinde 2008. Translation as Intercultural Transfer: The Case of Law. *SKASE Journal of Translation and Interpretation* 3/1 at <http://www.skase.sk/Volumes/JTI03/pdf_doc/2.pdf>.

Internet addresses

The UK Companies Act 2006 at <http://www.opsi.gov.uk/acts/acts 2006 /ukpga_20060046_ en _1>.

Zakon o trgovačkim društvima (Croatian Companies Act), NN 111/93 at <http://narodne-novine.nn.hr/clanci/sluzbeni/260024.html>.

Zakon o izmjenama i dopunama zakona o trgovačkim društvima (Act on Amendments to the Croatian Companies Act) at <http://narodne-novine.nn.hr/clanci/sluzbeni/329385.html>.

Legal Discourse across Cultures

Janet Ainsworth

Linguistic Ideology in the Workplace: the Legal Treatment in American Courts of Employers' 'English-only' Policies

1. Introduction

As the American workforce has become increasingly ethnically diverse in the past few decades, employers have faced challenges in managing their workplaces. In the course of maintaining their businesses, employers have responded to these challenges by adopting a variety of policies and practices to promote efficient and harmonious work environments. At times, however, employer attempts to regulate the workplace may cross the line and constitute legally impermissible discrimination. Under American civil rights law, workers are protected from discrimination in the workplace based on such categories as their race and national origin, but are not explicitly protected from discrimination resulting from the language they speak (Title VII of the Civil Rights Act of 1964). Of course, as an empirical fact, the use by a worker of a language other than English is often correlated with that worker's race or national origin (Perea 1994). Given that nexus between language usage and membership in a class protected under civil rights law, the question is whether it is legal for private employers to impose 'English only' requirements in the workplace and to discipline and even fire workers for speaking languages other than English.

These so-called 'English-only' rules are distinct from threshold English language competence requirements that might be imposed as job criteria. Clearly, many jobs can only be competently performed by workers with a degree of proficiency in English, and thus it is permissible to require a prospective employee to demonstrate an appropriate level of English language competence as a pre-condition to being hired for those jobs. That kind of employment qualification is not being questioned here. Rather, the 'English-only' rules at issue in this chapter are workplace rules that are imposed on workers already hired and performing on the job. In most cases, the jobs in question are low-skilled manual labour jobs, often in workplaces with a large number of workers whose first language is other than English. Under these 'English only' rules, workers are told that they must use English exclusively in the workplace or risk being disciplined or even fired. A worker using any other language in the workplace risks being summarily fired, even if the worker utters only a short phrase in that language. For example, in one reported case, an employee was fired for answering a question with *donde lo quieres?* [where do you want it?] in Spanish (Saucedo v. Brothers' Well Services 1979). In another case, a worker was dismissed for saying *no hay más* [there isn't any more] in Spanish (Garcia v. Gloor 1980). In some cases, workers were disciplined for using languages other than English even on their breaks or at lunch (Gonzalez v. Salvation Army 1991; Kania v. Archdiocese of Philadelphia 1998; EEOC v. Premier Operator Services 2000).

2. The expansive enforcement of 'English-only' rules in the contemporary American workplace

The proliferation of 'English only' policies appears to be of comparatively recent origin, with litigated cases by employees objecting to these policies beginning around 1980 and increasing dramatically in the past two decades (Rodriguez 2006: 1700). Court challenges to these rules are sometimes filed by fired or disciplined workers, and other times by workers seeking to prospectively enjoin the enforcement of these policies. In the earliest reported cases, federal district courts seemed sympathetic to the claim that penalizing foreign language use was tantamount to discrimination on the basis of race or national origin. In one early case, an Oregon federal district court held that an 'English only' policy could not be lawfully enforced against patrons in a tavern (Hernandez v. Erlenbusch 1973). In another early challenge to an 'English only' rule, the court found that the rule was unlawfully applied to a well driller by his employer (Saucedo v. Brothers' Well Services 1979). However, in recent years, federal appellate courts have become more hostile to such claims and have rejected employee arguments that 'English only' rules are prohibited under the Title VII civil rights law (Garcia v. Gloor 1980, Garcia v. Spun Steak 1993).

Federal courts have likewise upheld the enforcement of 'English only' rules in contexts beyond employment as well. Prison inmates have unsuccessfully challenged rules requiring that all sent or received mail be in English (Ortiz v. Fort Dodge Correctional Center 2004); that all inmate telephone calls be conducted in English (Boriboune v. Litscher 2003); and that inmates be barred from speaking languages other than English amongst themselves while working (Allah v. Poole 2009). Recently, a federal court in Kansas held that public schools could permissibly impose 'English only' rules on students – even in their playground and lunchtime conversations – and could suspend children for violations (Rubio ex rel. Z.R. v. Turner Unified School District No. 202 2006).

It is in the employment context, however, that most litigation over 'English only' policies has occurred. Such workplace policies have become increasingly common, often being enforced even in circumstances that seem counter-productive to workplace efficiency. For example, a Florida child welfare caseworker was disciplined for speaking Spanish on the job to a Spanish-speaking client. Despite the fact that an interview in Spanish was obviously the best way to serve that client, the caseworker's supervisor warned her, "Watch yourself, missy. I told you not to talk Spanish because we are in the United States" (Goitia v. Florida 2007: 37837). In another case, a taxi service implemented an 'English only' policy for its drivers even though one of its units, Taxi Latino, specifically catered to a Spanish-speaking clientele (Gonzalo v. All Island Transportation 2007). A New Jersey doctor's office hired a bilingual office manager specifically for her ability to speak Spanish, since their patients were overwhelming Spanish speaking, but fired her nonetheless for what her Anglophone supervisor felt was *excessive* Spanish speaking with the patients (Rosario v. Cacace 2001). The appeal of 'English only' policies to employers has been so irresistible that they are sometimes applied even in contexts such as these that would seem to be counter-productive.

3. Are 'English-Only' rules discriminatory?

Workers who face punishment and dismissal under the 'English only' rules have argued that these rules constitute covert forms of impermissible discrimination. It would be clearly unlawful for an employer to fire a worker for being of a particular ethnic origin or racial group. Punishing an employee for speaking a language associated with a race or ethnicity, if it were in fact a cover for employer animosity against that race or ethnic group, would then likewise be a civil rights violation. However, employees can seldom prove that the motivation of the 'English only' rule in their workplace is a pretext for actual racial or ethnic bias on the part of the employer. Instead, they argue that the enforcement of the rule, regardless of employer motivation, has a disparate impact on employees of a particular race or national origin. Because only those employees who speak a language other than English will be at risk of workplace discipline, the brunt of the rule falls on racial and ethnic minority workers. Under American civil rights law, once an employee demonstrates that a facially neutral workplace policy has a disparate negative impact on a protected category of workers – such as race or national origin – the employer must shoulder the burden to prove that the policy in question is justified by a compelling business necessity (Griggs v. Duke Power Company 1971; Albemarle Paper Company v. Moody 1975).

Appellate courts have, however, rejected the employees' claims that these rules operate to constitute direct race or ethnic discrimination, and go so far as to even deny that the enforcement of English-only rules has a disparate impact on workers based on their race or national origin. Despite the obvious linkage between language and ethnicity, American appellate courts have determined that these policies are nevertheless not impermissible discrimination. An examination of the courts' justifications for this determination reveals a judicial ideology about the nature of language and language use that underlies their analysis, an ideology that is inconsistent with the understanding of language derived from research in cognitive linguistics and sociolinguistics. Linguistic ideology – defined as "ideas about language [which] are implicated in the process by which any cultural ideas gain the discursive authority to become dominant" (Gal 1998: 321-322) – shapes judicial reasoning in these cases to the detriment of the claims of the bilingual workers. An unpacking of this linguistic ideology within the reasoning of the courts is essential to an understanding of why the appellate courts holdings in these cases are so fundamentally at odds with a linguistically informed perspective on the nature of communication and bilingualism.

4. Court rejection of worker claims of unlawful discrimination

In beginning their analyses of the workers' discrimination claims, the appellate court judges tend to be dismissive of the magnitude of the imposition on employees who are forced to communicate solely in a language which is not their first language. The centrality of speech in human interaction is ignored, with the Ninth Circuit characterizing speaking with fellow workers a mere privilege granted to workers through employer magnanimity. As with any other privilege, the court went on, employers are within their rights to condition the exercise of what they deem the privilege of worker communication on any whim or basis at all, since they had no obligation to grant the privilege of communication in the first place (Garcia v. Spun Steak 1993: 1487). The Fourth Circuit agreed, arguing that "the ability to converse on the job is a *privilege* of employment" (Long v. First Union Corporation 1996: 941, emphasis in original).

Not all courts have gone so far as to imagine that employers are so omnipotent that they could properly insist that workers do their jobs in absolute silence such that any lesser restriction on worker communication is automatically permissible. Even courts that take less extreme positions on employer power have, however, seriously underestimated the heavy burden placed on workers by requiring that all speech in the workplace be in English. Courts are able to trivialize this burden as a mere 'inconvenience', as the Ninth Circuit Court of Appeals put it, because of a mischaracterization of the nature of bilingual language users and usages, which in turn rests on their flawed linguistic ideology (Garcia v. Spun Steak 1993: 1488). Since the workers in question are described as being 'bilingual', the appellate judges characterize the rules as imposing no meaningful burden on them at all, since "it is axiomatic that the language a person who is multilingual elects to speak at a particular time is a matter of choice" (Garcia v. Spun Steak 1993: 1487). Therefore, since the workers in question could choose to speak in either their first language or in English, any apparent disparate impact on racial or ethnic minorities of the 'English only' rule is actually caused by the free choice of the workers to flout a rule that they could easily have complied with (Garcia v. Gloor 1980: 269-270; Garcia v. Spun Steak 1993: 1487). What these courts have considered a worker's "mere preference" to speak a particular language is thus unprotected by anti-discrimination law (Cosme v. Salvation Army 2003: 231).

5. Flawed linguistic assumptions in the courts' reasoning in 'English-only' rule challenges by employees

The courts' analysis in these cases rests on a number of unexamined assumptions about bilingual language use. First, it presumes that languages are transparent media of referential communication, such that there is nothing that cannot be as easily and effectively said in English as in the workers' native languages. Next, it presumes that bilingual workers by definition have sufficient facility in English to enable them to satisfy all of their communicative needs in either language, regardless of the context of the language use or the register of language performance. In that way, differences in the spectrum of linguistic competence among persons who could be called 'bilingual' are not seriously considered, and differences in an individual bilingual's linguistic competence depending on communicative context are minimized or flat-out ignored. Third, this analysis presumes that the particular language used by multilingual individuals is always a matter of conscious choice, so that it is fair and reasonable to hold bilingual speakers accountable whenever they 'choose' to use language other than pure English. Fourth, the courts' reasoning presumes that rules penalizing the use of a particular language are not the equivalent of rules discriminating against the ethnic or racial groups that typically use that language, since there is no necessary connection between language use and ethnic and racial identity. Each one of these four assumptions is highly questionable.

5.1. Law's false assumption that languages are transparent media of referential communication

This assumption focuses on the literal referential meaning of language and assumes that every language maps seamlessly onto every other language, without slippages or gaps. Linguists studying bilingualism have exposed the inadequacy of this assumption (Altarriba 2003). Although languages do appear to be substantially commensurable, linguistic research confirms what many people exposed to a foreign language intuitively realize: there are many shades of meaning that cannot be adequately represented in another language. For example, what is the English language equivalent to the Spanish term *machismo*? It is clearly not the same thing as either 'masculinity' or 'maleness.' In fact, because there is no good way to express the concept in English, English speakers familiar with the idea must make use of the Spanish word even in their English language discourse. These gaps and slippages between languages are ever-present, creating barriers to full equivalence in communication, even when a speaker is highly fluent in both languages. However, few multilingual speakers are in fact highly fluent in all of their languages, and problems in cross-linguistic communication are multiplied manifold under those circumstances.

5.2. Law's false assumption that, if persons are described as bilingual, they are capable of expressing themselves appropriately in either their first language or in English

In almost all of the reported cases, the workers in question are described as 'bilingual,' or competent in using English as well as their first language. However, the courts seldom go behind the label 'bilingual' to consider the *degree* of English language competence of the workers or the degree to which their competence varies according to domain of usage. Instead, the courts presume that bilingual speakers are fully fluent in each language, such that it is reasonable to require them to express themselves solely in English while on the job. Bilingual speakers are popularly imagined to be the equivalent of two monolinguals inhabiting the same speaking mind (Grosjean 1989).

In reality, the perfectly bilingual workers imagined by the courts are very much the exception rather than the rule among bilinguals. Bilingual proficiency exists on a continuum, with fully balanced bilinguals at one end of the spectrum, and those with extremely limited and context-specific ability at the other (Butler/Hakuta 2006: 118-125). Only rarely are bilinguals able to process and use their second language with anything approaching the fluency of their first language (Grosjean 1995). Given the fact that many of these 'English only' policies are imposed in workplaces involving low-skill, manual labour jobs, it is unsurprising that many of the workers would be able to perform their jobs effectively notwithstanding minimal English language competence. That is, the contextual domains in which such workers are conversant in English tend to be quite limited, likely sufficient for the demands of repetitive manual tasks but insufficient for other domains of ordinary communication. Thus, in order to be understood, such workers would have had no choice but to resort frequently to their first language, given their slight grasp of English vocabulary and syntax, even when they are attempting to speak in English. This phenomenon, called code-switching, involves the mixing of two languages within one discursive frame, and is a necessity for those whose second language is inadequate for ordinary communicative purposes. However, even highly fluent bilingual individuals tend to code-switch, sometimes because of the perceived inadequacy of a particular language to fully express the desired meaning. Code-switching can be intentionally performed by the speaker or it can be unconscious on the part of the speaker. When it is consciously done, code-switching serves a variety of linguistic functions: referential (when the speaker does not know the right word in the other language); expressive (invoking an identity indexed by language); phatic (invoking a change in register or tone of conversation); or metalinguistic (commenting on the language itself) (Appel/Muysken 1987: 118-120).

Neurolinguistic research has demonstrated that bilinguals appear to process language differently than do monolinguals, even when they are operating in monolingual mode (Fabbro 1999; Heredia/ Altarriba 2002). Psycholinguistic studies have explored the differences between bilingual and monolingual speakers in the linguistically constructed experience of the self (Pavlenko 2006). Thus, to presume that a bilingual speaker – even one with an exceptional degree of fluency in the acquired language – can and will use language in the way that a monolingual does is a mistake.

5.3. Law's false assumption that the language used by a bilingual person is always a matter of conscious choice on the part of the speaker

Courts have accepted employers' claims that employee use of foreign language is a kind of wilful insubordination deserving of punishment (Cosme v. Salvation Army 2003). Although some kinds of code-switching may be intentionally deployed by the speaker (Gumperz 1982; Myers-Scotton/Bolonyai 2001), much code-switching is in fact outside the conscious control of the code-switching speaker. In fact, it is well established by sociolinguistic researchers that bilinguals are often unaware that they have code-switched in their conversation (Poplack 1980: 601; Gal 1988: 245-46). When their code-switching is called to their attention, bilingual speakers will often blame it on a lapse of attention and will promise to pay better attention and avoid future code-switching. Despite their best intentions, however, they usually quickly resume code-switching in their discourse (Ritchie/ Bhatia 2006: 350-351). This may be a consequence of the fact that bilinguals cannot 'switch off' one language and operate solely in the other. As recent studies in neurolinguistic processing have revealed, both linguistic channels remain open regardless of the language being used at the moment (Grosjean 2006: 54-55).

One of the factors that has been identified as triggering this unconscious code-switching is the nature of the identity of the person being addressed, through a process referred to as accommodation (Myers-Scotton 2006: 154-158). Bilingual speakers are most likely to involuntarily code-switch when speaking with another who they know shares their linguistic background. To the extent that the workplaces in question are staffed by other ethnically identified workers, one would expect a high degree of involuntary code-switching to be triggered under those circumstances. This situation can be thought of as a form of functional interference, in which the lexicon or morphosyntactic structure of the speaker's dominant language is involuntarily mixed in with the second language being used (cf. Muysken 2006). In short, the belief that courts have expressed that bilinguals invariably have full conscious control over which language use in the workplace flies in the face of the psycholinguistic and neurolinguistic research on bilingualism.

5.4. Law's false conclusion that language use has no connection to the construction of ethnic identity

In determining that 'English only' workplace rules do not constitute impermissible discrimination on the basis of race or national origin, the courts distinguish between those markers of race and ethnicity that are immutable and consequently protected, and those that are merely incidentally associated with the protected categories of race and national origin such as language (Garcia v. Gloor 1980; Garcia v. Spun Steak 1993). Language use, these courts maintain, is not the same as the status of race or national origin because the user can make a conscious choice to use the language in question or not. According to this analysis, only those race or ethnic-linked traits that are immutable and not the product of choice should be protected by Title VII. Leave aside for a moment the fact that this reasoning would permit discrimination on the basis of religion, since the adoption or rejection of religious belief is the quintessential case of a voluntary choice rather than an immutable trait. The question remains: should the non-immutability of a trait associated with race or ethnicity render discrimination on the basis of that admittedly changeable trait impervious to legal redress?

On the face of it, it is certainly true that there is no invariable nexus between ethnicity and language use – some members of a particular ethnic group will not have command over the language traditionally associated with it, and likewise some out-group members will be fluent users of that language despite their lack of membership in the ethnic group. Nevertheless, it is beyond dispute that language serves a key role in the construction and maintenance of ethnic identity (Fishman 1977; Poplack 1980; Fishman 2001). Because the courts' linguistic ideology as already discussed accepts the concept that language is a transparent vehicle for the conveyance of referential meaning, the corollary – that language is nothing more than a transparent vehicle for reference – is but an easy step away. The insistence on this mechanistically instrumental view of language – divorced from any connection between language use and social identity – makes it difficult for courts to acknowledge that language usage has social meaning and that the semiotics of language use and language variation indexes social identity (Gumperz/Cook-Gumperz 1982) Having concluded that language usage does not invariably index ethnic identity, courts are led to conclude that punishing workers for violating an 'English only' rule does not support even an inference of discrimination on the basis of race or national origin (Velasquez v. Goldwater Memorial Hospital 2000; Magsanoc v. Coast Hotels and Casinos 2008; Pacheco v. New York Presbyterian Hospital 2009).

6. Are there compelling business reasons to justify 'English only' policies on the job?

The application by judges of these erroneous ideas about language in general and bilingualism in particular leads them to conclude that 'English only' rules are neither direct evidence of impermissible discrimination nor even the source of a disparate impact to the workers' non-Anglophone racial and ethnic groups. Having made that determination, appellate courts then hold that these workers have not made out the necessary *prima facie* case of unlawful discrimination to entitle them to relief under Title VI of the Civil Rights Act. Therefore, because the workers cannot show impermissible discrimination, it is not necessary that the courts go on further to determine whether the employers have a compelling business necessity to justify actions that have a disproportionate negative impact on racial or ethnic minorities on the job. Yet, some courts have continued their analysis to consider employers' claims that their particular 'English only' rules are justified due to their overriding business needs. Courts have been exceptionally deferential to employer arguments that their policies are based on legitimate business necessity. Almost any assertion of business necessity is accepted as justifying these policies – even a vague, conclusory claim that an 'English only' rule was needed so that the business would run 'smoothly and efficiently' was found to be sufficient to establish adequate business necessity to justify the policy in question (Long v. First Union Corporation 1996).

When pushed for specific justifications, employers have asserted two major business-related justifications for the imposition of 'English only' workplace rules. First, they are said to be needed to ensure a safe and efficient workplace. Second, the employers assert that these rules are necessary to promote racial and ethnic harmony on the job. The evidence in the cases, however, suggests strongly that, if employers did have the burden to justify these rules, they would be unable to do so.

The appeal to a monolingual workplace as promoting safety and efficiency is, at first blush, a persuasive argument. In an ideal world, a monolingual environment would result in more transparent communication among workers than would a multilingual workplace. But, as the testimony in the cases demonstrates, we do not live in that hypothetical ideal world. In the real world, workers with limited English competence will have a hard time understanding job instructions if they must be exclusively in English. Cooperation with co-workers will be often stymied when workers are prevented from discussing the job at hand in the language with which they have the greatest facility. Workers with limited English ability may be unable to fully understand safety warnings in English and may be unable to adequately inform fellow workers and supervisors of dangerous conditions that they happen to see on the job. In most of the litigated cases, the offending foreign language that resulted in worker discipline was used on the job between two workers who shared the fluent use of that language in question (Saucedo v. Brothers' Well Services 1979, Garcia v. Gloor 1980). Ironically, the required use of English in those cases might well have resulted in a less efficient and less safe workplace than simply permitting the workers to communicate in their shared first language.

If the appeal to workplace safety and efficiency turns out upon examination to be an inadequate rationale in most instances for the imposition of 'English only' rules on a linguistically diverse workplace, employers' attempts to justify 'English only' rules as promoting racial and ethnic harmony in the workplace are even less plausible. The asserted impetus for the imposition of English-only policies is often a claim that monolingual English workers fear that fellow workers are saying insulting things about them when they speak in other tongues (see, e.g., Hernandez v. Erlenbusch 1973; Gonzalez v. Salvation Army 1991; Garcia v. Spun Steak 1993; Kania v. Archdiocese of Philadephia 1998; Roman v. Cornell University 1999; Barber v. Lovelace Sandia Health Systems 2005; EEOC v. Sephora USA 2005). In none of the reported cases was there concrete evidence introduced that the non-English-speaking workers actually were making derogatory comments about their English-speaking co-workers. Apparently a belief on the part of monolingual speakers that those speaking in a foreign language are doing so in order to talk negatively about them is a common paranoid suspicion, regardless of whether it has any basis in fact. Such suspicion might well contribute to an ethnically divided environment in the workplace, but it could be better addressed by imposition of a policy forbidding insulting or harassing one's co-workers, whatever language is used to do so.

If the imposition of an 'English only' rule is supposed to overcome racial and ethnic tensions and promote racial and ethnic harmony in the workplace, the evidence from these cases shows that it badly backfires. Once workplaces adopt 'English only' rules, they tend to become more ethnically polarized and tense as a direct result of the newly imposed rules (see, e.g., Hernandez v. Erlenbusch 1973: 754; Gutierrez v. Municipal Court 1988: 1042-1043; EEOC v. Premier Operator Services 2000: 1070). Bilingual workers complain about being mocked for their use of accented or non-standard English (Gutierrez v. Municipal Court 1988: 1042-1043). They report that they are singled out by their supervisors and threatened with being fired if they slip and speak in their native languages, creating a tense atmosphere in which the possibility of termination looms constantly (Garcia v. Spun Steak 1993: 1486-87; Goitia v. Florida 2007: 37841). Unable to express themselves adequately in English in their workplace interactions, these workers report feeling humiliated and at a distinct disadvantage compared to their monolingual English co-workers (Garcia v. Spun Steak 1993: 1487). Yet courts have consistently rejected workers' assertions that the enforcement of 'English only' rules creates a hostile working environment for them that is tantamount to overt racial or ethnic discrimination. (see e.g. Tran v. Standard Motor Products 1998; Montes v. Vail Clinic 2007).

It is unsurprising, however, that non-Anglophone workers come to feel that their ethnic heritage itself is being directly denigrated by a policy that they see as specifically targeting their ethnic identity. In one case, a Spanish-speaking worker reported that her employer 'screamed' at her "go back to your own country" when she was overheard speaking Spanish to a fellow worker (Chen 1994: 162-163). Another worker testified that, when fired for violating the English-only policy at work, his supervisor told him to "go home and sit on his Puerto Rican bum" (Lopez v. Flight Services 2008). In another case, a worker who was told "We don't tolerate any 'Mesican' [sic] talk" on the job concluded that his Mexican heritage was being singled out for disrespect (Saucedo v. Brothers' Well Service 1979: 920). In fact, in another such case, the 'English only' policy was announced with a sign stating "Absolutely No Guns, Knives or Weapons of any kind are allowed on these Premises at any time! English is the official language of Premier Operator Services, Inc. All conversations on these premises are to be in English" (EEOC v. Premier Operator Services 2000: 1069-1070). It is easy to see why a policy apparently analogizing the speaking of foreign languages to the possession of deadly weapons was seen by the bilingual workers as a sign that they themselves were being demonized. Demoralized and alienated from employers and English-speaking fellow workers, the bilingual workers in these cases testify that these restrictions create an "atmosphere of inferiority, isolation, and intimidation" (Garcia v. Spun Steak 1993: 1486-1487). Far from ensuring a harmonious workplace, 'English only' rules appear to be a recipe for a tense environment in which racial and ethnic divisions between workers become amplified and sharpened, and inter-ethnic resentment and hostility fuelled.

7. Conclusion

As this chapter suggests, the imposition and justification of 'English only' rules in the workplace is facilitated by a form of language ideology that courts and lawyers unreflectively deploy. Because that ideology is not consciously articulated, it is largely impervious to direct challenge. Even when expert witnesses with linguistics training testify in these cases, courts too often elect not to seriously consider their testimony. Sadly, when expert scientifically-based knowledge clashes with judicial 'common sense' ideological beliefs, ideology tends to beat out science. The analysis of the English-only employment discrimination cases exposes one aspect of a linguistic ideological hegemony in the law. As a normative matter, this analysis further suggests the need for explicit legal protection for language rights as a civil rights issue because of the critical link between language and social identity.

References

Appel, Rene / Muysken, Pieter 2005. *Language Contact and Bilingualism.* Amsterdam: Amsterdam University Press.

Altarriba, Jeannette 2003. Does 'Cariño' equal 'Liking'? A Theoretical Approach to Nonequivalence between Languages. *International Journal of Bilingualism* 7, 305-322.

Butler, Yuko G. / Hakuta, Kenji. 2006. Bilingualism and Second-language Acquisition. In Bhatia, Tej K./ Ritchie, William C. (eds) *The Handbook of Bilingualism.* Malden, MA: Blackwell, 114-144.

Chen, Edward M. 1994. Garcia v. Spun Steak: Speak-English-only Rules and the Demise of Workplace Pluralism. *Asian Law Journal* 1, 155-188.

Fabbro, Franco 1999. *Neurolinguistics of Bilingualism.* East Sussex, UK: Psychology Press.

Fishman, Joshua A. 1997. *In Praise of the Beloved Language: A Comparative View of Positive Ethnolinguistic Consciousness.* Berlin: Mouton de Gruyter.

Fishman, Joshua A. (ed.) 2001. *Handbook of Language and Ethnic Identity.* New York: Oxford University Press.

Gal, Susan 1988. The Political Economy of Code Choice. In Heller, Monica (ed.) *Codeswitching: Anthropological and Sociolinguistic Perspectives.* Berlin: Mouton de Gruyter, 245-262.

Gal, Susan 1998. Multiplicity and Contention among Language Ideologies. In Schieffelin, Bambi B. / Wooland, Kathryn A. / Kroskrity, Paul V. (eds) *Language Ideologies: Practice and Theory.* New York: Oxford University Press, 317-331.

Grosjean, Francois 1989. Neurolinguists Beware! The Bilingual is Not Two Monolinguals in One Person. *Brain and Language* 36, 3-15.

Grosjean, Francois 1995. A Psycholinguistic Approach to Code-switching: The Recognition of Guest Words by Bilinguals. In Milroy, Lesley / Muysken, Pieter (eds) *One Speaker, Two Languages: Cross-disciplinary Perspectives on Code-switching.* Cambridge: Cambridge University Press, 259-275.

Grosjean, Francois 2006. Studying Bilinguals: Methodological and Conceptual Issues. In Bhatia, Tej K. / Ritchie, William C. (eds). *The Handbook of Bilingualism*. Malden, MA: Blackwell, 32-63.

Gumperz, John J. 1982. Conversational code switching. In Gumperz, John J. *Discourse Strategies*. Cambridge: Cambridge University Press, 55-99.

Gumperz, John J. / Cook-Gumperz, Jenny (eds) 1982. *Language and Social Identity*. Cambridge: Cambridge University Press.

Heredia, Roberto R. / Altarriba, Jeannette (eds) 2002. *Bilingual Sentence Processing*. Amsterdam: Elsevier Science.

Muysken, Pieter 2006. Two Linguistic Systems in Contact: Grammar, Phonology, and Lexicon. In Bhatia, Tej K. / Ritchie, William C. (eds) *The Handbook of Bilingualism*. Malden, MA: Blackwell, 147-168.

Myers-Scotton, Carol / Bolonyai, Agnes 2001. Calculating Speakers: Codeswitching in a Rational Choice Model. *Language in Society* 30, 1-28.

Myers-Scotton, Carol 2006. *Multiple Voices: An Introduction to Bilingualism*. Malden, MA.: Blackwell.

Pavlenko, Anna. 2006. *Bilingual Minds: Emotional Experience, Expression, and Representation*. Clevedon, UK: Multilingual Matters.

Perea, Juan F. 1994. Ethnicity and Prejudice: Re-evaluating 'National Origin' Discrimination under Title VII. *William and Mary Law Review* 35, 805-870.

Poplack, Shana 1980. Sometimes I'll Start a Sentence in Spanish y Termino en Espanol: Toward a Typology of Code-switching. *Linguistics* 18, 581-618.

Ritchie, William C. / Bhatia, Tej K. (2006). Social and Psychological Factors in Language Mixing. In Bhatia, Tej K / Ritchie, William C. (eds) *The Handbook of Bilingualism*. Malden, MA: Blackwell, 336-352.

Rodriguez, Cristina M. 2006. Language Diversity in the Workplace. *Northwestern University Law Review* 100, 1689-1773.

Cases and statutes cited

Albemarle Paper Company v. Moody, 422 U.S. 405 (1975).
Allah v. Poole, 506 F.Supp. 2d 174 (W.D. N.Y. 2009).
Barber v. Lovelace Sandia Health System, 409 F. Supp. 2d 1313 (D. N.Mex. 2005).
Boriboune v. Litscher, 91 Fed. Appx. 498 (7th Cir. 2003).
Cosme v. Salvation Army, 284 F. Supp. 2d 229 (D. Mass. 2003).
EEOC v. Premier Operator Services, 113 F. Supp. 2d 1066 (N.D. Tex. 2000).
EEOC v. Sephora USA, 419 F. Supp. 2d 408 (S.D.N.Y. 2005).
Garcia v. Gloor, 618 F.2d 264 (5th Cir. 1980).
Garcia v. Spun Steak, 998 F.2d 1480 (9th Cir. 1993).
Goitia v. Florida, 2007 U.S. Dist. LEXIS 37837 (M.D. Fla. 2007).
Gonzalez v. Salvation Army, 1991 WL 11009376 (M.D. Fla 1991).
Gonzalo v. All Island Transportation, 2007 U.S. Dist. LEXIS 13069 (E.D.N.Y. 2007).
Griggs v. Duke Power Company, 401 U.S. 424 (1971).
Gutierrez v. Municipal Court, 838 F.2d 1031 (9th Cir. 1988), reh'g denied 861 F.2d 1187 (9th Cir.), cert. granted and judgment vacated as moot, 490 U.S. 1016 (1989).
Hernandez v. Erlenbusch, 368 F. Supp. 752 (D. Or. 1973).
Kania v. Archdiocese of Philadelphia, 14 F. Supp. 2d 730 (E.D. Pa. 1998).
Long v. First Union Corporation, 83 F.3d 1151 (4th Cir. 1996).
Lopez v. Flight Services, 2008 WL 203028 (W.D. N.Y. 2008).
Magsanoc v. Coast Hotels and Casinos, 293 Fed. Appx. 454 (9th Cir. 2008).
Montes v. Vail Clinic, 497 F.3d 1160 (10th Cir. 2007).
Ortiz v. Fort Dodge Correctional Center, 368 F.3d 1024 (8th Cir. 2004).
Pacheco v. New York Presbyterian Hospital, 593 F.Supp. 2d 599 (S.D.N.Y. 2009).
Roman v. Cornell University, 53 F. Supp. 2d 223 (N.D. N.Y. 1999).
Rosario v. Cacace, 767 A. 2d 1023 (N.J. Super. Ct. App. Div. 2001).
Rubio ex rel. Z.R. v. Turner Unified School District No. 202, 453 F. Supp. 2d 1295 (D. Kan. 2006).
Saucedo v. Brothers' Well Service, 464 F. Supp. 919 (S.D. Tex. 1979).
Tran v. Standard Motor Products, 10 F. Supp. 2d 1199 (D. Kan. 1998).
Title VII, Civil Rights Act of 1964, as amended 42 U.S.C. 2000e (1994).
Velasquez v. Goldwater Memorial Hospital, 88 F.Supp. 2d 257 (S.D.N.Y. 2000).

WILLIAM BROMWICH

Discourse Practices and Divergences in Legal Cultures in Employment Tribunals*

1. Introduction

This chapter takes as its starting point the insights provided by a number of authors (Swales 1990, 1996, 2004; Drew/Heritage 1992; Bhatia 1993, 2002, 2004; Maley 1994; Goodrich 1988; Candlin/Bhatia/Jensen 2002; Bhatia *et al.* 2003; Garzone 2003; Gotti 2003; Tessuto 2003; Bhatia/Gotti 2006) to examine discourse and professional practices in employment tribunals first in a national and then in an international context. With a view to investigating legal discourse in different legal systems, the chapter examines the institutional constraints on discourse processes in employment cases at Employment Tribunals in the UK, the European Union Civil Service Tribunal in Luxembourg, and the International Labour Organization Administrative Tribunal (ILOAT) in Geneva. Although in all cases the pragmatic function is the presentation of complaints by employees against their employers for the purpose of obtaining compensation or reinstatement, the procedural rules shaping the discourse are strikingly different, with consequent variation in generic structure and lexical content. In examining the institutional procedures and case materials, it is argued that Employment Tribunals in the UK, standing firmly in the common law tradition, provide for courtroom hearings in which the parties present their evidence orally, following the classic sequence of *examination-in-chief* and *cross-examination*. On the other hand, at the European Union Civil Service Tribunal (where cases may be heard in

* The author wishes to acknowledge support from the Marco Biagi Foundation, University of Modena and Reggio Emilia.

any of the 23 official languages of the EU, depending on the language of the application) and at the ILOAT, the proceedings (in English or French) bear a stronger resemblance to the civil law tradition, with most or all of the discourse taking the form of written pleadings. The jurisdiction of the EU Civil Service Tribunal is supranational, and that of the ILOAT international, dealing with complaints lodged by staff members respectively of EU and UN organizations. In the case of the European Union Civil Service Tribunal, written pleadings may be accompanied by hearings. However, in the case of the ILOAT, the holding of courtroom hearings would require the parties to travel from all over the world. Partly due to this constraint, the discourse is structured in an entirely different manner compared to the national tribunal, with claims presented and argumentation constructed almost exclusively on the basis of written documents, in a genre chain (Fairclough 2003: 31) consisting of the *complaint*, the *defendant's reply*, the *complainant's rejoinder*, the *defendant's surrejoinder*, and finally the *judgment*. This enables the ILOAT to deal with cases entirely on the basis of written pleadings, with applications for hearings seldom allowed. An examination of the terminology in English in the three Tribunals, one national, one supranational,[1] and one international, reveals significant divergences in legal cultures, as the parties seek to construct and interpret meanings while complying with the institutional constraints prevailing in each of the systems.

1 As regards Supranational Law, "Practically speaking, there is only one supranational legal order – the European Union". University of California, Berkeley, <http://www.law.berkeley.edu/library/classes/iflr/basicsguide.html> (This and all subsequent websites in this chapter last accessed 30-09-09).

2. The Employment Tribunal

Two of the key characteristics of Employment Tribunals in Great Britain (not including Northern Ireland, which has its own separate provisions)[2] are reported to be their accessibility and informality:

(1) You can represent yourself and the Employment Tribunal will try to make things clear for you. The procedures are quite informal.[3]

This point was emphasized by the part-time Chairman of an Employment Tribunal in London (*The Guardian,* The Common Good: March 20 2001):

(2) The employment tribunal is uniquely a court for ordinary people, which is what attracted me to it. The ethos is that it should be accessible and as informal as possible.[4]

The level of informality extends to allowing unrepresented claimants to represent themselves in the Tribunal, rather than instructing a solicitor, and as a result the Chairman of the Tribunal may be called upon to provide assistance to the unrepresented party (*The Guardian,* Public Voices: March 21 2002):

(3) The work we do is challenging and can include complex questions of law, assisting an unrepresented party and some very high value claims.[5]

There is a tension between the need to guarantee access to the Tribunal, and the need to avoid inflating the number of claims, taking account of the fact that in all 151,000 claims were accepted by the

---

2 Northern Ireland has Industrial Tribunals and the Fair Employment Tribunal.

3 Information taken from government website DirectGov: <http://www.direct.gov.uk/en/Employment/ResolvingWorkplaceDisputes/Employmenttribunals/DG_173242>.

4 <http://www.guardian.co.uk/society/2003/mar/20/publicvoices5>.

5 <http://www.guardian.co.uk/society/2003/mar/20/publicvoices5>.

Employment Tribunals in 2008-2009.[6] The attempt to facilitate access to the Tribunal is reflected in the language used on the DirectGov website to explain the workings of Employment Tribunals to the general public:

(4) An Employment Tribunal deals with disputes to do with work. Before applying to an Employment Tribunal see *if you can resolve your problem another way* and check *if you are entitled* to make an Employment Tribunal claim. (Emphasis added here and in all subsequent examples)[7]

The use of the second person pronoun in example (4) is intended to signal an informal conversational tone rather than a formal bureaucratic voice, while the use of technical terms is generally avoided. In example (5) even the term 'Tribunal' is explained, and the judge and the lay members are referred to simply as 'people'.

(5) Cases are usually heard by a panel of three people, called a 'Tribunal'. It is made up of a legally qualified Employment Judge, and two 'lay members' that represent the employee and employer sectors. The lay members use their experience to bring balance to the proceedings.[8]

The DirectGov website description of the workings of Employment Tribunals places an emphasis on informality:

(6) Employment Tribunals hear cases involving employment disputes. They are less formal than a court.[9]

At the same time a particularly important institutional constraint on discourse in the Tribunal is highlighted:

---

6 Tribunals Service, *Employment Tribunal and EAT Statistics (GB), 1 April 2008 to 31 March 2009*, <www.tribunals.gov.uk>.

7 See the explanatory material posted on the DirectGov website: <http://www.direct.gov.uk/en/Employment/ResolvingWorkplaceDisputes/Employmenttribunals/DG_10028122>.

8 *ibid.*

9 *ibid.*

(7) However, you give evidence under an oath or affirmation, and if you lie you can be convicted of perjury.[10]

The parties to the proceedings, and the witnesses they call to give evidence in support of their claims, are thus made aware of this constraint, even in cases in which they do not have legal representation.

DirectGov also provides guidance for claimants in the transition from the world of everyday experience to the world of legal discourse, with the transformation of the verb phrases of practical experience into the noun phrases of legal terminology, as shown in the following examples from the DirectGov website:[11]

PRACTICAL EXPERIENCE	LEGAL CONCEPT
a panel of three people	a Tribunal
not being paid	unlawful deduction from wages
your employer treats you less favourably because you are disabled	disability discrimination

Table 1. From the world of practical experience to the world of legal discourse.

In this process the language becomes more highly nominalized, facilitating the flow of the discourse.

2.1. Preliminary sites of engagement: mediation, conciliation and arbitration

In spite of the alleged informality and accessibility of the Employment Tribunal, in most cases there are substantial legal costs and making a legal claim is undoubtedly a challenging experience. For this reason, employees are encouraged to seek alternative dispute resolution, which brings to mind the discourse of international arbitration law in the world of commerce (Bhatia/Candlin/Gotti 2003). The advice is to seek redress through internal procedures initially, then to consider mediation, conciliation or arbitration at a later stage:

---

10 *ibid.*
11 *ibid.*

(8) It is often better to sort out problems informally with your employer before going to an Employment Tribunal. In most cases you should try to resolve the problem through your employer's grievance or disciplinary process before you make a claim. You could also try the help of a third party (mediator or conciliator). [...] If your dispute is likely to turn into an Employment Tribunal case, Acas (the Advisory, Conciliation and Arbitration Service) may be able to offer you a free conciliation service.[12]

The Advisory, Conciliation and Arbitration Service (Acas) has a duty to take an even-handed stance to resolving disciplinary and grievance issues at work, providing guidance to both employers and employees, and in support of its mission it publishes an 80-page guide to *Discipline and grievances at work – The Acas Guide.*[13] Mediation, conciliation and arbitration are seen as a way of avoiding the substantial costs associated with hearings at the Employment Tribunal, in the same way that international arbitration is intended to reduce the costs of dispute resolution in commercial matters. "Arbitration is intended to be an efficient, economical and effective alternative to litigation" (Bhatia 2007: 396): in the employment field the three distinct options of mediation, conciliation and arbitration are intended to perform the same function. Arbitration is presented as one of a number of alternatives in order to avoid recourse to the Employment Tribunal:

(9) *What arbitration is*
In arbitration, you and your employer allow an independent and impartial outsider (the arbitrator, or arbiter in Scotland) to determine the outcome of your problem. Arbitration differs from conciliation and mediation because the arbitrator acts like a judge, making a firm decision on a case.
If you and your employer agree to go to an arbitrator, it may be a quick way of resolving a problem without the stress and expense of an Employment Tribunal. Arbitration is faster and less formal than an Employment Tribunal.[14]

If the parties opt for mediation rather than arbitration, the mediators may be Acas employees (internal mediators), or external mediators, working either individually or in pairs, as co-mediators. The mediator

---

12 *ibid.*

13 <www.acas.org.uk>.

14 <www.direct.gov.uk/en/Employment/ResolvingWorkplaceDisputes/index. htm>.

is not intended to judge but to facilitate the reaching of a settlement between the parties. Mediation can be used:

(10) (i) for conflict involving colleagues of a similar job or grade, or between a line manager and their staff;
(ii) at any stage in the conflict as long as any ongoing formal procedures are put in abeyance, or where mediation is included as a stage in the procedures themselves;
(iii) at any stage in the conflict as long as any ongoing formal procedures are put in abeyance, or where mediation is included as a stage in the procedures themselves;
(iv) to rebuild relationships after a formal dispute has been resolved;
(v) to address a range of issues, including relationship breakdown, personality clashes, communication problems, bullying and harassment.[15]

However, it is recommended that mediation should not be used as a *first resort*: rather, "people should be encouraged to speak to each other and talk to their manager before they seek a solution via mediation".[16] The first stage of dispute resolution is to follow internal procedures, the second stage is mediation, co-mediation (mediators working as a pair), conciliation or arbitration, and the third and final stage is the filing of a claim with the Employment Tribunal. Any consideration of discursive practices at the Tribunal needs to take account of this overall context, in which Acas professional practices play a significant role. In addition, the *Acas Code of Practice on disciplinary and grievance procedures*[17] provides a 'soft law' basis for dispute resolution, and Employment Tribunals expect parties to comply with the provisions of this Code:

(11) An Employment Tribunal will look at whether you and your employer have followed the principles in the Acas Code of Practice on disciplinary and grievance procedures (the Code). The Code sets out the principles you and your employer should follow to achieve a reasonable standard of behaviour in handling grievance and disciplinary cases.[18]

---

15 <www.acas.org.uk> *Discipline and grievances at work – The Acas guide, p.7.*
16 <www.acas.org.uk> *Discipline and grievances at work – The Acas guide, p.8.*
17 <www.acas.org.uk> *Discipline and grievances at work – The Acas guide, p.23.*
18 See DirectGov, footnote 8, *supra.*

The use of the hedging device 'reasonable' to describe the 'standard of behaviour' in a site of engagement of this kind introduces an element of vagueness into the discourse, previously investigated with reference to legislative texts (Bhatia *et al.* 2005) but which also plays a key role in this 'soft law' context. Similar considerations apply to the terms 'unreasonable' and 'unreasonably':

(12) An Employment Tribunal will consider whether a failure to follow the principles in the Code was unreasonable. It can choose to adjust awards by up to 25 per cent if it considers that you or your employer acted unreasonably.[19]

Although the Code of Practice counts only as 'soft law', failure to comply with its provisions can clearly give rise to material consequences in the world of 'hard law'. A further reference to 'reasonable' behaviour is to be found in connection with the awarding of costs in cases in which the claimant's behaviour is deemed to be 'unreasonable':

(13) Unlike other courts, Employment Tribunals don't usually order either side to pay costs unless either:
- they decide you or your employer acted unreasonably in bringing the case,
- or any representatives at the hearing behave unreasonably.[20]

2.2. Investigating discursive practices at the Employment Tribunal

The investigation of discursive practices at the Employment Tribunal presents significant methodological difficulties in the sense that audio and video recordings of the proceedings are not permitted, transcripts are not published, and participant observation is required to gain insight into the institutional and interpersonal dynamics. In order to examine the multiple discourses, actions and voices in employment cases, for the present study the author attended hearings in two separate cases at the central London Employment Tribunal, in 2007 and 2008, making a written record of some of the most salient exchanges.

---

19 See footnote 8, *supra*.

20 <http://www.direct.gov.uk/en/Employment/index/htm> Employment Tribunals.

Information was also obtained from the participants in the proceedings, taking account of the evident limits of ethnographic research findings. In addition, information about discourse processes at the Tribunal was obtained from the Employment Tribunals (Constitution and Rules of Procedure) Regulations 2004.[21] In particular, with regard to accessibility, the right of the parties *to give evidence, to call witnesses, to question witnesses and to address the tribunal* appear to be a particularly significant feature of discursive practice at the Employment Tribunal, as clearly stated in the Regulations:

(14) What happens at the Hearing
27. - (1) The President, Vice President or a Regional Chairman shall fix the date, time and place of the Hearing and the Secretary shall send to each party a notice of the Hearing together with information and guidance as to procedure at the Hearing.
(2) Subject to rule 14(3), at the Hearing a party shall be entitled to give evidence, to call witnesses, to question witnesses and to address the tribunal.
(3) The tribunal shall require parties and witnesses who attend the Hearing to give their evidence on oath or affirmation.[22]

The Regulations are characterized by a higher level of formality than the advice posted on the DirectGov website cited above, which was intended for the general public, and characterized by a conversational tone, the use of the second person pronoun, verb phrases and the limited use of legal terminology. On the other hand, the Regulations are aimed at members of the specialized discourse community, even though the level of complexity does not equal that of legislative provisions (Bhatia 1994: 137). The sentence in example (15) below is over 70 words long, with a formal tone, the use of the third person, and formal legal terminology, such as *proceedings, a pre-hearing review, the chairman, the party, the contentions, make an order* and *as a condition of.* However, it achieves the objective of transparency and lack of ambiguity:

---

21 The Employment Tribunals (Constitution and Rules of Procedure) Regulations 2004, Article 27 <http://www.opsi.gov.uk/si/si2004/20041861. htm>.

22 The Employment Tribunals (Constitution and Rules of Procedure) Regulations 2004, Article 20 <http://www.opsi.gov.uk/si/si2004/20041861. htm>.

(15) Requirement to pay a deposit in order to continue with proceedings 20. - (1) At a pre-hearing review if a chairman considers that the contentions put forward by any party in relation to a matter required to be determined by a tribunal have little reasonable prospect of success, the chairman may make an order against that party requiring the party to pay a deposit of an amount not exceeding £500 as a condition of being permitted to continue to take part in the proceedings relating to that matter.[23]

In addition, the Regulations clearly state the consequences of persisting with a vexatious or unfounded claim:

(16) An order made under this rule, and the chairman's grounds for making such an order, shall be recorded in a document signed by the chairman. A copy of that document shall be sent to each of the parties and shall be accompanied by a note explaining that if the party against whom the order is made persists in making those contentions relating to the matter to which the order relates, he may have an award of costs or preparation time made against him and could lose his deposit.[24]

In semiotic terms, the courtroom conveys clear signals about the authority and power relations to the parties as they take their places in this "strange and alien setting":

> [The] courtroom is, for most people, a strange and alien setting. Anyone who visits a court for the first time and witnesses a typical day or even an hour's proceedings is usually someone overcome by a sense of having ventured into an arcane […] world. […] Semiotically, the strongest meanings communicated by the physical setting of the room and behaviour of those in it are those of hierarchical power. The physical layout of the room expresses, as it is intended to, a 'symbolic representation of the authority of the court' (Goodrich 1988: 143). The judge or magistrate(s) occupies a dominant, focal position, usually (in England or Australia) sitting under an insignia-topped canopy which marks their position as a representative of sovereign justice. The opposing parties, each represented by counsel face the judge or magistrate (the 'bench'), each occupying a delimited area and space of table. Of the chief participants, only the counsel move freely in the inner space […] of the court. (Maley 1994: 32)

23 *ibid.* Article 20(1).
24 *ibid.* Article 20(1).

By means of a kind of interdiscursivity (Fairclough 2003: 218) between professional domains, the Employment Tribunal reproduces many of these courtroom features, with the members of the Tribunal (the Employment Judge and the two lay members) seated in a dominant position facing the rest of the courtroom. The counsel for the claimant and the defendant sit diagonally opposite the Chairman of the Tribunal, accompanied by their respective clients, while members of the public are seated at the back.

Although the parties are required to present any relevant documentary evidence (pay slips, letters of dismissal, written records of any disciplinary procedures) seven days before the hearing, written pleadings are not required:

(17) If a party wishes to submit written representations for consideration at a hearing (other than a case management discussion) he shall present them to the Employment Tribunal Office not less than 7 days before the hearing and shall at the same time send a copy to all other parties.[25]

Standing firmly in the common law tradition, the argumentation takes place as an oral trial, regardless of whether or not the claimant has appointed a legal representative. The centrality of the oral trial as a site of engagement in common law systems is underlined by Maley:

> The oral trial is the centrepiece of the adversary system (Devlin 1979: 54) and the rules which regulate the oral proceedings are essentially verbal: they are the rules of evidence and other exclusionary rules which constrain the semiotics of the situation. These are the rules which are implied by the adversary system and which are intended to make it not only workable but equitable. They stipulate what must be said, what may be said – and of course by whom and in what order (Maley and Fahey 1991: 3). That is to say, the ideational, interpersonal and textual meanings of this discourse type are strictly constrained. (Maley 1994: 33)

At this stage of the analysis, the claim that the interdiscursivity between Employment Tribunals and law courts *strictu senso* is established by a comparison of the courtroom settings may appear to stand

25 The Employment Tribunals (Constitution and Rules of Procedure) Regulations 2004, Article 14(5) <http://www.opsi.gov.uk/si/si2004/20041861.htm>.

on shaky ground, as there is indeed a lower degree of formality in Employment Tribunals, also due to the absence of uniformed (or even plain-clothes) police officers in Employment Tribunals. However, in taking the analysis a step further, and considering discursive practices in the Tribunal, the claim seems to stand on firmer ground when considering the cross-examination of the parties and witnesses.

In particular, the practice of examination of the witness by counsel for one party, followed by cross-examination of the witness by counsel for the opposing party, is a significant institutional constraint leaving the witnesses with limited room for manoeuvre. In many cases cross-examination is aimed at undermining witness credibility rather than at simply ascertaining the facts of the case or the order in which they took place. In particular, double-bind questions can have a damaging impact on the credibility of the witness in the eyes of the jury (in criminal cases) and of the Chairman and lay members of the Tribunal (in employment cases). Drew argues that:

> In the adversarial Anglo-American criminal-justice system, cross-examination is essentially hostile. Attorneys test the veracity or credibility of the evidence being given by the witnesses with questions which are designed to discredit the other side's version of events, and instead to support his or her own side's case. When being cross-examined, witnesses are, of course, conscious of this purposefulness behind the questions they are asked. They are alive to the possibility that a question or a series of questions may be intended to expose errors or inconsistencies in their evidence, and hence to challenge and undermine it. This awareness on the part of the witness is manifest in the guarded and defensive ways in which they answer certain questions. (Drew 1992: 470)

At least one significant instance in which a witness gave a guarded response to hostile cross-examination was recorded during participant observation of a case at the Central London Employment Tribunal in 2007. The witness was a teenager, a young man who was giving evidence against a fellow employee in a restaurant who had brought a claim for unfair dismissal. The claimant actually lost her case since at the end of the hearing she was found by the Tribunal to have been dismissed with just cause, as she had been taking money from the till at the end of each evening, an act of dishonesty that she attempted to conceal by pretending to give substantial refunds to dissatisfied customers who complained about the quality of their meals. Such complaints were only recorded at the end of shifts worked by this particular employee, and this counted against her. The teenager giving evidence gave the impression of being an honest young man who had the courage to give a detailed first-hand account of the facts of the case, even though his testimony was clearly damaging to the employee who had been engaging in repeated acts of dishonesty. However, he was subjected to extremely hostile cross-examination by counsel for the claimant, who in concluding a series of hostile questions, asked him in a brusque manner: "You're a cheeky young chap, aren't you?" This was a double-bind question since confirmation would have resulted in a loss of face for the witness, whereas a denial that challenged the veracity of the claim would only have confirmed that he was indeed cheeky, revealing a tendency to 'answer back' to his 'elders and betters'. In this case, the teenage witness was well aware of the pragmatic force of the question, and avoided falling into that particular trap by maintaining a dignified silence. In this way, without uttering a single word, he managed to refute the claim that had been put to him.

This particular exchange exemplifies the transfer of discursive practices from the domain of litigation to the employment domain. In Bhatia's terms this transfer could be said to be a form of 'colonization' of discourse processes, with practices transplanted from one professional domain to another, in particular with "the importation of typical litigation processes and procedures" (Bhatia 2007: 397). He underlines the need for "the study of interdiscursivity where two rather different professional practices, each one well-established in its own right, interact with each other, creating a perfect environment for the 'colonization' of one practice by the other" (Bhatia 2007: 397). From the point of view of the witness, this hostile cross-examination imported from the domain of litigation was evidently an intimidating experience, in contrast with claims that discourse practices in the Employment Tribunal are characterized by 'informality' and 'accessibility'. Alternative forms of dispute resolution – mediation, conciliation and arbitration – can clearly play a role.

3. The European Union Civil Service Tribunal

In the multilingual and multicultural context of the 27 Member States in the European Union, the discourse practices and procedures in the EU Civil Service Tribunal are not modelled on the practices and procedures in the Employment Tribunal examined above, but have developed autonomously in the civil law tradition. The Rules of Procedure of the Tribunal provide evidence that the institutional framework is that of the European Court of Justice, in existence since 1953,[26] and the Court of First Instance, set up in 1989 with a view to reducing the number of staff cases referred to the ECJ. The European Union Civil Service Tribunal came into operation in 2005 to perform the same function, with the paradoxical result that the Court of First Instance no longer acts as the court of first instance in staff cases, but as the court of appeal. However, in discourse and procedural terms there is a strong 'family resemblance' between the three judicial bodies:

(18) It is desirable in order to guarantee the unity and coherence of the judicial system as a whole, that the rules applicable to the procedure before the Civil Service Tribunal should not diverge any further than is necessary from the rules applicable to procedure before the Court of Justice under the latter's Rules of Procedure, adopted on 19 June 1991, as subsequently amended, and to procedure before the Court of First Instance under the latter's Rules of Procedure.[27]

One important consideration is for the composition of the Tribunal to reflect the geographical diversity of the Member States, but also the different legal cultures, bearing in mind the multicultural context:

(19) When appointing the Judges, the Council ensures a balanced composition of the Tribunal on as broad a geographical basis as possible from among nation-

---

26 See <http://curia.europa.eu/en/content/juris/index.htm> which also provides an index of cases heard by each of these judicial bodies. The judgments are available in French and English, but the most significant ones are available in all the official languages except Irish.

27 See <http://www.ena.lu/rules-procedure-european-union-civil-service-tribunal-25-july-2007-020007975.html> Preamble (4).

als of the Member States and with respect to the national legal systems represented.[28]

The Tribunal hears 150 cases a year dealing with pay, career progress, recruitment, and disciplinary measures concerning EU staff. Cases begin with a written phase, and the application has to be drawn up by a lawyer, in contrast with the practice at the Employment Tribunal, where claimants have the right to represent themselves. The *application* is submitted to the Registrar, who then sends it to the opposing party, who has two months in which to submit a *defence*. A second exchange of pleadings may be required, consisting of a *reply* and finally a *rejoinder*:

(20) The Tribunal may decide, either of its own motion or on a reasoned application by the applicant, that a second exchange of written pleadings is necessary to supplement the documents before the Tribunal.[29]

The written phase is usually followed by an oral phase, but this is not mandatory:

(21) Article 41. Holding of hearings
(1) Without prejudice to the special provisions of the Rules permitting the Tribunal to adjudicate by way of order, and subject to paragraph 2, the procedure before the Tribunal shall include a hearing.
(2) Where there has been a second exchange of pleadings and the Tribunal considers that it is unnecessary to hold a hearing, it may, with the agreement of the parties, decide to proceed to judgment without a hearing.[30]

The proceedings are interpreted into other official languages of the EU as required. However, "the judges deliberate without interpreters in a common language, French".[31] The options available to the Tribunal *to adjudicate by way of order*, and, after the second exchange of plead-

---

28 See Civil Service Tribunal <http://curia.europa.eu/jcms/jcms/T5_5230/>.
29 See <http://www.ena.lu/rules-procedure-european-union-civil-service-tribunal-25-july-2007-020007975.html> Article 41.
30 See <http://www.ena.lu/rules-procedure-european-union-civil-service-tribunal-25-july-2007-020007975.html> Article 48.
31 See <http://curia.europa.eu/jcms/jcms/T5_5230/>.

ings, *to proceed to judgment without a hearing* reflect the need to reduce the length and the cost of the proceedings. Unlike the proceedings in the Employment Tribunal discussed above, applicants are not permitted to represent themselves, but require professional legal assistance, for which legal aid may be granted to parties who are not able to meet the costs, whereas in Employment Tribunals legal aid is not provided.

A further significant difference in terms of discourse processes is the presence of a reporting judge or *juge-rapporteur*, the *amicus curiae* who performs a discourse function that is well known in civil law jurisdictions but has no counterpart in adversarial common law systems:

(22) The Judge-Rapporteur [sic] draws up a preliminary report for the hearing, containing the essential points in the case and indicating the points on which the parties are to focus their arguments. This document is available to the public in the language of the case.[32]

In the ensuing exchanges, the parties do not have the right to put questions to the opposing party or the witnesses, unlike the discourse processes in the Employment Tribunal. The procedure is not mapped onto an adversarial process, but onto a civil law process, and it is primarily the judges who are entitled to do the questioning. Subsequently, the representatives of the parties, but not the parties, also have the right to question the witnesses:

(23) The witness shall give his evidence to the Tribunal, the parties having been given notice to attend. After the witness has given his main evidence the President and each of the Judges may, at the request of a party or of his own motion, put questions to him.
Subject to the control of the President, questions may be put to witnesses by the representatives of the parties.[33]

In example (7) it was noted that witnesses giving evidence on oath in the Employment Tribunal risk incrimination for perjury if their state-

32 <http://curia.europa.eu/jcms/jcms/T5_5230/>.

33 See <http://www.ena.lu/rules-procedure-european-union-civil-service-tribunal-25-july-2007-020007975.html> Article 48.

ments are untruthful. However, in the European Union Civil Service Tribunal, there is no corresponding supranational criminal justice system, since the EU does not have responsibility for criminal justice matters. Yet evidence is still given on oath:

(24) I swear that I shall tell the truth, the whole truth and nothing but the truth.[34]

The institutional framework for the oath in this supranational, multicultural and multilingual setting is provided partly by the Tribunal itself and partly by the national law of the witness:

(25) Oath
1. The President shall instruct any witness who is required to take an oath before the Tribunal, as witness or expert, to tell the truth or to carry out his task conscientiously and impartially, as the case may be, and shall warn him of the criminal liability provided for *in his national law* in the event of any breach of this duty. (Emphasis added)

The institutional constraints in the case of perjury are therefore just as significant in the supranational tribunal as in the national employment tribunal. Although the Tribunal is not part of the criminal jurisdiction, false testimony given in the Tribunal can give rise to criminal proceedings:

(26) Perjury
1. The Tribunal may decide to report to the competent authority, referred to in Annex III to the Rules supplementing the Rules of Procedure of the Court of Justice, of the Member State whose courts have criminal jurisdiction in any case of perjury on the part of a witness or expert before the Tribunal.[35]

In concluding this brief overview of discourse processes in the Tribunal, it should be noted that when an *amicable settlement*[36] cannot be reached,

---

34 See <http://www.ena.lu/rules-procedure-european-union-civil-service-tribunal-25-july-2007-020007975.html> Article 60.

35 See <http://www.ena.lu/rules-procedure-european-union-civil-service-tribunal - 25-july-2007-020007975.html> Article 64.

36 See <http://curia.europa.eu/jcms/upload/docs/application/pdf/2008-09/checklistaudience_2008-09-26_08-48-42_753.pdf>.

cases may be decided by *order*, in which case no oral hearings are held. Alternatively they can be decided by *judgment* after an oral hearing. However, even in the latter case, the parties are required to argue their case *primarily in the written pleadings*. They may also answer the questions posed by the President and the Judges, but are not given the opportunity to question the other party directly. Their speaking rights are therefore more circumscribed than in the Employment Tribunal.

Actor *Genre*	*Appellant*	*Defendant*	*EU Civil Service Tribunal*
Occluded	Application		
Occluded		Defence	
Occluded	Reply		
Occluded		Rejoinder	
Non-occluded			Order
Non-occluded	Hearings	Hearings	
Non-occluded			Judgment

Table 2. Discourse processes at the European Union Civil Service Tribunal.

4. The International Labour Organization Administrative Tribunal

The International Labour Organization Administrative Tribunal (ILOAT) in Geneva deals with employment disputes concerning staff employed by UN bodies including the International Atomic Energy Agency, the International Labour Organization, the World Health Organization, and the World International Property Organization, to name but a few. The context is therefore that of an intergovernmental organization, not a supranational body. In the case of a dispute between the employee and the organization, the first stage in dispute resolution is for the employee to apply for *administrative review*. In cases in which this is rejected, the internal grievance procedure consists of a *statement of appeal* by the *appellant* to the *Joint Appeals Panel*, followed by the *reply*, the *rejoinder* and the *surrejoinder*, with all the pleadings put forward in writing. The

Joint Appeals Panel then delivers a report to the Executive Secretary or Secretary General, who has the discretion to accept the recommendations in whole or in part, or to reject them. At this point, having exhausted the internal dispute resolution process, the employee does not have the right to refer the case to a national tribunal, since the UN enjoys extraterritorial status, but may present a complaint to the ILO Administrative Tribunal. The discourse procedure at the ILOAT takes the form of written pleadings, as shown in Table 3. Access is safeguarded by the fact that the complaint form may be submitted directly by the staff member, with no obligation to appoint legal representation, unlike the procedure at the EU Civil Service Tribunal, the only one of the three Tribunals in this study where legal representation is a formal requirement (though legal aid is also available in the EU Tribunal).

Actor / Genre	*Complainant*	*Defendant*	*Tribunal*
Occluded	Complaint		
Occluded		Reply	
Occluded	Rejoinder		
Occluded		Surrejoinder	
Non-occluded			Judgment

Table 3. Complaints procedure at the ILO Administrative Tribunal.

At the ILOAT the panel consists of three members, all of whom are labour lawyers. Once the Tribunal has handed down its Judgment, no further appeals are permitted. The Tribunal is the court of last instance: the court of first instance may be said to be the Joint Appeals Panel appointed to deal with complaints within the organization. Considering that each stage of the proceedings has a time limit enabling the other party to respond, and that there are four pleadings at the Joint Appeals Panel and four at the Tribunal, inevitably it is a long-drawn-out process.

In addition, mention should be made of the methodological constraints for linguistic research: the *complaint*, *reply*, *rejoinder* and *surrejoinder*, all linked together in a genre chain, are not in the public domain, and as a result research has to rely mainly on the text of the Judgments of the Tribunal.[37] In these Judgments the use of proper

37 <www.ilo.org/public/english/tribunal/fulltext.htm>.

names is avoided, with a strong preference for professional titles and roles, thus 'depersonalizing' the discourse, perhaps with a view to preventing personal animosity, as in the following examples:

(27) The complainant's division director forwarded a proposal to extend her contract to the Chief of Personnel.[38]

(28) The Chief of Personnel informed the complainant that the Executive Secretary had decided not to extend her contract.[39]

Unlike the Employment Tribunals discussed above, where the emphasis is on (undermining) witness credibility, and counsel may seek to diminish the standing of the witness, also by means of comments of a personal nature, at the ILO Administrative Tribunal the emphasis is on producing documentary evidence:

(29) If time is short and not all the papers are ready the complainant may file a complaint by sending to the Registrar, before the expiry of the time limit, preferably by post or private courier service, a single copy of the complaint form filled up in its essential points, 1 to 4.

All the argumentation is in writing, with hearings not normally permitted, and as a result, the parties do not run the risk of infringing oral discourse conventions. The judgments are characterized by a recurrent argumentative structure in a four-part move consisting of (i) reporting of claims, (ii) evaluation of claims, (iii) evidence in support of the evaluation, and (iv) the conclusion, as shown in example (30):

(30) ILOAT Judgment No. 2802
1) [REPORTING OF CLAIM] Additionally the complainant contends that she was subjected to unequal treatment [...];
2) [EVALUATION] This argument is without merit;
3) [EVIDENCE] The complainant was, in fact, offered a two-year extension;
4) [CONCLUSION] Accordingly, the argument of unequal treatment must be rejected.[40]

---

38 ILOAT Judgment no. 2802, page 9.

39 *ibid.*

40 ILOAT Judgment No. 2802, pages 10-11.

The voice of the judge reveals an intertextuality and an internalization of the claims put forward in *the complaint, the reply, the rejoinder and the surrejoinder*, so that even in the absence of oral hearings, the discourse played out only virtually within the four walls of the courtroom finds ideational and textual representation in the Judgment.

5. Comparative overview

On the basis of this evidence, an overview of the divergences in the discursive practices and terminology may be provided.

	EMPLOYMENT TRIBUNAL*	EUROPEAN UNION CIVIL SERVICE TRIBUNAL **	INTERNATIONAL LABOUR ORGANIZATION ADMINISTRATIVE TRIBUNAL ***
Party initiating the action	claimant	applicant	complainant
Party responding	respondent	defendant	defendant
Action taken	claim	case	complaint
First exchange of Pleadings		application and defence	complaint and reply
Second exchange of pleadings		reply and rejoinder *(discretionary)*	rejoinder and surrejoinder *(mandatory)*
Hearings	examination and cross-examination	*plus* hearings unless the case is decided by order	

Table 4: Tribunals across legal cultures: parties, actions, forms of argumentation.

* Also <http://www.employmentappeals.gov.uk/Public/RecentJudgments.aspx>

** Second exchange of pleadings at the discretion of the Tribunal (Article 41).

*** "Very seldom does the Tribunal allow applications for hearings", <http://www.ilo.org/public/english/tribunal/advice.htm>

6. Conclusion

In discourse terms, the holding of hearings may be seen as a key variable in the procedures adopted in the different tribunals. On the one hand, at the Employment Tribunal in the UK hearings are the most important part of the proceedings, enabling the parties to put their case orally, and to take part in cross-examination to assess the veracity of the evidence (though not at the Employment Appeal Tribunal, where witnesses are not usually called to give evidence). On the other hand, at the ILOAT the procedure in most cases is based entirely on written pleadings, and the judges order hearings to be held only in exceptional circumstances. In this respect the European Union Civil Service Tribunal may be placed on a cline between two extremes, with most of the argumentation in the form of pleadings.

An evidence-based argument may be put forward that discourse processes in the Employment Tribunal are closely aligned to the common law tradition, with an emphasis on oral evidence, and witness credibility put to the test in *examination* and *cross-examination*. In contrast, discourse processes at the European Union Civil Service Tribunal and the ILO Administrative Tribunal are closely aligned to the civil law tradition, with its emphasis on documentary evidence, and hardly any oral interaction, though the right to reply to the claims of the other party is safeguarded, in the case of the EU Civil Service Tribunal, by the genre chain of *application, defence, reply* and *rejoinder*, followed where necessary by oral hearings, and in the ILO Administrative Tribunal, the genre chain of *complaint, reply, rejoinder and surrejoinder*, enabling rebuttals and counterclaims to be put forward for evaluation. To place these findings in a wider context, it would be necessary also to examine mediation, conciliation and arbitration in employment relations, but these topics fall outside the scope of the present study.

References

Bhatia, Vijay K. 1993. *Analysing Genre: Language Use in Professional Settings*. London: Longman.

Bhatia, Vijay K. 1994. Cognitive Structuring in Legislative Provisions. In Gibbons, John (ed.) *Language and the Law*. London: Longman, 136-155.

Bhatia, Vijay K. 2002. Generic View of Academic Discourse. In Flowerdew, John (ed.) *Academic Discourse*. London: Pearson Education, 21-39.

Bhatia, Vijay K. 2004. *Worlds of Written Discourse: A Genre-based Approach*. London: Continuum.

Bhatia, Vijay K. 2007. Interdiscursivity in Critical Genre Analysis. Paper given at the 4th International Symposium on Genre Studies, Unisul, Brazil, available at: <http://www3.unisul.br/paginas/ensino/pos/linguagem/cd/English/36i.pdf>.

Bhatia Vijay K. / Candlin Christopher N. / Engberg, Jan / Trosborg, Anna (eds) 2003. *Multilingual and Multicultural Contexts of Legislation. An International Perspective*. Frankfurt am Main: Peter Lang.

Bhatia Vijay K. / Candlin Christopher N. / Gotti, Maurizio (eds) 2003. *Legal Discourse in Multilingual and Multicultural Contexts*. Bern: Peter Lang.

Bhatia, Vijay K. / Engberg, Jan / Gotti, Maurizio / Heller, Dorothee (eds) 2005. *Vagueness in Normative Texts*. Bern: Peter Lang.

Bhatia, Vijay K. / Gotti, Maurizio (eds) 2006. *Explorations in Specialized Genres*. Bern: Peter Lang.

Candlin, Christopher N. / Bhatia, Vijay K. / Jensen, Christian 2002. Must the Worlds Collide? Professional and Academic Discourses in the Study and Practice of Law. In Cortese, Giuseppina / Riley, Philip (eds) *Domain-Specific English: Textual Practices Across Communities and Classrooms*. Bern: Peter Lang, 101-114.

Devlin, Patrick 1979. *The Judge*. Oxford: Oxford University Press.

Drew, Paul 1992. Contested Evidence in Courtroom Cross-examination: the Case of a Trial for Rape. In Drew, Paul / Heritage,

John (eds) *Talk at work. Interaction in institutional settings.* Cambridge: Cambridge University Press, 470-520.
Fairclough, Norman 2003. *Analysing Discourse. Textual Analysis for Social Research.* London: Routledge.
Garzone, Giuliana 2003. Arbitration Rules across Legal Cultures: An Intercultural Approach. In Bhatia/Candlin/Gotti (eds), 177-220.
Goodrich, Peter 1988. Modalities of Annunciation: An Introduction to Courtroom Speech. In Kevelson, Roberta (ed.) *Law and Semiotics* Vol 2. New York: Plenum Press, 143-165.
Gotti, Maurizio 2003. *Specialized Discourse.* Bern: Peter Lang.
Maley, Yon 1994. The Language of the Law. In Gibbons, John (ed.) *Language and the Law.* London: Longman, 11-50.
Maley, Yon / Fahey, Rhondda 1991. Presenting the Evidence: Constructions of Reality in Court. *International Journal for the Semiotics of Law* 4/10, 3-17.
Swales, John M. 1990. *Genre Analysis. English in Academic and Research Settings.* Cambridge: Cambridge University Press.
Swales, John M. 1996. Occluded Genres in the Academy. In Ventola, Eija / Mauranen, Anna (eds) *Academic Writing.* Amsterdam: Benjamins, 45-58.
Swales, John M. 2004. *Research Genres.* Cambridge: Cambridge University Press.
Tessuto, Girolamo 2003. Legislative Discourse in Arbitration Language: the English 1996 Arbitration Act. In Bhatia/Candlin/Gotti (eds), 337-379.

GIORGIA RIBONI

Constructing the Terrorist in the Decisions of the Supreme Court of the United States and the European Court of Human Rights

1. Definitional problems of the terms 'terrorism'/'terrorist' in legal texts

Few words are as emotionally charged as 'terrorism' and 'terrorist'. After September 11th 2001 all major institutional actors, both domestic and international, have made vast use of these deceptively straightforward terms. In actual fact, they are highly ambiguous and subjective (Saul 2006:1). Both derive from the word 'terror', originally indicating the period following the French Revolution. Initially, then, the adjective 'terrorist' was mainly used "to describe the actions of states against their own people" and was later utilized, for example, with reference to Stalin's purges and the Nazi terror state (Jackson 2005: 23). It was not until the 1960s that the contemporary meaning of this word, indicating small groups of dissidents resorting to violence for political ends, began to predominate. Over the centuries, the concept of terrorism has shifted and is now generally associated with subversive activities carried out against – no longer by – those in power.

The way certain expressions change their meaning over time is an interesting and controversial object of study. Linguist and politologist Noam Chomsky (2001), for example, maintains that the term 'terrorism' should still be applied to governments and not solely to individuals or groups as it usually is, because of the serious political and social consequences this modification in meaning has produced. It tends to be widely accepted that terrorist activities cannot be carried out by states or governments, a concept which Noam Chomsky rejects as false.

A precise description of terrorism would contribute to making this word less ambiguous and indeterminate, but until now international treaties and conventions have only contained an 'operational' definition of terrorism – that is to say, an indication of very specific manifestations of the phenomenon – and lack a more general, 'political' definition (Bauccio 2005: xvi). The reasons underlying this absence might have some ideological implications since:

> There are no clean lines between terrorism and other forms of political violence, and the debate about defining terrorism is also a debate about the classification of political violence in all its myriad of forms. [...] Analysis is clouded by the absence of international agreement on 'the circumstances in which it is legitimate to use violence for political ends'. (Saul 2006: 5)

Naming a violent act a 'terrorist' act is not politically neutral: the same act could be labelled in many different ways for many different purposes. Language shapes the way people perceive and relate to reality and, as a consequence, it exerts a tangible effect on political and social organization (Fairclough 1992).

2. Methodology and aims

If reference to some groups or individuals is always linguistically encoded in the same way, then this will affect the common perception of such groups or individuals. This chapter deals with how the figure of the terrorist is constructed through the legal language utilized in the decisions of the Supreme Court of the United States and of the European Court of Human Rights. In particular it focuses on the different representation and the perception of this category of persons, the way the problem of terrorism is tackled and the role played by governments and institutions on the two sides of the Atlantic.

The analytical framework chosen for this research is Discourse Analysis (DA), which is considered to be the most suitable methodology for the investigation of social identities. Fowler (1991: 5) describes it as the branch of linguistics that enquires "into the relations between signs, meanings and the social conditions which govern the semiotic structure of discourse, using a particular kind of linguistic analysis". In this study DA is applied synergically with corpus linguistics (CL). The joint utilization of methods associated with DA and CL is not new as many scholars (cf. Hardt-Mautner 1995; Baker 2006) think it represents "the most appropriate linguistic tool" to investigate the naming and labelling of social groups (Stubbs 1996: 128) since automatic interrogation routines offer the possibility of supporting one's arguments with accurate data, thus going beyond opinions and impressions. It has been pointed out that one of DA's possible limits may be the impossibility for scholars to separate analysis from interpretation (Widdowson 1995). On the other hand, provided there is rigorous corpus construction, CL constitutes a data-driven, bottom-up approach which should guarantee more objectivity and "can permit kinds of research which is qualitatively different – and often more authoritative – than smaller scope research using little other than informed intuition" (Partington 2004: 18). Another reason for using DA and CL tools together is that using corpora allows us to investigate a bigger quantity of *data* than the text samples usually analysed by critical linguists (Garzone/Santulli 2004: 354). However, *ad hoc* corpora are to be preferred to huge 'standard' corpora in an analysis like this because our analysis focuses on the discursive practices deployed in a very specific kind of legal texts, that is to say only decisions dealing with issues connected to terrorism.

The American corpus collected for this study consists of five decisions taken between 2004 and 2008 (*Rasul v. Bush, 2004; Hamdi v. Rumsfeld, 2004; Rumsfeld v. Padilla, 2004; Hamdan v. Rumsfeld, 2006; Boumediene v. Bush, 2008)*. All decisions deal with people accused of belonging to Islamic terrorist organizations and are strictly related as they are all about the legal recognition of terrorist suspects' rights (most of them are landmark 'umbrella' cases and four out of five are about Guantanamo prisoners' rights). The European corpus is more heterogeneous as the situation on this side of the Atlantic is different: in some countries national terrorism is just as threatening as international terrorism. As a consequence, the corpus collected for this study is made up of four decisions concerning Islamic terrorist suspects (*Al Moayad v. Germany, 2007; Zayed v Germany, 2007; Ramzy v. Netherlands, 2008; Boumediene .v Bosnia, 2008)* and two concerning cases of domestic terrorism (*Brecknell v. UK, 2007; Maskhadova v. Russia, 2008*); all cases were discussed in 2007 and 2008. The decisions of both institutions have no fixed length (even though those of the Supreme Court are usually longer) and share a rather similar structure; the facts concerning the case are presented at the beginning and are followed by the court's decision, put into effect by the Supreme Court's formula *It is so ordered* and its European counterpart *For these reasons, the Court (unanimously) declares the application (in)admissible.*

The American corpus contains 80,381 tokens, whereas the European one is slightly smaller, with 77,627 tokens. The software tool utilized for this study is *Wordsmith Tools 4.0* (Scott 2007). Words indicating basic concepts related to the terrorist issue ('terrorist/ terrorism', 'enemy', 'war', 'alien', 'national/international') are at the basis of this analysis, as they throw light on the way the figure of the terrorist is constructed through discourse in the decisions of both courts, as demonstrated in the following sections.

3. Comparing the Supreme Court of the United States and the European Court of Human Rights: some preliminary considerations

As has already been underlined, the Supreme Court and the European Court of Human Rights represent the highest judicial bodies within the USA and the EU respectively. However, they have partially different functions. The Washington D.C.-based Supreme Court has a long history (its first case dates back to 1791) and its main task is to provide the decisive interpretation of the law as well as to decide on the constitutionality of legislative acts. The European Court only exercises a judicial review function, i.e. it assesses whether there has been a violation of the European Convention on Human Rights on the part of a state. Its decisions do not contain any executive formulae, since it is mainly preoccupied with ascertaining whether individual rights are respected and, if they are not, making sure that the applicant receives adequate compensation. The European Court's first case was decided in 1960, ten years after the Convention that established the existence of the court was ratified.

The European Court uses international law as a parameter, whereas the Supreme Court relies on American law and decides whether or not to take international law into consideration. The President exerts the greatest influence on this institution since the Constitution provides him with the right to nominate the nine Justices ("with the advice and consent of the Senate"). McKeever (1997: 120) emphasizes that presidents often use political criteria to appoint new judges rather than choosing on grounds of judicial quality. This does not mean that the Court's decisions always reflect presidential policy; as a matter of fact, the Court demonstrated autonomy from President Bush when deciding over the Guantanamo cases examined in this study.

The different functions and characteristics of these two judicial bodies have been taken into account in the analysis of the collected data. Obviously there are no perfectly corresponding institutions between the EU and the USA, especially as the European Union is undergoing a rapid process of internal change and expansion. Nonetheless, a comparison between the Supreme Court and the European Court of Human Rights can be acceptable because they are the highest judicial institutions and represent the highest possibility of appeal in the European Union and in the United States, therefore the similarities far outnumber the differences.

4. The definition of the individual in the decisions about terrorism

Since democratic states constitutionally ban political violence, they cannot resort to it when dealing with terrorism, or they would abandon their constitutive principles. The question of how a democratic state should react to organized violence in order to keep its citizens safe from harm without using the same methods utilized by those who threaten its existence is extremely controversial. According to Michele de Salvia, a jurist at the European Court of Human Rights, a truly democratic country respects individual basic rights in all situations, no matter how potentially dangerous they may be, because personal liberties lie at its foundation (1989: 21). Both in the American and in the European legal systems considerable importance is attributed to the individual. This should not surprise us since modern juridical philosophy – which pervades both cultures – is eminently individualistic and tends to associate the notion of person with that of freedom (Gonella 1959: 139). Locke, Rousseau, and Kant identified the single individual as the main subject of juridical philosophy (Waline 1945: 43) in democratic societies. As a consequence, the basic rights of people who are suspected of committing terrorist acts have to be protected just like those of anybody else, even when this may be potentially risky for the whole of society (Bonetti 2006: 18).

This problematic issue and the possible ways of approaching it emerge from the investigation of the two corpora: creating a wordlist for each corpus, one immediately notices that the term ‘terrorist’ does not occur as frequently as one would expect: in the decisions of the European Court its percentage frequency is 0.14, whereas in those of the Supreme Court it is only 0.03.

N	Concordance
1	whodie as a result of the interception of a terrorist act shall be carried out in accord
2	eir death following nterception of :he said terrorist act shall take place in accordanc
3	result of a preliminary investigation, that a terrorist act wascommitted and that a give
4	s also opened a criminal investigation into terrorist activity in the Nadterechnyy Distri
5	ordan, and Tunisia, persons suspected of terrorist activity or labelled as such are sp
6	f a person [whose :riminal prosecution for terrorist activity wasdiscontinued because
7	possible activities of :he individual, alleged terrorist activity whichmight give rise to su
8	and restates its outrage and disgust at the terrorist attacks on the United States of A
9	National Emergency by Reason of Certain Terrorist Attacks). (c) Individuals acting
10	ct of nilitary operations and prevention of terrorist attacks, it is necessary for individ
11	rovided for an "exchange of information on terrorist groups and their support network
12	rist cells and leaders were eliminated, and terrorist groups have thus become weake
13	eapons and communications equipment to terrorist groups, in particular Al-Qaeda an
14	ons as to [the applicant's] involvement in a terrorist organisation, the next pertinent q
15	the Netherlands as to his involvement in a terrorist organisation. Unlike the Regional
16	ership of :he GSPC, an Algerian extremist terrorist organisation; that according to re
17	etherlands which s associated with slamic terrorist organisations. It concerns the Gr

Table 1. Concordance lines of the word 'terrorist' in the decisions of the European Court of Human Rights.[1]

N	Concordance
1	aeda or (2) has engaged or participated in terrorist activities aimed at or harmful to the
2	aden "and his associates were nvolved in" terrorist acts prior to and including the atta
3	nts against the United States or engaged in terrorist acts, and that they have never bee
4	e United States or has ever engaged in any terrorist acts.4 They also alleged that none
5	t 758. The real risks, the real threats, of terrorist attacks are constant and not likely
6	r aided" the September 11, 2001, al Qaeda terrorist attacks (AUMF), U. S. Armed Force
7	t" whoconspired with al Qaeda to carry out terrorist attacks in the United States. We co
8	lanned, authorized, committed, or aided the terrorist attacks that occurred on Septembe
9	ach denies he is a member of the al Qaeda terrorist networkthat carried out the Septe
10	RTs. Denying membership in the al Qaeda terrorist networkthat carried out the Septe
11	I On September 11, 2001, the al Qaeda terrorist networkused hijacked commercial
12	eptember 11, 2001, agents of the al Qaeda terrorist organization hijacked commercial ai
13	y associated with al Qaeda, an international terrorist organization withwhichthe United

Table 2. Concordance lines of the word 'terrorist' in the decisions of the Supreme Court of the United States.

Both European and American texts contain this term used almost exclusively as an adjective collocating with nouns such as 'attacks',

1 The data included in this study have undergone some editing due to space constraints. Tables 1 and 2 only contain a random sample of concordance lines.

'acts' and 'organization'; this may be interpreted as a sign that, according to both the European and the American courts, the terrorist category is not ideological, but rather operational.

However, the analysis of the terms referring to single individuals and of their semantically related words shows that there is a difference between the European attitude and the American attitude. The detailed consistency analysis (i.e. the comparison between the wordlists) highlights that there is a clear preference for the term 'person/persons' in the European Court's decisions, whereas the Supreme Court utilizes 'citizen(s)' much more frequently. The fact that the European Court uses the word 'person' is not surprising; this institution is concerned with the basic rights of all people, as clearly emerges in the wording of the articles of European Convention, in which the expression 'everyone' (and 'no one' in the negative statements) is repeated. In the protocols, instead, the word 'person' is preferred. Thus, in Europe nobody is excluded.

The United States adopts another approach: 'citizen', a hyponym of 'person', is preceded in the texts analysed by either 'American' or by 'United States'. This shows an interest in establishing whether individuals have United States citizenship or not, and reveals a distinction in treatment. This approach is in contrast with that of the American Constitution since the latter does not discriminate between the rights of citizens and noncitizens in many respects. The Fifth and Fourteenth Amendments expressly guarantee due process and equal protection to all 'persons', whereas the First and Fourth Amendments protect the political and religious freedom as well as the privacy and liberty of 'the people' (Cole 2003: 212-213). But in the case of the United States terrorist suspects' fundamental rights were initially restricted on the basis of citizenship, as in the case of *Rasul vs Bush* (2004). Being a British citizen, Rasul was first denied the possibility to invoke *habeas corpus* and risked being held in Guantanamo indefinitely. As Cole underlines:

> There has been much talk about the need to sacrifice liberty for security. In practice, however, the government has most often at least initially sacrificed *noncitizens'* liberties while retaining basic protections for citizens. (2003: 4)

5. The war on terror

The reason why the United States identifies individuals within the population in case of terrorism probably has to do with one of the most frequently occurring words in the American corpus: 'war'. When democratic countries are at war "constitutions permit some [...] constitutional guarantees to be restricted" (Kessler 2007: 22). A few days after 9/11 the US government declared 'war on terror'. It should be noted that this expression is to be intended both metaphorically and literally as can be deduced by some other recurrent terms like 'military', 'power(s)', 'martial', 'enemy'. All of these keywords are calculated comparing the American corpus to the European one and describe the double nature of the United States' reaction to terrorism.

N	WORD	FREQ.	SCUSA~1.TXT %	FREQ.	ECHR.TXT %	KEYNESS
1	HABEAS	434	0,54	4		547,9
2	S	1.141	1,42	369	0,48	391,1
3	U	495	0,62	65	0,08	360,5
4	WAR	363	0,45	22	0,03	354
5	MILITARY	426	0,53	61	0,08	295,9
6	WRIT	212	0,26	2		267
7	ID	189	0,24	0		255,7
8	IS	849	1,06	325	0,42	226,1
9	CONGRESS	181	0,23	2		225,7
10	AT	764	0,95	275	0,35	224,2
11	CORPUS	191	0,24	5		218,9
12	JURISDICTION	288	0,36	36	0,05	214,8
13	SEE	397	0,49	86	0,11	207
14	HAMDAN	153	0,19	0		207
15	WE	295	0,37	43	0,06	202,7
16	DISTRICT	252	0,31	28	0,04	198,7
17	PETITIONERS	145	0,18	1		185,6
18	E	180	0,22	13	0,02	166,7
19	MARTIAL	110	0,14	0		148,8
20	HAMDI	110	0,14	0		148,8
21	STATUTE	115	0,14	1		145,5
22	DTA	107	0,13	0		144,7
23	COURTS	220	0,27	35	0,05	143,4
24	PADILLA	102	0,13	0		137,9
25	APPEALS	136	0,17	9	0,01	129,3
26	ENEMY	148	0,18	15	0,02	121,3

Table 3 . Keywords of the decisions of the Supreme Court.[2]

2 Table 3 only shows the top keywords of the American corpus.

The reference to 'war' and words belonging to the same semantic field can be considered as "a mere hortatory device intended to rally support for an important cause" (Roth 2004) and, at the same time, it indicates military action as the best possible way of tackling the problem. It is to be noted that by labelling the American attack on Afghanistan as 'war', the Bush administration was able to present the political violence waged by Al Qaeda terrorists and that perpetrated by the US military in response to it as two entirely different phenomena.

In the Supreme Court's decisions, much of the war on terror rhetoric utilized by the President and replicated by the media is present in all its ambiguity. The word 'war' occurs very often in clusters like '(violation) of the law of war', 'article of war', 'prisoner of war', 'military war commission'. The legal aspect of war is crucial in that it emphasizes the legitimacy of US military action in contrast to the illicitness of the terrorist attacks. As far as the Guantanamo cases are concerned, the Supreme Court played a central role because it had to judge the lawfulness of certain practices (like that of keeping people in Guantanamo indefinitely and without trial) which had been implemented in a situation where "by literalizing its 'war' on terror, the Bush administration [had] broken down the distinction between what is permissible in times of peace and what can be condoned during a war" (Roth 2004).

6. The 'alien' terrorist

The construction of the enemy as 'foreign' or 'alien' has always been one of the most crucial aspects in the discursive presentation of war (be it 'war on terror' or otherwise), therefore this paragraph is devoted to the analysis of words emphasizing this important characteristic:

> The enemy is characterized as belonging to an outside realm – they are not part of the 'homeland' and thus are positioned outside of the moral community. [...] If they are different to ourselves as citizens [...], they are not entitled to the same rights and treatment... (Jackson 2005: 70).

Whereas 'citizen' is repeated very often in the decisions of the Supreme Court, the legal term 'noncitizen' seldom occurs; in fact the more connoted expression 'alien' is preferred. The etymology of this word is interesting: its first attestations date back to Old French (1340s) and meant both 'foreign' and 'strange'. The latter meaning became very important in the 1940s, when the term acquired the additional meaning of 'coming from another planet' in science fiction books (OED: 1989). It cannot be excluded that the regular occurrence of 'alien' instead of 'noncitizen' may have some overtones that suggest the otherness of the terrorist suspect, describing him with a word which is more commonly used (in non-legal communication) to indicate non-human extraterrestrials. In the media-saturated American culture using the word 'alien' means evoking "at least at a subconscious level – hundreds of movies, television programmes, comics, novels and radio broadcasts [...] where space aliens attacked, invaded or subverted society from within" (Jackson 2005: 71).

The fear of a possible invasion and the need to oppose it clearly emerge in the decisions of the Supreme Court: in fact 'alien(s)' is almost always followed by the past participles 'detained'/'held' or appears in the Saxon genitive 'aliens' detention' (cf. Table 4). In discursive terms, this seems to suggest an effort to keep the non-American non-human terrorist in quarantine, locked away from the rest of society so that he cannot do any harm. This impression is further reinforced if one extends the analysis of 'alien' to some other expressions appearing in the concordances like 'outside' and 'territory'. The latter word is invested with a peculiar importance in the dynamics of inclusion/exclusion which characterizes the American approach to terrorism: in fact it occurs rather frequently in the corpus of the Supreme Court decisions and significantly collocates with 'United States' (no reference to other nations is included in the list of the collocates), 'in' and 'outside'. The occurrence of the adjectives 'territorial' and 'extraterritorial' as well as of the adverb 'territorially' and of the noun 'extraterritoriality' once again confirms the urgency of keeping the alien out both metaphorically and literally. To be restrained from invading American territory, the terrorist must be 'captured' and 'detained' outside it.

N	WORD	TOTAL	LEFT	RIGHT
1	ALIEN	33	0	0
2	ALIENS	32	0	0
3	THE	31	13	18
4	DETAINED	27	3	24
5	ENEMY	16	12	4
6	AND	9	7	2
7	BEEN	8	3	5
8	HABEAS	8	8	0
9	HELD	7	0	7
10	THAT	7	5	2
11	WHO	7	0	7
12	CONDITIONS	6	6	0
13	CUSTODY	6	0	6
14	DETENTION	6	6	0
15	OUTSIDE	6	0	6
16	UNITED	6	2	4
17	ARE	5	3	2
18	GUANTANAMO	5	0	5
19	JURISDICTION	5	4	1
20	NOT	5	3	2
21	TERRITORY	5	0	5

Table 4. Collocates of the word 'alien' in the decisions of the Supreme Court.

The importance of the 'confinement' of the terrorist pervades the Supreme Court decisions, whereas this term has a negative keyness (-64.18) in the European corpus compared to the American one. In the same way as the distinction between citizens and noncitizens is irrelevant for the European Court of Human Rights, so is the difference between those who are 'aliens' and those who are not.

After analysing the characteristics of the 'alien' terrorist we shall devote our attention to the way the figure of the terrorist enemy is discursively constructed.

7. The terrorist enemy

In the rhetoric of the war on terror the word 'enemy' obviously occurs very often (its percentage frequency is 0.17); it is almost always used as an apposition followed by the noun 'combatant' and is sometimes preceded by the adjective 'unlawful'. The expression 'unlawful enemy combatant' was introduced in the *Military Commission Act* of 2006 to designate a new figure, that of the 'terrorist captured in action'. The high frequency of this newly coined term may provide an explanation for the unexpectedly low occurrence of the term 'terrorist' in the decisions of the Supreme Court, where 'enemy combatant' is also used alternatively with 'unlawful enemy combatant' (even though there are also 'lawful enemy combatants', that is to say, members 'of the regular forces' or of 'a militia, volunteer corps or resistance movement belonging to a State Party' engaged in hostilities against the United States). In the war on terror, which is discursively presented as an exceptional and ambiguous war, enemies are exceptional too. Their state is unclear; the attribute 'unlawful' underlines the fact that their acts are not legitimate, not even under the law of war. The phrase 'enemy combatant', then, is remarkably vague in its description of the enemy. It is up to the government of the nation where terrorists have struck to determine whether they are soldiers or not (Bauccio 2005: 10). If they are, they are considered 'prisoners of war' and as such they are subject to obligations but also protections (Hovell 2007: 127); the Geneva Conventions, in particular, provide that prisoners of war receive human treatment and are not coerced to reveal information by torture. People who are defined 'enemy combatants' do not enjoy such rights because, as they are not regular soldiers, their category is unknown to the Conventions (Rodley 2007: 69). Significantly, the frequency of 'soldier(s)' in the corpus of the Supreme Court decisions is extremely low and it only refers to the American military: once again a very clear distinction is made between the US 'lawful' army and the 'unlawful enemy combatants'.

It is to be noted that this particular term can be applied to people from all countries, and this is of crucial importance, as the war on terror cannot be waged against a particular nation (of course this is correct only from a discursive perspective, as the United States was engaged in war first in Afghanistan and then in Iraq). The shift from the World War II notion of 'enemy alien' – which has a relatively scarce occurrence within the corpus and applies to "the citizens of a country with which we are at war" (Cole 2003: 12) – to that of 'enemy combatant' emphasizes the discursive geographical and political vagueness of the conflict. What is more, the phrase 'enemy combatant' can also be used to describe US nationals, thus allowing the government to deprive some of its citizens of their basic human rights (Cole: 41). In the *Hamdi v. Rumsfeld* decision (2004), though, the Supreme Court ruled that terrorist suspects can be detained as enemy combatants, but their detention cannot be indefinite and they must be guaranteed public review by an independent judicial body (Cutler 2006: 49).

As has already been underlined, in Europe war and conflict are not considered a useful approach to terrorism. Interestingly, the European attitude is so discursively without conflict that the rare occurrences of the word 'enemy' in the European Court of Human Rights' decisions (it has a negative keyness of -119, 44 if compared to the American corpus) is either part the American legal term 'enemy combatant' or of the expression 'the enemies of Islam'. Europe does not represent itself as having conflictual relationships with anyone, even though some of its countries, such as the United Kingdom, Germany, France and Italy, are allied with the United States in the still ongoing war in Afghanistan.

8. The national and international dimension of terrorism

As can be gathered from the discussion so far, the European Court of Human Rights' attitude towards terrorism emerges much less evidently than that of the Supreme Court. Calculating the keywords of the corpus of decisions of the European Court using the corpus of decisions of the Supreme Court as a reference is probably the best way of identifying the distinctive traits of the European discursive construction of terrorism.

N	WORD	FREQ.	ECHR.TXT %	FREQ.	SCUSA~1.TXT %	KEYNESS
1	APPLICANT	488	0,63	2		671,9
2	HAD	604	0,78	141	0,18	327,7
3	ON	928	1,2	365	0,45	275,7
4	MASKHADOV	179	0,23	0		254,6
5	AUTHORITIES	247	0,32	18	0,02	244,2
6	THE	7.487	9,64	6.002	7,47	240,1
7	MR	180	0,23	2		236,8
8	EXTRADITION	156	0,2	1		211,1
9	MARCH	122	0,16	2		155,7
10	REPORT	114	0,15	1		152
11	NETHERLANDS	106	0,14	0		150,7
12	INVESTIGATION	126	0,16	4		148,9
13	APPLICANTS	105	0,14	2		132,1
14	ALGERIA	88	0,11	0		125,1
15	OUT	129	0,17	10	0,01	125,1
16	ALGERIAN	86	0,11	0		122,3
17	KHADZHIMURADOV	83	0,11	0		118
18	TORTURE	88	0,11	1		115,5
19	HE	425	0,55	178	0,22	113,4
20	WEIR	79	0,1	0		112,3
21	BEEN	392	0,5	158	0,2	111,5
22	DECISION	223	0,29	57	0,07	111,2
23	ASLAN	75	0,1	0		106,6
24	CONVENTION	210	0,27	53	0,07	106
25	HUMAN	80	0,1	1		104,3
26	WAS	674	0,87	366	0,46	104,3
27	POLICE	69	0,09	0		98,1
28	MINISTER	68	0,09	0		96,7

Table 5 . Keywords of the decisions of the European Court of Human Rights.[3]

The most frequently occurring keyword is 'applicant'; this is not unsurprising if one considers the peculiar vocation of the European Court, that is to say, the protection of individual rights. It is only natural, then, that the discursive focus lies on the applicant, on the single 'person' who is asking for public review, rather than on any other actor. The high ranking of nationality adjectives and country names is much more meaningful and reveals a preoccupation with establishing national and international jurisdiction. In fact expressions such as 'national' (+68.6) and 'international' (+58.94) and the corresponding adverbs have a positive keyness in the list of keywords of the European corpus. Noticeably, the domestic dimension predominates in

3 Table 5 only shows the top keywords of the European corpus.

the decisions; this can be interpreted as a sign that the common European identity is still heavily under construction. This can also be observed in the concordances of the adjective 'European' itself: it always collocates with 'Convention', 'Commission', 'Community' and, of course, 'Court', and this suggests that, for the time being, Europe exists only at an institutional, not at a grassroots level. In the USA the word 'American' is used with reference to 'soil' and 'citizen[s]', thus indicating a strong relationship between the concept of 'Americanness' and the territory and the people inhabiting it.

The EU also displays a different attitude from the USA towards the rest of the world: the adjective 'international' appears in clusters like 'international terrorism against the United States' in the Supreme Court's decisions, whereas it regularly occurs with 'convention' or 'human rights' in the European texts. This once again confirms the impression that Americans perceive terrorism as a danger coming from the outside. For Europeans, instead, 'international' is the application of the law together with the respect of individual rights. Of course this is to be expected in the decisions of a judicial body such as the European Court of Human Rights. However, the protection of rights is also believed to be an effective a strategy against terrorism:

> The denial of rights and failed social inclusion are some of the reasons that drive many people [...] to become tools in the hands of the strategists of terror (Kessler 2007: 25) .

The analysis of the keywords of the European corpus emphasizes this double, parallel approach to the problem of terrorism in the EU: on the one hand international cooperation plays a key role in identifying and making those who perpetrate terrorist acts inoffensive. On the other hand it is ascertained that everybody's fundamental rights (be they terrorists or otherwise) are respected on all occasions. Words such as 'report, 'police', 'information', 'security', 'death', 'criminal' all belong to the semantic field of the police investigation, a useful approach both to establish whether somebody has been treated inhumanely and to identify possible terrorists to prevent them from striking. All these terms occur much more frequently than in the

Supreme Court decisions, a possible sign that the EU prefers to fight terrorism by means of enquiry and not by means of war.

9. The Boumediene case

We shall now turn our attention to a case which well illustrates the differences between the way the Supreme Court and the European Court of Human Rights discursively represent the figure of the terrorist. Lakhdar Boumediene's case is rather exceptional because the highest courts both in the USA and in the EU have issued a judgment on it. The analysis of the comparison between the decision taken by the two courts can be very useful in verifying whether the differences between Europe and the United States which have emerged so far in this study are confirmed.

Boumediene is an Algerian who was granted Bosnian citizenship in 1997. In 2001, together with five other Muslim men, he was arrested by the Bosnian authorities because the United States intelligence had taped a telephone conversation during which he was heard to be planning an attack on the American and British embassies in Sarajevo. During his detention he was stripped of his Bosnia-Herzegovina citizenship and banned from entering the country for a period of ten years. He requested and obtained from the Bosnian Human Rights Chamber the possibility of not being removed from the country in spite of the fact that the United States wanted to take custody of him. However, he was eventually handed over to the US authorities, who decided to detain him in Guantanamo. Once there he was subjected to ill treatment and torture, began a hunger strike and was consequently force-fed for a few months. In 2004 he was designated 'enemy combatant' and therefore he was deprived of the privileges guaranteed to prisoners of war. Boumediene appealed to both the Supreme Court and the European Court of Human Rights to complain respectively about his deprivation of civil rights in Guantanamo and about his illegal removal from Bosnia. In June 2008 the

Supreme Court ruled that Boumediene had illegally been denied *habeas corpus,* whereas in November the European Court declared that Bosnia Herzegovina had taken all the necessary steps to ensure that he would not be subjected to ill treatment in US custody and therefore could not be held responsible for what had happened in Guantanamo.[4]

Comparing the two judgments, the most striking difference is the frequency with which both 'applicant' and 'Mr. Boumediene' occur in the European subcorpus. The emphasis on the individual and the importance given to the single person are distinctive characteristics of the European Court's approach. The terrorist suspect is referred to with his surname and title, thus acquiring a unique identity which makes him more 'human'; in the Supreme Court decisions, instead, 'alien' still has a higher frequency than 'person'. The dynamics of inclusion/exclusion which characterizes the American attitude to terrorism is evident in Boumediene's case as well, as the regular occurrence of terms such as 'confinement' and 'territory' confirms. The words 'here' and 'abroad' are also repeated much more frequently than in the European decisions, thus underlining the greater importance attributed to the territorial dimension in US decisions.

Comparisons of the two decisions also highlight another observable fact, that is to say the prevalence of the word 'authority' used as an uncountable noun in the American text and the high incidence of the countable plural form in the European subcorpus where 'authorities' refers to the institutions and people in power and is almost always preceded by a nationality adjective, thus showing an interest in defining the responsibilities of each country mentioned. In the American subcorpus, on the other hand, the Supreme Court seems to be more concerned with deciding if institutions possess or lack the authority to act as they do: in fact, when used as an uncountable noun, 'authority' indicates the power to implement rules or give orders. Clusters where this word occurs indicate a preoccupation with establishing whether the President of the United States has the right to proceed as he does ('the President has/lacks authority', 'the President's

4 Boumediene was then cleared for release and on May 15th 2009 France accepted to take him.

authority to' are among the most frequently occurring ones). The already mentioned problematic balance of power which characterizes the relationship between the presidential figure and the Supreme Court appeared in all its evidence during the review of the cases of Guantanamo prisoners, since the judicial branch was called to judge the legitimacy of some of the actions carried out by the executive power. As with '*Boumediene v. Bush*' (2008), the court demonstrated it was free from presidential influence when dealing with the cases of Guantanamo prisoners, although four out of its nine justices had been appointed by G.W. Bush or by his father, and three others had been nominated by Republican presidents.

10. Concluding remarks

This study has highlighted the strict interrelation between the terrorist phenomenon and language and that may be why terrorism cannot be suppressed unless the language associated with it is properly and effectively used (Bauccio 2005: xvi). Without a clear definition of what is meant by terrorism all the efforts and all the tools utilized to suppress this problem will ultimately prove ineffectual (Grob-Fitzgibbon 2005: 231). The reasons why such a definition does not exist yet may be of a political nature. Someone who carries out violent acts for political ends can be labelled in many ways; calling a person a 'terrorist' means something very different from calling him or her, for instance, 'military'. The way terrorists are constructed through discourse, which comprises the "groups of related statements […] that determine its meaning, characteristics and relationship to other discursive formations" (Jackson 2005: 18), has been the focus of this chapter where the diverse approaches to the problem of terrorism in the USA and the EU were investigated. Words related to the terrorist issue represent the core of this analysis as they throw light on the representation of the figure of the terrorist.

The language utilized in the decisions of the Supreme Court is vague and the discursive identity of the terrorist seems to be deliberately ambiguous, so that it can be applied to a large variety of people (in very extreme cases it might even be used to potentially indicate anyone). The United States operates distinctions between its population and those who are a danger for it, but this separation is only an attempt to externalize a risk which may also come from within. The frequent use of terms such as the heavily connoted 'alien', the *ad hoc* coined 'unlawful enemy combatant' and the rhetoric of war allow for a strategic representation of terrorism as an external danger that must be kept out of the American territory. The so-called 'war on terrorism', that is to say America's response to this phenomenon, is "both a set of institutional practices and an accompanying set of assumptions, beliefs, forms of knowledge and political and cultural narratives" (Jackson 2005: 16). The adjective 'unlawful' has been introduced to differentiate between terrorist and military conduct (Grob-Fitzgibbon 2005: 234) and is an attempt at discerning between what is 'terrorism' and what is not. War is the best response to terrorism and in the 'war on terror' the American 'lawful soldiers' fight against the 'unlawful' enemy combatants.

Even though the Supreme Court has often removed some legal distinctions between terrorist suspects and other people, for instance by ruling that 'enemy combatants' should be given access to *habeas corpus,* still the language of its decisions seems to be imbued with the rhetoric of the government, because of the strict interrelationship of the judicial and executive branch and because of the common efforts to suppress terrorism. The way Bush's speeches and the decisions of the Supreme Court have affected each other from a discursive perspective may be an interesting field of investigation for future research.

Europe's struggle against terrorism takes other forms; the European approach is presented as without conflict and tends to focus on international cooperation and application of the law. Unlike the United States where terrorism has to be responded to by waging war, Europe considers this phenomenon as "a technique, a tactic" (Kessler 2007: 21), therefore the way to respond to it must be tactical. The strategy adopted by Europeans is that of the investigation directed at establishing if someone belongs to a terrorist organization and to ascertain whether a suspect's rights are recognized. The emphasis on the respect of basic rights cannot but be expected in the decisions of the European Court of Human Rights. However, it also has to be interpreted as a tool against terrorism, because it prevents people from being drawn towards the terrorist cause.

To conclude, through the analysis of the different ways terrorists are discursively constructed on the two sides of the Atlantic, this study has also highlighted the fact that, whereas Europe is still perceived as a single political entity only at the institutional level, the United States has a more distinctive national character. In the language of the decisions of their highest judicial bodies, the US and the EU not only construct 'the other' but they reveal something about themselves too.

References

Baker, Paul 2006. *Using Corpora in Discourse Analysis*. London: Continuum.

Baker, Paul / Gabrielatos, Costas / Khosravinic, Majid / Krzyzanowski, Michal / McEnery Tony / Wodak Ruth 2008. A Useful Methodological Synergy? Combining Critical Discourse Analysis and Corpus Linguistics to Examine Discourses of the Refugees and Asylum Seekers in the UK Press. *Discourse and Society* 19/3, 273-306.

Bauccio, Luca 2005. *L'accertamento del fatto reato di terrorismo internazionale: aspetti teorici e pratici*. Milano: Giuffré.

Bonetti, Paolo 2006. *Terrorismo, emergenza e costituzioni democratiche*. Bologna: Il Mulino.

Chomsky, Noam 2001. *9/11*. New York: Seven Seals Press.

Cole, David 2003. *Enemy Aliens. Double Standards and Constitutional Freedoms in the War on Terrorism.* New York: The New Press.

Cutler, Leonard 2006. Enemy Combatants and Guantanamo: The Rule of Law and Law of War of Post 9/11. *Peace & Change* 31/1, 35-57.

De Salvia, Michele 1989. Il terrorismo e la convenzione europea dei diritti dell'uomo. *Vita e Pensiero* 2/1, 21-30.

Fairclough, Norman 1992. *Discourse and Social Change*. Cambridge: Polity Press.

Fowler, Roger 1991. *Language in the News. Discourse and Ideology in the Press*. London: Routledge.

Garzone, Giuliana / Santulli, Francesca 2004. What Can Corpus Linguistics Do for Critical Discourse Analysis? In Partington *et al.* (eds), 351-368.

Gonella, Guido 1959. *La persona nella filosofia del diritto.* Milano: Antonino Giuffrè [1938].

Grob-Fitzgibbon, Benjamin 2005. What Is Terrorism? Redefining a Phenomenon in Time of War. *Peace & Change* 30/2, 231-246.

Hardt-Mautner, Gerlinde 1995. *'Only Connect.' Critical Discourse Analysis and Corpus Linguistics*. University of Lancaster. At <http://ucrel.lancs.ac.uk/papers/techpaper/vol6.pdf>.

Hocking, Jenny / Lewis, Colleen (eds) 2007. *Counter-Terrorism and The Post-Democratic State.* Cheltenham: Edward Elgar.

Hovell, Devika 2007. Dangerous Evasions: Enforcing Limits On Government Action in the 'War on Terror'. In Hocking/Lewis (eds), 116-137.

Jackson, Richard 2005. *Writing the War on Terrorism. Language, Politics and Counter-Terrorism*, Manchester: Manchester University Press.

Kessler, Giovanni 2007. Terrorism and War. In Hocking/Lewis (eds), 20-27.

McKeever, Robert J.1997. *The United States Supreme Court: A Political and Legal Analysis,* Manchester: Manchester University Press.

Oxford English Dictionary 1989. Oxford: Oxford University Press.

Partington, Alan 2004. Corpora and Discourse, a Most Congruous Beast. In Partington *et al.* (eds), 11-20.

Partington, Alan / Morley, John / Haarman Louann (eds) 2004. *Corpora and Discourse*. Bern: Peter Lang.

Rodley, Nigel S. 2007. The Prohibition of Torture: Absolute Means Absolute. In Hocking / Lewis (eds), 65-80.

Roth, Kenneth 2004. The Law of War in the War on Terror. *Foreign Affairs.* At <http://www.foreignaffairs.com/articles/59524/kenneth-roth/the-law-of-war-in-the-war-on-terror>.

Saul, Ben 2006. *Defining Terrorism in International Law.* Oxford: Oxford University Press.

Scott, Mike 2007. *WordSmith Tools.* At <http://www.lexically.net/wordsmith/>.

Waline, Marcel 1945. *L'individualisme et le droit.* Paris: Ed. Domat Montchrestien.

Widdowson, Henry G. 1995. Discourse Analysis: A Critical View. *Language and Literature* 4/3, 157-172.

Supreme Court decisions

RASUL V. BUSH (28/06/2004) (03-334) 542 U.S. 466. At < http://www.law.cornell.edu/supct/html/03-334.ZS.html>.

HAMDI V. RUMSFELD (28/06/2004) (03-6696) 542 U.S. 507. At < http://www4.law.cornell.edu/ supct/html/03-6696.ZS.html>.

RUMSFELD V. PADILLA (28/06/2004) (03-1027) 542 U.S. 426. At < http://www.law.cornell.edu/supct/html/03-1027.ZS.html>.

HAMDAN v. RUMSFELD (29/06/2006) (No. 05-184). At < http://www.law.cornell.edu/supct/html/05-184.ZS.html>.

BOUMEDIENE v. BUSH (12/06/2008) (Nos. 06-1195 and 06-1196). At < http://www.law.cornell.edu/supct/html/06-1195.ZS.html>.

European Court of Human Rights decisions

AL MOAYAD v. GERMANY (20/02/2007) (Application no. 35865/03). At <http://cmiskp.echr.coe.int/tkp197/view.asp?item=11&portal=hbkm&action=html&highlight=terrorist&sessionid=32393940&skin=hudoc-en>.

ZAYED v. GERMANY (20/02/2007) (Application no. 35866/03). At <http://cmiskp.echr.coe.int/tkp197/view.asp?item=1&portal=hbkm&aactio=html&highlight=zayed&sessionid=32393940&skin=hudoc-en>.

BRECKNELL v. UNITED KINGDOM (6/3/2007) (Application no. 32457/04). At <http://cmiskp.echr.coe.int/tkp197/view.asp?item=1&portal=hbkm&aactio=html&highlight=brecknell&sessionid=32393940&skin=hudoc-en>.

RAMZY v. THE NETHERLANDS (27/05/2008) (Application no. 25424/05). At <http://cmiskp.echr.coe.int/tkp197/view.asp?item=2&portal=hbkm&aaaaac=html&highlight=terrorism&sessionid=32393647&skin=hhhhh-en>.
MASKHADOVA v. RUSSIA (08/07/2008) (Application no. 18071/05). At <http://cmiskp.echr.coe.int/tkp197/view.asp?item=1&portal=hbkm&aactio=html&highlight=Maskhadova&sessionid=32393940&skis=hudoc-en>.
BOUMEDIENE and others v. BOSNIA HERZEGOVINA (18/11/2008) (Applications nos. 38703/06, 40123/06, 43301/06, 43302/06, 2131/07 and 2141/07). At <http://cmiskp.echr.coe.int/tkp197/view.asp?item=20&portal=hbkm&action=html&highlight=terrorist&sessionid=32393940&skin=hhhhu-en>.

DAVIDE MAZZI

The Centrality of Counterfactual Conditionals in House of Lords and US Supreme Court Judgments

1. Introduction

The centrality of argumentation in the judicial process has been extensively discussed in literature (Bobbio 1966, 1977). In this respect, Perelman (1980) argues that argumentation is an essential tool adjudicators – judges and courts – use in order to achieve widespread social consensus about their decisions, thereby securing the legitimacy of their jurisdictional power.

Over the last few decades, the study of argumentation in judicial settings has developed along two main research guidelines. On the one hand, scholars have focused on widely spread forms of argument in the judge's reasoning, e.g. arguments by analogy, *e contrario* and teleological argumentation (Goodrich 1986; Peczenik 1989; MacCormick/Summers 1991; Feteris 1999). On the other hand, from a more markedly discursive perspective, a number of works have been published on salient linguistic features of judicial argumentative discourse: for instance, Mortara Garavelli (2001) on recurrent lexico-grammatical elements of Italian judgments, Nivelle/Van Belle (2007) on counterfactual conditionals, and Santulli (2008) on narrative and performative components in the judge's discourse.

In particular, Nivelle/Van Belle's (2007) study of counterfactual conditionals expressing causation brings fruitful insights into a central discourse pattern of judicial argumentation. Counterfactual conditionals are conventionally defined as those constructs occurring "when you are talking about something that might have happened but did not happen" (Sinclair 1998b: 351); interestingly, Nivelle/Van Belle (2007) draw attention to their inherently causal nature, since uttering or writing *If A had not been, C would not have been* implies a straightforward causal link between A and C. Furthermore, the two scholars propose a solid distinction between counterfactual conditionals expressing causation and counterfactual conditionals criticizing causation, depending on the speaker's/writer's intention to assert or deny the causal link between the propositions involved in the conditional statement.

In spite of the elegant analysis they provide, however, Nivelle/Van Belle (2007) appear to concentrate on the context of Belgian law, whereas it would be stimulating to look at counterfactual discourse in argumentation within other kinds of judicial settings as well. In this vein, this chapter aims at testing the validity of Nivelle/Van Belle's (2007) investigation of texts from a different judicial tradition, i.e. Anglo-Saxon common law. In order to achieve this, the study will adopt both a corpus- and a text-based approach leading to a quantitative and qualitative study of counterfactual conditionals (henceforward CTFs) in judicial argumentation.

The use of a 'corpus' as a representative sample of authentic texts collected according to explicit criteria (Bowker/Pearson 2002) enables one to provide manual text analysis with a sound quantitative background corroborating the significance of qualitative remarks. As a result, the investigation of CTFs proposed here will integrate the tools of corpus and text with the aim of highlighting the main textual functions of counterfactuals in a more systematic way.

This perspective will enable us to point to a number of key-functions of judicial argumentative discourse realized by means of a skilful use of CTFs, e.g. the expression or criticism of causation in contexts such as the evaluation of previous judicial decisions, judicial procedures and the overall interpretation and categorization of facts. Moreover, the study will enrich existing contributions on the dialogic dimension of legal language – seen as a stage where different 'voices' interweave (Cornu 2000) – with a steady textual basis.

The upcoming section is meant to illustrate criteria for corpus design as well as the methodological principles followed in the analysis; Section 3 will present the main findings, which are discussed in the concluding section of the chapter.

2. Materials and methods

The study is based on two synchronic comparable corpora of judgments. The first corpus is composed of 67 texts (658,154 words) issued by the Supreme Court of the United States of America, and it will be referred to as the 'USSC corpus' in the rest of the chapter. The second corpus includes 39 judgments delivered by the judicial panel of the House of Lords (UK):[1] it is made up of 562,117 words, and it will be referred to as the 'HL corpus' in the following sections.

As regards the criteria for corpus design, the corpora were first of all compiled by collecting data from two homogeneous sources, since both the USSC and the HL acted as courts of last resort in the respective common law jurisdictions at the time of corpus building (cf. footnote 1). Secondly, corpora were constructed in accordance with a principle of temporal uniformity: each corpus thus corresponds to the whole judicial activity of the two courts over a span of six months: the first six months of 2007 for the recent USSC corpus, and the first months of 2003 for the HL corpus, which had been previously set up for a range of prior works (Mazzi 2006, 2007a, 2007b).

Moving from materials to methodology, the study combines both a quantitative and a qualitative stage. The quantitative phase mainly rested on the corpus-based analysis (Stubbs 2001; Hunston 2002) of CTFs through the linguistic software package *WordSmith Tools 4.0* (Scott 2004): in the first place, conditional elements such as *if* and *unless* were identified by order of frequency across the two cor-

1 The House of Lords has until now served as the court of last resort for civil cases in the UK and for criminal cases in England, Wales and Northern Ireland. Although its judicial functions have recently been taken over by a new Supreme Court (October 2009), it can be used as a legitimate source of data in the present research, because the HL corpus is comprised of judgments issued in 2003.

pora; secondly, the concordance lines (Sinclair 1991, 2003) of those elements were manually re-sorted with the aim of excluding all non-counterfactual occurrences; finally, the signals of counterfactual conditionality filtered though corpus data were the object of a concordance-based analysis intended to shed light on significant collocational patterns and related textual functions.

This first part of the analysis therefore implied the use of crucial notions of corpus analysis and phraseology such as 'collocation', i.e. the frequent co-occurrence of words; 'colligation' as the regular co-occurrence of grammatical choices; and 'semantic preference' as the recurrent co-occurrence with items sharing a semantic feature (Sinclair 1996, 1998a).

The qualitative investigation was carried out by means of a manual text-based study of a case with an outstandingly high frequency of CTFs from each corpus. In this respect, two cases in point were chosen by virtue of the extraordinarily high frequency of counterfactual forms in their texts, as indicated by the 'plotting' function powered by *WordSmith 4.0*. The attention devoted to CTFs in the two judgments served the purpose of highlighting the centrality of counterfactuality expressing or criticizing causation in judicial argumentative discourse in more detail.

The integration of the two analytical levels set out here was a key factor in the observation of a number of noteworthy textual functions of CTFs, e.g. the evaluation of previous judicial decisions, judicial procedures and the overall interpretation and categorization of facts, along with the recurrent dialogic flavour of judicial argumentation. The main findings of the study will be presented in the next section.

3. Results

The quantitative corpus-based analysis highlights a relatively restricted range of textual signals of counterfactual conditionality across USSC and HL judgments. More specifically, corpus data reveal that the discursive realization of counterfactuality mainly rests on *if* and the more formal construct '*had* + Subject + Past Participle'. Counterfactual signals are listed in Table 1 with their raw frequency: as anticipated, the table only includes counter-factual occurrences of the linguistic elements indicated, as a result of the concordance-sorting process preliminary to their in-depth qualitative study (cf. Section 2):[2]

Counterfactual signals	*US Supreme Court*	*House of Lords*
IF	73	208
HAD + Subject + PP	31	48
UNLESS	0	0
SHOULD + Subject + HAVE + PP	0	0

Table 1. Counterfactual signals in US Supreme Court and HL judgments and related raw frequency.

Table 1 points to the even distribution of '*had* + Subject + Past Participle' across the two types of judgments considered here (31 and 48 occurrences in USSC and HL texts respectively). By contrast, the overall predominance of counterfactual *if* is more accentuated in HL than in USSC texts (208 v. 73 occurrences). In addition, no counterfactual usages are attested for *unless* and *should* – cf. the construct '*should* + Subject + *have* + Past Participle' – in either of the corpora.

With the exception of *unless* and '*should* + Subject + *have* + Past Participle', the counterfactual signals outlined in Table 1 were analysed at both a quantitative concordance-based level and from a more qualitative text-based perspective focusing on the two cases in point. The salient findings of the two-part analysis designed at the outset will now be illustrated in subsections 3.1 and 3.2 respectively.

2 Apart from the straightforwardly counterfactual construct '*had* + Subject + Past Participle', the general corpus frequency for *if* is 1,318 in USSC texts and 1,731 in HL judgments; *unless* occurs 168 times in the USSC corpus, and 157 times in the HL corpus; furthermore, the entries for *should* are 1,012 and 603 in HL and USSC texts respectively.

3.1. Concordance-based analysis of CTFs

The concordance-based study of counterfactual signals provides strong evidence that Nivelle/Van Belle's (2007) classification of CTFs applies to the common law judicial texts analysed here. Therefore, the two categories of CTFs expressing causation and CTFs criticizing causation may be recognized across USSC and HL texts alike. This aspect becomes apparent if we compare the following two examples:[3]

(1) There is no dispute that these standards would have been satisfied <u>if</u> petitioner had taken the final step of refusing to make royalty payments under the 1997 license agreement. (USSC, Medimmune v. Genentech)

(2) <u>Even if</u> he had been sober, he would still probably have killed Nicholas Davies. (HL, Regina v. Dietschmann)

In (1), the judge establishes a straightforward causal link between the petitioner's refusal to make royalty payments on the one hand, and the failure to comply with relevant legal standards on the other. On the contrary, the judge's argument in (2) is aimed at denying any causal link between the defendant's drunkenness and his ascertained murder of Nicholas Davies; in fact, the HL judge here suggests that even if circumstances had been the complete opposite – i.e. if the defendant had been sober – the killing would have occurred anyway. As a result, *if* in (1) introduces a CTF expressing causation, whereas *even if* in (2) paves the way to a CTF criticizing causation.

More importantly, corpus data do not simply confirm the veracity of Nivelle/Van Belle's (2007) insights, but they also enable us to identify four main textual functions of CTFs expressing or criticizing causation, i.e. constructing the judge's stance first of all with reference to previous judicial opinions; secondly, in relation to adopted judicial procedures; thirdly, with regard to the interpretation and categorization of facts. Finally, CTFs may be observed to contribute to the dialogic dimension of judicial argumentative discourse. Let us now consider each one of the four analytical levels to which the closer examination of data leads.

---

3 In all numbered examples, emphasis, underscoring and bold typeface are mine.

To begin with, CTFs can underlie the judge's intention to express or criticize causation with reference to previous judicial opinions. This is of particular relevance in the context of the common law, where the centrality of precedents generally steers the court's argument to the in-depth discussion of analogous past cases. When judges make CTFs in this context, counterfactual signals mainly collocate with elements such as *Court*, *jury*, *order*, *require* and *instruct* as in (3) below:

(3) We have never held that no instruction is capable of curing the *Penry* problem with the 'special issues'. Indeed, we have suggested that the problem could have been avoided if the trial judge had not instructed the jury to give a false answer to one of the 'special issues', but had instead taken the course discussed in *Penry* – defining the term 'deliberately' as used in the first 'special issue' in a way that was broad enough to permit consideration of the relevant mitigating evidence. (USSC, Smith v. Texas)

In (3), the issue clearly revolves around the correct interpretation of the controversial term *deliberately*. The use of the CTF serves to highlight the judge's view on the issue, notably that the *trial judge*'s decision to instruct the jury *to give a false answer* is what caused the *problem*, i.e. the persistent nature of the dispute itself. The judge's stance is that no problem would ever have arisen had the trial judge adopted the right line of argument to be derived from the court's *dictum* in *Penry*, a case where – the USSC judge argues – an appropriate definition of *deliberately* was provided.

In the second place, CTFs may indicate the judge's standpoint about judicial procedures. Reasoning often delves into these facets of the judicial process, because opting for one procedure rather than another is indeed likely to have serious consequences for either of the parties involved. When CTFs are employed in this pragmatic framework, they predominantly colligate with verbs denoting procedures such as *hear* (*testimonies*), *proceed*, *omit*, *expire* (e.g. with regard to *time limits*) and *seek* (*an extension*):

(4) indeed, although I have not heard argument on the point, there is every indication that, if the Crown had sought an extension of the custody time limits the defendants would have had difficulty in resisting it. However the

fact remains that, although Mrs Radford fired a warning shot on 5 October 2001 when the prosecution could still have applied for an extension of the limit, no application was made. (HL, In re Kanaris)

In (4), the judge asserts that the nature of proceedings was deeply affected by the *Crown*'s failure or reticence to make an application to request an extension of the *time limits* at stake. As it happens, the Crown's choice is admittedly what determined the position of advantage in which the defendants came to find themselves. In the passage, therefore, the CTF draws attention to the crucial effects of the Crown's strategy: the defendants' ease in wriggling out, as it were, of the obligations that might have been imposed on them by virtue of the extension of time limits.

In the third place, CTFs can signal the judge's position with regard to the interpretation and categorization of evidence. This textual function bears on a turning point of judicial argumentation, since the attribution of the facts of the case to the convenient normative context is a very delicate operation which deserves to be well secured at a discursive level too, as can be appreciated in (5) and (6):

(5) California reads this language to suggest that for a specific occupant of the car to be seized he must be the motivating target of an officer's show of authority, see Brief for Respondent 12, as if the thrust of our observation were that Brower, and not someone else, was "meant to be stopped." But our point was not that Brower alone was the target, but that officers detained him "through means intentionally applied;" <u>if</u> the car had had another occupant, it would have made sense to hold that he too had been seized when the car collided with the roadblock. (USSC, Brendlin v. California)

(6) <u>Had</u> the work <u>been carried out</u> by the landlord, he would either have charged a premium or an increased rent. Thus the work must be taken to have been carried out by the tenant in return for the grant of the tenancy at a reduced rent and without a premium, in other words at the expense of the landlord: see Rosen v Trustees of Camden Charities [2002] Ch 69, CA. 38. <u>Even if</u> this had not been the case, however, and the work had been carried out by the tenant at his own expense, the result would have been the same. It may be assumed that, when the work of subdivision was originally carried out, it did increase the value of the property. (HL, John Lyon's Charity v. Shalson)

In (5), the CTF is intended to cast light on an important point of the body of evidence ascertained by the court, i.e. who was onboard a car which *collided with the roadblock*; in this respect, the judge emphasizes that the sole presence of Mr Brower in the car (*if the car* ***had had*** *another occupant...*) causes him to be the only person to be considered as *seized*, namely deliberately and purposefully detained by the police. Conversely, if we focus on the CTFs in the second part of (6) (*even if this...*) we readily note that its goal is to refute the argument that the tenant's involvement in the *works* would have had any legal consequences at all (*the result would have been the same*). Both the CTF expressing causation in (5) and the CTF criticizing causation in (6) play a significant role in the judge's reconstruction of the facts of the case as well as in the ensuing identification of liabilities and the eventual verdict.

The use of CTFs documented earlier on generally implies the co-occurrence of counterfactual signals with factual verbs such as *occur* and *commit*, or with the noun *evidence*. In the light of the important function of CTFs discussed here, it may be worth introducing two further specifications as to the co(n)texts in which CTFs are attested to occur in this capacity. For example, the opportunity of resorting to CTFs in the interpretation of facts may originate from the judge's attempt to determine the burden of proof that is to be ascribed to one of the parties. In this case, counterfactual elements typically colligate with the verbs *prove*, *disclose* and *show*, which contribute to an overall semantic preference of 'evidentiality':

(7) If the appellant had proved that she had been discriminated against by Superintendent Laird on the ground of her sex, I consider, for the reasons given by my noble and learned friend Lord Hope of Craighead, that she would have been entitled to a finding that she was subjected to a detriment and that the judgment of the Court of Appeal on this point, delivered before the judgment of this House in Chief Constable of the West Yorkshire Police v Khan [2001] 1 WLR 1947, should not be followed. (HL, In re Shields)

The hub of the Law Lord's argumentation in (7) is the explicit formulation of the burden of proof falling upon the defendant: it was up to her to successfully prove that she had been discriminated against (*if...had proved*) in which case she would have received due lawful recognition that she had been *subjected to a detriment*, thereby discouraging judges from following the judgment delivered by the Court of Appeal.

Alternatively, CTFs can be observed to lie at the heart of judicial categorizations of facts based on the judges' attempt to disclose the purpose behind the relevant law in force. As far as these so-called teleological interpretations of the law (MacCormick/Summers 1991) are concerned, judges set out to reconstruct the original genuine reasons that moved legislators to lay down the law the way they did: from a discursive point of view, this is often done by means of CTFs typically collocating with *Congress* or *Parliament* in USSC and HL judgments respectively, and the verb *intend* along with the nouns *statute*, *section* or *Act*:

(8) At bottom, this case is not about the validity of the city's title to immovable property, or even the validity of its automatic prejudgment lien. Rather, it is a dispute over a foreign sovereign's tax liability. If Congress had intended the statute to waive sovereign immunity in tax litigation, I think it would have said so. Accordingly, I respectfully dissent. (USSC, Permanent Mission of India v. City of New York)

In (8), the judge points out that the lack of references to the willingness by the legislature to *waive sovereign immunity in tax litigation* in the letter of the contested statute is the element that renders any interpretation in that sense dispreferred. The passage represents the concluding stage of the judge's reasoning, where he/she makes use of counterfactuality to create a straightforward causal association between such a conspicuous absence in the body of law and his/her resolution to dissent from any concurring opinion upholding an arguably erroneous reconstruction of the Congress's intents.

As was mentioned in the first part of this section, one final perspective offered by the concordance-based analysis reviewed here rests on the dialogic dimension of judicial argumentative discourse to which CTFs contribute. Dialogism is a pervasive phenomenon of judicial textuality in that the judge's argument often appears to embed and confront other voices at play in the judicial process.

On the one hand, the judge's voice sets up a dialogue with the parties and/or other judges in present or past proceedings, thus activating a backward orientation of his/her discourse, as in (9):

(9) So *Mr Gordon said that* another approach to the construction of the Act would be to concentrate less upon the fact that cloned embryos were embryos and more on the fact that they were cloned. The policy shown by section 3(3)(d) means that one cannot simply assume that cloned embryos would have been regulated like ordinary fertilised embryos. They might have been prohibited like the cloning of fertilised embryos already in existence. 35. My Lords, I can see that this argument might have created a genuine dilemma if Mr Gordon had been able to take the next step and put forward, as an alternative construction, a reading of the Act which brought cloned embryos within the prohibition in section 3(3)(d). It would then have been necessary to decide which of these alternative constructions was supported by the better arguments. But Mr Gordon, rightly in my opinion, felt unable to do so. (HL, Regina v. Secretary of State for Health)

The extract illustrates this facet of dialogism very well: the Law Lord overtly refers to the arguments put forward by one of the parties (*Mr Gordon said that...*) and then he goes on to reject the main thrust of his reasoning by centring his own counter-discourse on the CTF *if Mr Gordon had been able to....* The function of the CTF is to demonstrate that Mr Gordon's incapability to offer an alternative reading of the disputed *Act – Mr Gordon...felt unable to do so* later on – rules out the relevance of his line of argument, which by consequence creates no *dilemma* at all.

On the other hand, the judge's voice can respond to arguments that may foreseeably be addressed to him/her, accordingly anticipating on possible reactions to his/her argumentation. In contrast with the backward orientation of discourse noted above in (9), the judge's discourse here takes on a distinctively forward orientation exemplified in (10):

(10) Finally, *it might be argued that* the saving clauses preserve only state law rights and remedies. This argument has no textual basis. If Congress had intended to limit the clauses to state law, it surely would not have phrased them to preserve 'any and all' rights and remedies. Other provisions in both Acts, including a later sentence in the section containing the Securities

> Exchange Act's saving clause, suggest that Congress explicitly referred to States when it intended to impose a state law limitation. (USSC, Credit Suisse Securities v. Billing)

In (10), the USSC judge figures out a potential objection to his argumentation (*it might be argued that*...) which he promptly intends to refute – *This argument has no textual basis*. From this point of view, the judge uses a CTF to show that that argument is untenable: in particular, he argues that the phrasing of the law is what inevitably causes one to believe that the Congress was unwilling to limit *the clauses* to state law. The CTF *if Congress had intended*... brings us back to the teleological flavour of judicial reasoning discussed earlier on (cf. 8), yet it adds to it by way of the dialogic nature characterizing the judge's discourse in this case.

Table 2 below provides the bi-partite classification of dialogic argumentative discourse observed so far with a sound quantitative background. As such, the table displays the frequency of backward- and forward-oriented dialogic forms of CTFs across our two corpora:

Dialogic forms of CTFs	*USSC*	*HL*
Backward-oriented	37	86
Forward-oriented	7	34

Table 2. Raw frequency of backward- and forward-oriented dialogic forms of CTFs in USSC and HL judgments.

Table 2 suggests that the dialogic use of CTFs prevails in HL texts (120 occurrences altogether v. 44 of USSC judgments), whereas the outstanding incidence of backward-oriented dialogic forms seems to be shared by both types of common law judgments considered. A closer look at the dialogic implications CTFs may have in judgments concludes the presentation of findings related to the concordance-based study of counterfactuals. The next section will shed more light on the centrality of CTFs in judicial argumentative discourse through a more qualitative text-based study of two cases in point extracted from each corpus.

3.2. A qualitative text-based study of CTFs

The important role of CTFs in judicial argumentation will be investigated in this section by means of a genuinely text-based analysis of two cases. These were selected because an automatic survey of data indicated that they are the two judgments with the highest frequency of CTFs in the USSC and the HL corpus respectively. The chosen judgments are *Scott v. Harris*, issued by the USSC on 30 April 2007, and *Regina v. Dietschmann*, delivered by the HL on 27 February 2003.

Beginning with the American case, the dispute in *Scott v. Harris* was essentially about the serious consequences following the police pursuit of the defendant, Mr Harris. He was driving his car in a drunken state, thus putting the lives of all passers-by at great risk. Mr Scott, the petitioner, was a police officer on duty: he drove off to pursue Mr Harris's car, which he eventually rammed off the road by applying a push bumper – a well-known technical device employed by the police to seize offenders – to the rear of the vehicle. The officer's action, however formally legitimized by the law, caused Mr Harris to crash and to remain quadriplegic for the rest of his life.

Moving from the ascertained facts of the case to the core of the argumentative analysis of interest here, we may observe that the question at the crux of controversy is formulated by Justice Scalia precisely through the CTF reported in (11) below:

(11) couldn't the innocent public equally have been protected, and the tragic accident entirely avoided, <u>if</u> the police had simply ceased their pursuit?

The question in (11) enables the judge to discuss what kind of causal relationship there might be between the defendant's pursuit by the police, and the protection of innocent people on the road as well the pre-emption of the tragic accident which befell Mr Harris. The conclusion drawn by Justice Scalia and approved of by the majority of the USSC was that Mr Scott's operation was correct, as can be seen in (12):

(12) We think the police need not have taken that chance and hoped for the best. Whereas Scott's action – ramming respondent off the road – was certain to eliminate the risk that respondent posed to the public, ceasing pursuit was not.

What is most interesting to note is that this outcome relies on a fairly commonsensical yet very effective piece of causal reasoning pivoting around the CTF in (13):

(13) First of all, there would have been no way to convey convincingly to respondent that the chase was off, and that he was free to go. Had respondent looked in his rear-view mirror and seen the police cars deactivate their flashing lights and turn around, he would have had no idea whether they were truly letting him get away or simply devising a new strategy for capture. Perhaps the police knew a shortcut he didn't know, and would reappear down the road to intercept him, or perhaps they were setting up a roadblock in his path. Cf. Brower, 489 U.S. at 594. Given such uncertainty, respondent might have been just as likely to respond by continuing to drive recklessly as by slowing down and wiping his brow.
Second, we are loath to lay down a rule requiring the police to allow fleeing suspects to get away whenever they drive so recklessly that they put other people's lives in danger. It is obvious the perverse incentives such a rule would create: every fleeing motorist would know that escape is within his grasp if only he accelerates to 90 miles per hour, crosses the double-yellow line a few times, and runs a few red lights. The Constitution assuredly does not impose this invitation to impunity earned by recklessness.

The somewhat dense passage reproduced above has its focal point in the CTF *had respondent looked...and seen...he would have*, which projects the judge into a thorough assessment of the effects arising out of the potential decision on the police's part to give up on pursuing the offender. Obviously, this is not what actually took place, but the argumentation *ad absurdum* elaborated by the judge has the advantage of illustrating the definitely undesirable adverse effects that would certainly have arisen had Mr Scott resolved to cease the pursuit: on the one hand, the defendant could simply have kept on driving recklessly – *he would have had no idea whether they were truly letting him get away or simply devising a new strategy for capture*; on the other hand, such an interpretation of the officer's duties would lay down a dangerous rule securing the impunity of motorists blatantly breaching the highway code, by reason of the life-threatening effects which may be caused by a seizure – *every fleeing motorist would know that escape is within his grasp if only he accelerates to 90 miles per hour.*

However controversial and far from expected, Justice Scalia's argumentation is very hard to reverse, which may explain why the majority of his peers shared his view that *Scott's attempt to terminate the chase by forcing respondent off the road was reasonable, and Scott is entitled to summary judgment*, as we read as a gloss to Scalia's opinion.

Moving from the USSC to the House of Lords, the *Regina v. Dietschmann* case represents the last stage of a long judicial story crying out for a prominent place in recent British crime news. The defendant in the dispute, Mr Dietschmann, admitted he had killed a man called Nicholas Davies in a savage attack. The killing occurred when the defendant was heavily intoxicated by alcohol consumption and at the same time was suffering from a certified mental abnormality.

On these grounds, the basic question on which the proceedings ended up turning was whether the defendant's deliberate intention to kill Mr Davies was the decisive factor (possibly in association with drunkenness), in which case it would come to a categorization of the ascertained facts as 'murder'; or whether the defendant's mental impairment could pave the way to a configuration of Mr Dietschmann's liability in terms of 'manslaughter' and resulting diminished responsibility:

(14) The question [...] is as follows:
Does a defendant seeking to prove a defence of diminished responsibility under section 2(1) of the Homicide Act 1957 in a case where he had taken drink prior to killing the victim, have to show that if he had not taken drink
(a) he would have killed as he in fact did; and
(b) he would have been under diminished responsibility when he did so?

Once again, as in *Scott v. Harris*, the judge uses a CTF in order to articulate the question, this time stressing that the core of adjudication lies in determining what role, if any, drunkenness might have had in the killing in comparison with mental disorders – *Does a defendant...have to show that* ***if*** *he had not taken drink...*

Lord Hutton's opinion about the issue is that regardless of the effects of drinking on Mr Dietschmann's wrongful deeds, mental impairment still had the upper hand among the plausible causes of the killing, as we read from the bit of counterfactual reasoning reported in (15):

(15) I think that in referring to substantial impairment of mental responsibility the subsection does not require the abnormality of mind to be the sole cause of the defendant's acts in doing the killing. In my opinion, even if the defendant would not have killed <u>if</u> he had not taken drink, the causative effect of the drink does not necessarily prevent an abnormality of mind suffered by the defendant from substantially impairing his mental responsibility for his fatal acts.

It is interesting to note that Lord Hutton carves his argumentation out of the well-credited psychiatric examination by Dr El Azra, the real 'warrant' (Toulmin 1958) by which the judge concludes that the causal link between the defendant's drunkenness and the killing of Mr Davies needs to be excluded (cf. 16). For the sake of visual clarity, the warrant provided by the psychiatric report is in bold, whereas the CTF serving as the argument in Lord Hutton's reasoning is underlined as in prior examples:

(16) **He [Dr. El Azra] was of the opinion that** the appellant had been in a transient psychotic state at the time of the incident. **In his opinion the appellant perceived that** the breaking of the watch was an abuse of Sarah's memory and it took him out of the boundaries of reality. **He falsely believed that** Nicholas Davies had been urinating on Sarah's grave. **The fact that** the appellant was under the influence of alcohol **did not explain** what had happened. <u>Even if</u> he had been sober, he would still probably have killed Nicholas Davies.

The judge's line of argument, cunningly crafted from the interplay of competing causal elements and discursively anchored through the reiterated use of CTFs observed above, then expectedly leads Lord Hutton to issue a verdict requesting the previous conviction for murder to be quashed and substituted by one for manslaughter:

(17) Accordingly, for the reasons which I have given, I would remit the case to the Court of Appeal for that court to decide whether to allow the appeal and quash the conviction for murder and order a new trial or to substitute a verdict of guilty of manslaughter for the verdict of murder found by the jury and to pass an appropriate sentence for that offence.

4. Conclusions

The results illustrated over the previous section suggest that there is much room for the applicability of Nivelle/Van Belle's (2007) research framework to common law judicial texts as well. Indeed, the spread of counterfactuality expressing or criticizing causation in the argumentative style of common law judges could altogether be traced back to the Anglo-Saxon origins of the legal thought about causation, as pointed out by Hart/Honoré (1959) and acknowledged by Nivelle/van Belle (2007) themselves. As a matter of fact, causality as a key-principle of reasoning, already present in Bacon's discussion of inductive logic within the *Novum Organum*, was also thoroughly dealt with by Hume. In his *Enquiry Concerning Human Understanding*, the Scottish philosopher pointed to 'causes' as the governing principle determining such essential relationships between objects as proximity, distance, temporal sequence and necessary connections. In addition, Hume drew up an inventory of eight rules to evaluate causes and effects: he thus postulated, for instance, that there must be spatio-temporal proximity between causes and effects; there must be some common traits between objects provoking the same effects; and conversely, the heterogeneous effects brought about by similar objects must lie in their underlying difference.

In this vein, the view that great care should be placed in determining the core of causal links in argumentation was taken up by legal theory as well. In that respect, scholars such as Hart and Honoré (1959) argued that under specific circumstances a causally relevant factor is a necessary component of a range of conditions jointly sufficient for the harmful outcome. What is more, they add, the judicial duty to ascertain whether a particular outcome would have been produced in the absence of the agency at stake is closely linked with the formulation of counterfactual calculations.

Still, this research appears to do more than simply confirm previous analytical insights by law and argumentation scholars. First of all, the investigation reported here adds to prior examinations of counterfactuality by enriching them through the rigour and systematicity provided by corpus insights. The interplay of a quantitative and a qualitative perspective, the integration of corpus and text enabled us to disclose the actual discursive fabric of CTFs: accordingly, the analysis brought first-hand empirical evidence that the expression and criticism of causation is closely linked to distinctive contexts, specific passages in argumentation whereby judges perform key acts such as the review of previous judicial opinions, the assessment of relevant procedures and the categorization of facts with regard to the burden of proof to be ascribed to parties as well as the interpretation of the goals behind the law. Furthermore, the approach adopted in the chapter substantiates prior research in that it relates CTFs with the dialogic dimension often associated with judicial argumentation (Section 3.1).

Finally, the findings of the text-based analysis documented in Section 3.2 show how deeply integrated CTFs may be in the argumentative discourse of judges, who are often called upon to disclose the cause-effect dynamics underlying judicial disputes. The corpus and text-based examination of CTFs designed here is thus meant to be illustrative of the diversified types of discursive anchoring and of counterfactual reasoning within the judge's argumentation.

Further research appears to be needed in order to set up a comparative framework involving the study of judgments produced by different courts within the same legal system: this would amount to moving beyond the overview of frequency data to embrace a fine-grained observation of the similar or distinctive places that CTFs may occupy in the argumentative devices courts set in motion. For instance, the texts produced by a common law court such as the House of Lords – let alone the recently-established English Supreme Court – could interestingly be compared with those delivered by an equity body like the Chancery Division of the High Court of England and Wales (cf. Bondi/Mazzi 2008 for a preliminary survey of data).

References

Bobbio, Norberto 1966. Preface to Perelman, Chaïm / Olbrechts-Tyteca, Lucie *Trattato dell'argomentazione. La nuova retorica*, Torino, Einaudi.

Bobbio, Norberto 1977. *Dalla struttura alla funzione. Nuovi studi di teoria del diritto*. Milano: Edizioni di Comunità.

Bondi, Marina / Mazzi, Davide 2008. The Words of Equity: an Analysis of a Corpus of Judgments. In Carpi, Daniela (ed.) *Practising Equity, Addressing Law. Equity in Law and Literature*. Heidelberg: Winter, 425-446.

Bowker, Lynne / Pearson, Jennifer 2002. *Working with Specialized Language. A Practical Guide to Using Corpora*. London: Routledge.

Cornu, Gérard 2000. *Linguistique juridique*. Paris: Montchrestien.

van Eemeren, Frans H. / Grootendorst, Rob / Snoek Henkemans, Franciska (eds) 1996. *Fundamentals of Argumentation Theory*. Mahwah: Lawrence Erlbaum.

Feteris, Eveline 1999. *Fundamentals of Legal Argumentation*. Dordrecht: Kluwer.

Goodrich, Peter 1986. *Reading the Law: a Critical Introduction to Legal Method and Techniques*. Oxford: Blackwell.

Hart, Herbert L.A. / Honoré, Tony 1959. *Causation in the Law*. Oxford: Clarendon Press.

Hunston, Susan 2002. *Corpora in Applied Linguistics*. Oxford: Oxford University Press.

MacCormick, Neil / Summers, Robert S. (eds) 1991. *Interpreting Statutes: A Comparative Study*. Aldershot: Dartmouth.

Mazzi, Davide 2006. 'This is an attractive argument, but...': Argumentative Conflicts as an Interpretive Key to the Discourse of Judges. In Bhatia, Vijay / Gotti, Maurizio (eds) *Explorations in Specialised Genres*. Bern: Peter Lang, 271-290.

Mazzi, Davide 2007a. The Construction of Argumentation in Judicial Texts: Combining a Genre and a Corpus Perspective. *Argumentation* 14/1: 21-38.

Mazzi, Davide 2007b. *The Linguistic Study of Judicial Argumentation. Theoretical Perspectives, Analytical Insights*. Modena: Il Fiorino.

Mortara Garavelli, Bice 2001. *Le parole e la giustizia. Divagazioni grammaticali e retoriche sui testi giuridici italiani*. Torino: Einaudi.

Nivelle, Nele / Van Belle, William 2007. The Use of Counterfactual Conditionals Expressing Causation in Legal Discourse. In van Eemeren, Frans H. / Blair, J. Anthony / Willard, Charles A. / Garssen, Bart (eds) *Proceedings of the Sixth Conference of the International Society for the Study of Argumentation*. Amsterdam: SicSat, 989-996.

Peczenik, Alexander 1989. *On Law and Reason*. Dordrecht: Kluwer.

Perelman, Chaïm 1980. *Justice, Law and Argument*. Dordrecht: Reidel.

Santulli, Francesca 2008. La sentenza come genere testuale: narrazione, argomentazione, performatività. In Garzone, Giuliana / Santulli, Francesca (eds) *Il Linguaggio giuridico. Prospettive interdisciplinari*. Milano: Giuffrè, 207-238.

Scott, Mike 2004. *WordSmith Tools Version 4.0*. Oxford: Oxford University Press.

Sinclair, John 1991. *Corpus, Concordance, Collocation*. Oxford: Oxford University Press.

Sinclair, John 1996. The Search for Units of Meaning. *Textus* 9/1: 75-106.

Sinclair, John 1998a. The Lexical Item. In Weigand, Edda (ed.) *Contrastive Lexical Semantics: Current Issues in Linguistic Theory*. Amsterdam: John Benjamins, 1-24.

Sinclair, John [11]1998b. *Collins Cobuild English Grammar*. London: Harper Collins.

Sinclair, John 2003. *Reading Concordances. An Introduction*. London: Longman.

Stubbs, Michael 2001. *Words and Phrases: Corpus Studies on Lexical Semantics*. Oxford: Blackwell.

Toulmin, Stephen 1958. *The Uses of Argument*. Cambridge: Cambridge University Press.

IGNACIO VÁZQUEZ ORTA

A Genre-based View of Judgments of Appellate Courts in the Common Law System: Intersubjective Positioning, Intertextuality and Interdiscursivity in the Reasoning of Judges

1. Introduction and overview

In the common law, judgments of appellate courts are extremely important texts, because they contain the judges' declarations on a case-by-case basis and are therefore a source of law. On a practical level, a judgment is the final decision in a legal dispute, which is argued and settled in a court of law representing an order of the court determining winners and losers. However, the function of a judgment goes beyond the settlement of specific disputes. Judgments also provide a public account of the judges' reasoning processes. They validate one form of argument and reasoning, one way of looking at the world over others. They are instances of legal arguments and ways of reasoning which are characteristic of the legal context. This makes judgments important texts also in legal education.

In spite of the importance of judgments for the two reasons mentioned, very little linguistic research has been carried out on this genre. Some research has been done on its macrostructure (Maley 1985), on the realization of its communicative purposes through language and on the intertextual characteristics of judgments and the consequences of this for teaching reading in English for Academic Purposes (Bhatia 1989). A generic structure of judgments has been identified (Maley 1985; Bhatia 1993) as well as a relationship between the structural elements and the communicative functions of declaring and justifying. At the micro level, modality has been found to play an important role in the justifying function of judgments (Maley 1989).

In this study I am concerned with judgments of appellate courts in order to illustrate how these texts express judges' intersubjective positioning when they write their judgments: firstly, by highlighting the specific forms of negotiating alternative positions and, secondly, by focusing on how texts (or rather the judge as the writer) negotiate past decisions, integrate these texts into their own texts and align themselves with these past decisions. Furthermore, I will argue that legal reasoning and interpretation is not primarily and exclusively an exercise of conclusive and unassailable logic leading to inevitable outcomes, as claimed by traditional legal theory, but that legal reasoning is an exercise in intersubjective positioning and making choices, although not totally unrestricted choices. Central to these arguments will be the idea of *dialogue* and *negotiation*. In a judgment, the writer enters into a number of dialogues with previous texts: with the evidence, argument and submissions made by the litigants in court, with the decision, which is being appealed against, and with similar decisions in the past (precedent). The writer also enters into a dialogue with possible future texts: a possible appeal against his/her decision and judges and lawyers who will be involved in similar cases in the future. And finally, writers may enter into a dialogue with their colleagues on the bench who may decide a case differently.

Section 2 will set out the theoretical foundations for this study: Legal discourse, Critical Discourse Analysis and Systemic Functional Linguistics. This chapter will focus on the relationship between language, context and social practice. Section 3 will develop a textual analysis of the resources for legal reasoning and for dialogue in judgments. This section will be concerned with the social construction of facts as well as the declaratory and justifying function of appellate judgments. The argument here will be that all structural elements of an appellate judgment are dialogic but different elements draw on different kinds of dialogues and to different degrees. Section 4 will draw some conclusions from the previous analysis and will discuss legal discourse as a discourse of power and solidarity and some of the implications of this.

2. Theoretical framework

To the extent that judgments are representative of a legal discourse they represent a different type of discourse from the everyday discourse of actions and events. In fact, my hypothesis here will be that the discourse of the social world is semiotically reconstructed as the abstract discourse of legal categories and legal rules which is represented in appellate judgments. Appellate judgments are the product of a multiplicity of long and complex processes of negotiation, re-contextualization and discursive reconstruction. The common law system is an adversarial system, where competing versions of facts need to be negotiated, reconstructed and re-contextualized along the litigation process. An event in the external world, or the 'real' world, happens and causes harm to another person. This may be a physical act such as a car crashing into other cars and, as a result, hurting people or damaging property. It may also be a verbal event: somebody says something causing harm to another person, such as a threat: "I am going to my mate's house. He will really fix you up", or it may be someone omitting to say something they should have said, as in the case of an operation, where a surgeon fails to inform his/her patient beforehand of a very specific and very rare risk.

These events are *re-constructed* discursively by the litigants in conference with their lawyers; they are further *re-contextualized* in lawyers' submissions to the court, by the evidence given in court, and by the arguments made and precedents cited by the lawyers on behalf of their clients. The final step in the litigation process is for the judge, after having considered the arguments and the evidence, to make a decision and to justify it in writing, further *re-contextualizing* what he/she read and heard in court.

The outcome of all this, the judgment, bears the traces of these various discursive events, some overtly and explicitly, some tacitly and implicitly. After publication in law reports, the judgment becomes a part of the body of the common law and will, in turn, leave its traces in arguments and decisions to be made in the future. This process is represented in Figure 1.

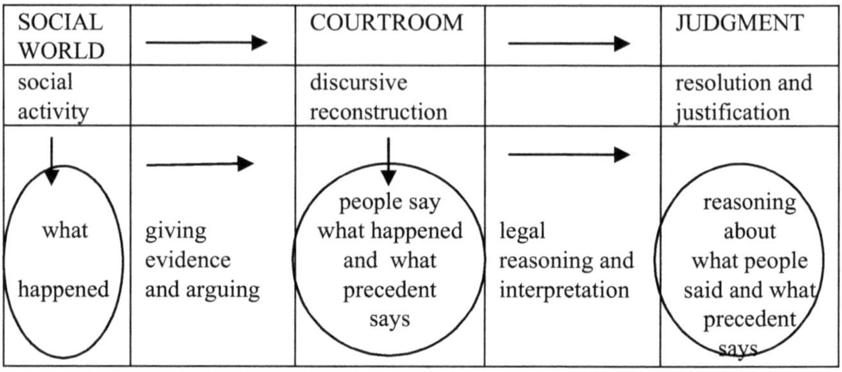

Figure 1. Discursive reconstructions of reality.

The traces of the discursive reconstructions and re-contextualizations that appear in judgments can be followed through Bakhtin's (1981) notion of 'dialogism' and 'heteroglossia' and through what Fairclough (1992) has termed 'manifest intertextuality' and 'constitutive intertextuality' (or interdiscursivity). Manifest intertextuality tells us something about the origins of a text, the various voices that have some stake in the text. Interdiscursivity is concerned with translating the discourse of social reality into legal discourse.

Thus, it will become clear that the language of judgments is functionally motivated by the very nature and the practices of the common law itself. Our premise here is that law is a discourse, that is, a social practice which is tied to institutions and which involves language. An implication of this is that both law and language are a part of society, not separate from society, as claimed by traditional legal reasoning. Social practices result in specific texts and an analysis of these texts can tell us something about the social practices which constitute a discourse. Thus, through the analysis of texts it is possible to gain an understanding of broader social processes.

The central argument is that legal reasoning is primarily concerned with intersubjective positioning, and this involves choice, that is, acknowledging alternative positions and choosing one alternative over another. This is both reflective of and constitutive of legal discourse. In the adversarial system of the common law, competing facts are presented by the litigants, and conflicting legal rules and principles may be available to be applied to the facts.

Furthermore, interpretation involves the choice of one possible meaning over other possible meanings. It will be my argument in this study that the interpretation of 'ambiguity' is not necessarily due to the inability of language to convey precise meanings but that the need for interpretation arises from certain discursive practices in legal reasoning: rules can be stated at different levels of generality by the same judge in the same text, and by different judges in different texts, which means that there can be alternative versions of the rule within a text as well as across texts and from these alternatives one has to be chosen as the 'correct' one.

The theoretical framework for the analysis of appellate judgments will be informed by Bakhtin's (1981) notion of dialogism[1] and heteroglossia as stated above. For the actual textual analysis we will use the notion of 're-contextualization' as a tool for discourse analysis (Fairclough 1992, 1995 and Bhatia 2004), which will be applied to a corpus of four appellate judgments taken from the collection of House of Lords Appellate Judgments:[2]

1. Austin (FC) (Appellant) v. Commissioner of Police (Respondent), 28 January 2009 (Austin v Co).
2. Agassi (Respondent) v. Robinson (Her Majesty's Inspector of Taxes) (Appellant), 17 May 2006 (Agassi v Ro).
3. Burton (Respondent) (Her Majesty's Collector of Taxes) v. Melham Ltd (Appellant), 15 February 2006 (Burton v Mel).
4. Dunnachie (Respondent) v. Smith and Kingston-upon-Hull Council (Appellants), 15 July 2004. (D v S).

---

1 In *The Dialogic Imagination* Bakhtin contrasts the 'dialogic' and the 'monologic' work of literature. The dialogic work carries on a continual dialogue with other works of literature and other authors. It does not merely answer, correct, silence, or extend a previous work, but informs and is continually informed by the previous work. Dialogic literature is in communication with multiple works. The term 'dialogic', however, does not just apply to literature. For Bakhtin, all language – indeed, all thought – appears dialogic.

2 <http://www.publications.parliament.uk/pa/ld/ldjudgmt.htm>.

The research questions for the present chapter are:

1. What choices from the linguistic system are made as the judgment unfolds?
2. How does the writer engage in a dialogue with other texts and with alternative possibilities?
3. How does the writer move between the common-sense discourse of everyday reality and the abstract discourse of the law?

3. Textual analysis

3.1. A genre-based study

My approach to the study of appellate judgments as a genre takes a functional standpoint. According to Maley (1994), judgments have two functions: the *justifying* function (judgments provide a public account of the reasoning process which leads to a judge's decision) and the *declarative* one (a judgment is the final decision in a legal dispute). I accept Maley's (1985) work on the generic structure of appellate judgments, where the following structural elements have been proposed:

1. Facts
2. Issue
3. Reasoning
4. Conclusion and Order/Finding.

Of these, Issue, Reasoning, Conclusion and Order/Finding are obligatory. Facts is an optional element, and when individual judgments are delivered they are present in the leading judgment but may be omitted in the others. Of course, judges are free to write their own account of the facts if they wish to do so. The justifying function is realized in *Issue* and *Reasoning*, while the declarative function is realized in *Conclusion* and *Order*.

My basic assumption in carrying out the textual analysis is that all structural elements of a judgment are highly dialogic. There is dialogue with other texts, where alternative meanings are attributed to external voices (extra-vocalization). There is dialogue about alternative meanings where the alternatives are inscribed in the writer's own words, and there is dialogue about degrees of experimental and interpersonal meanings. I exclude any other possible dialogues beyond the interplay of precedent decision, counsel's arguments and the appellate decision. This can be taken as a statement of the limitation of this study but my intention is to focus on those aspects more specifically, thus accepting the chapter's limitation in aim. These dialogues unfold throughout a judgment: facts are not 'found' but are socially constructed. There is a delicate balance here between monoglossic utterances assuming reader alignment and heteroglossic[3] utterances acknowledging alternative positions. I shall start, first of all, with the social constructions of facts.

3.2. The social construction of facts

The argument here is that facts in a legal judgment are not 'discovered' as pre-existing entities. Facts are socially constructed or, in Fairclough's terms, they are highly intertextual and interdiscursive. One important aspect here is that in appellate judgments, facts not only relate to the construction of events in the 'real' world, but they *construct* the discursive history of a case through the court system.

3.2.1. Negotiating the discursive history of a case

The history of a case is generally found at the beginning of a judgment and contextualizes the 'reasoning' and 'decision' that follows. The

---

3 Any language, in Bakhtin's view, stratifies into many voices: social dialects, characteristic group behaviour, professional jargons, generic languages, languages of generations and age groups, tendentious languages, languages of the authorities, of various circles and of passing fashions. This diversity of voice is, Bakhtin asserts, the defining characteristic of the novel as a genre. And this can be applied to any text whatsoever.

case history typically negotiates intertextual aspects such as: what happened before the case came before this court? What were some of the main arguments? What was the outcome of previous proceedings and appeals? What did the judges decide at each stage? What decisions did the litigants take in response to a court's decision? Thus, a judgment is firmly established as a dialogic text, responding to previous decisions and arguments. What this means is that a variety of external texts are introduced into the writer's text. To achieve this, external voices play a major role. In interdiscursive terms, legal discourse dominates here. The following are extracts from the four appellate cases in this study.

(1) (D v S: Buckmaster: 1-9) (legal discourse in SMALL CAPS, extra-vocalization values <u>underlined</u>)

1. My Lords, the facts of this case are simple.
2. On August 26, 1928, THE APPELLANT drank a bottle of ginger beer, manufactured by THE RESPONDENT, which a friend had bought from a retailer and given to her.
3. The bottle contained the decomposed remains of a snail which were not, and could not be, detected until the greater part of the contents of the bottle had been consumed.
4. AS A RESULT <u>SHE ALLEGED</u>, AND AT THIS STAGE <u>HER ALLEGATIONS</u> MUST BE ACCEPTED AS TRUE, that she suffered from shock and severe gastro-enteritis.
5. SHE ACCORDINGLY INSTITUTED THE PROCEEDINGS AGAINST THE MANUFACTURER WHICH HAVE GIVEN RISE TO THIS APPEAL.
6. <u>THE FOUNDATION OF HER CASE IS</u> THAT THE RESPONDENT, AS THE MANUFACTURER OF AN ARTICLE INTENDED FOR CONSUMPTION AND CONTAINED IN A RECEPTACLE WHICH PREVENTED INSPECTION, OWED A DUTY TO HER AS CONSUMER OF THE ARTICLE TO TAKE CARE THAT THERE WAS NO NOXIOUS ELEMENT IN THE GOODS, THAT HE NEGLECTED SUCH DUTY AND IS CONSEQUENTLY LIABLE FOR ANY DAMAGE CAUSED BY SUCH NEGLECT.
7. AFTER CERTAIN AMENDMENTS, WHICH ARE NOW IMMATERIAL, THE CASE CAME BEFORE THE LORD ORDINARY, WHO <u>REJECTED THE PLEA</u> IN LAW OF THE RESPONDENT AND ALLOWED A PROOF.
8. HIS INTERLOCUTOR WAS RECALLED BY THE SECOND DIVISION OF THE COURT OF SESSION, FROM WHOSE <u>JUDGMENT</u> THIS APPEAL HAS BEEN BROUGHT.

(2) (Austin v Co: White: 1-6)

1. THIS IS AN APPEAL BY A COMPLAINANT AGAINST <u>THE DISMISSAL BY A MAGISTRATE OF A COMPLAINT.</u>

2. THE APPELLANT IS AN ASSISTANT POLICE PROSECUTOR.
3. HE LAID A COMPLAINT AGAINST THE RESPONDENT (THE DEFENDANT) ALLEGING that the defendant had assaulted a named young woman, occasioning her actual bodily harm.
4. THE MAGISTRATE HELD THAT THE DEFENDANT'S CONDUCT DID NOT CONSTITUTE AN ASSAULT AND FOR THAT REASON HE DISMISSED THE COMPLAINT.
5. THE ONLY GROUND OF APPEAL IS THAT THE MAGISTRATE ERRED IN LAW IN HOLDING THAT THE DEFENDANT'S CONDUCT DID NOT CONSTITUTE AN ASSAULT.

In all four appellate cases of this study the judgments are contextualized by presenting an overview of the development of the case in the lower courts. Case histories are characterized by attributing alternative meanings to external voices. Furthermore, at this stage alternative meanings are not represented through quoted speech but all external voices are assimilated into the writer's own text. Among the assimilation choices made, there is predominantly strong assimilation, that is, the external texts are assimilated into the writer's own text to a very high degree and quite often the words of the external texts are no longer represented in any way, for example:

(3) My Lords, this is an appeal from a judgment of the Court of Appeal reversing a decision of Oliver J. (Agassi v Ro: 40)

It is nowhere stated what Oliver J's decision actually said and what the judgment of the Court of Appeal actually said. There are only a few instances where external texts are represented as reported speech:

(4) The magistrate held that the defendant's conduct did not constitute an assault. (Agassi v Ro: 41)

In the data for this study, intra-vocalization values are very rare in the construction of a text's discursive history. If this option is chosen, heteroglossic alternatives, which might be inferred by the reader, are generally closed down. Responsibility is taken by the writer in (5):

(5) The respondent brings an action for damages against the committee and members of the club – the striker of the ball is not a defendant. (Burton v Mel: 32)

Monoglossic utterances, allowing no alternative positions, are also rare in the construction of a text's discursive history. They give information that is obvious, such as litigants' names and their role in previous proceedings. This kind of information need not be attributed to external sources: the writer takes responsibility for these propositions:

(6) The appellant is an assistant police prosecutor. (Austin v Co: 21)

3.2.2. The social construction of facts and the negotiation of interdiscursivity

Courtroom discourse is a hybrid of two discourses – the discourse of the 'real' world, that is, the discourse of specific events involving specific people in circumstances, and the abstract discourse of legal categories and rules. In the resolution of a legal conflict, these two disparate discourses are brought together when lay people and law people interact with each other. In the lawyer's office and in the courtroom, this happens through *dialogue* (Maley *et al.* 1995; Gibbons/Hale 1997). In a judgment, these two discourses must be negotiated by the writer. He must bring the everyday discourse of the lay people within the domain of the discourse of law. He presents what people said in court as facts and then applies the law to the facts. This makes judgments a prime site of manifest intertextuality, as well as constitutive intertextuality or interdiscursivity (Fairclough 1992).

In the discursive history of a case it is the semiotic reality of the law that is foregrounded through assimilating previous texts into the writer's own and through assigning a technical legal value to assimilated texts: *the case, amendments, plea, judgment, decision, injunction, evidence, complaint, allegation.* At this stage, the commonsense discourse of the 'real' world is either absent, as in *D v S: Buckmaster* (legal discourse in SMALL CAPS in example 1), or it is very much backgrounded and either projected or embedded.

In conclusion, the discursive construction of events in the 'real' world is highly dialogic. In the social construction of facts, a dynamic has been identified from quoted or reported speech to nominalization:

X said that Y was nominalized to *statement, evidence, decision.*

This particular dynamic made it possible (i) to move the statement of facts forward and (ii) to assign technical values to utterances, which, in turn, was a means for evaluating the external text.

3.3. Statement of issue: the dialogic construction of legal issues

Issue is that part of a judgment where the events in the 'real' world which are the cause of a dispute in a court of law are recast as a legal problem, as legal categories. It is here where the everyday discourse of actions and events is semiotically constructed as the abstract discourse of legal categories and legal rules. The construction of legal issues is also highly dialogic but in a different way. Here it is interdiscursivity that comes into play. Everyday social actions are translated into the categories of the law. Legal issues are often constructed in terms of alternative categories, and can also be constructed in terms of degree. Because the legal issues are determined by the facts, Issue follows Facts.

I am putting the relationship between Facts and Issue in dialogic terms, highlighting the intertextual as well as the interdiscursive nature of legal issues. I see legal issues as dialogic because they are a response to previous texts – evidence, arguments and conclusion of the lower courts – as they have been negotiated in the construction of facts and in the discursive history of the case. In that sense, the Issue is a link in a chain of previous texts and the judge's reasoning that follows. In addition, I see legal issues as dialogic because they form a link between the problems in the 'real' world and the solution of the law. Legal issues are the translation of the everyday discourse of the 'real' world into the abstract and specialized discourse of legal rules and categories. In that sense, Issue is the link between the social discourse of events in the 'real' world and legal discourse.

3.3.1. Legal issues and intertextuality

It is important to note that the Issue follows from the evidence, arguments and decisions of the lower courts. In dialogic terms this means that the Issue is linked to the discursive history of the case (external voices in SMALL CAPS.)

(7) [Discursive history of the case] (D v S: 9-10; 1-3)

IN THE ACTION AND ON APPEAL THE RESPONDENT CONTENDED AS STATED ABOVE →	that the appellants were negligent or guilty of creating a nuisance in failing to take any sufficient precautions to prevent the escape of cricket balls from the ground and the consequent risk of injury to persons in Beckenham Road.
IN HER SUBMISSION →	it was enough that a ball had been driven into the road even once.
Such an event gave the appellants WARNING →	that a ball might be hit into the road, and the appellants, knowing this, must, as reasonable men, also know that an injury was likely to be caused to anyone standing in the road or to a passer-by.
THE ARGUMENT, AS SHE SAID, →	"was, however" strengthened when it was remembered that a ball had been driven over the fence from time to time even though at somewhat remote intervals. Such an event was known to the appellants to have occurred, and, if they had considered the matter, they ought to have envisaged the possibility of its repetition.

The question, however, remains: is it enough to make an action negligent to say that its performance may possibly cause injury or must some greater probability exist of that result ensuing in order to make those responsible for its occurrence guilty of negligence? The judge's statement of the issue takes up the arguments made by the appellant previously and recasts these arguments as the question to be answered, the legal problem to be solved. This is both reflective of and constitutive of the discourse of law. In adversarial proceedings, the issues are raised by the litigants, not by the judge. Therefore, in the judgment, the judge has to deal with the issues as they have been raised and argued by the litigants. The intertextual nature of addressing legal issues has been strongly emphasized by judges themselves, although not in terms of intertextuality but in terms of fairness:

> I think it is most unfair if a judge in the House of Lords puts forward a proposition of law which has never been advanced either in the courts below or in counsel's arguments. It is unfair to the courts below, it's unfair to counsel and it's most unsatisfactory, because very often if he [sic] had put forward this point to counsel, counsel would have had an answer and maybe would have cited a case which would have shown that he [sic] was wrong. It's a dangerous practice. (Law Lord, cited in Paterson 1982: 39)

To summarize, the statement of Issue forms intertextual links with a variety of previous texts. It forms a link with evidence, arguments and conclusions in the same case in the lower courts, it forms links with principles stated in precedents, and it forms a link between the facts of the case and the following reasoning and conclusion.

3.3.2. Legal issues and interdiscursivity

In a dispute before a court of law a problem in the 'real' world has to be translated into a legal problem. The Issue is the site where these two discourses meet – an everyday, commonsense discourse and the specialized, abstract discourse of the law. Interdiscursivity may be negotiated in a number of ways. Essentially, the translation of everyday discourse into legal discourse is not a straightforward process with one-to-one relationships between the two discourses, as in $x = 2$, or '*chien' means dog*. In the following I will discuss the different stages of the process. As a first step, a relationship between the two discourses could be established in an identifying relational clause.

(8) (D v S: 133)

The defendant's conduct	constituted	an assault.
Token		*Value*
'real' world discourse		legal discourse

Here a relationship between the two discourses is established in a monoglossic Token/Value clause. However, this does not seem to be an acceptable solution in legal judgments. In the data for this study, no such monoglossic Token/Value proposition construing legal issues has been found. If this construction occurs, it is attributed to an external source.

THE MAGISTRATE HELD →	*that the defendant's conduct*	*constituted*	*an assault.*
extra-vocalize	Token		Value
legal discourse →	'real' world discourse		legal discourse

This can be made further negotiable by attributing this extra-vocalization value to yet another source:

THE APPELLANT ARGUES →	THAT THE MAGISTRATE ERRED IN HOLDING →	*that the defendant's conduct*	*constituted*	*an assault*
extra-vocalize	extra-vocalize	Token		Value
legal discourse →	legal discourse →	'real' world discourse		legal discourse

To make this utterance further negotiable, an intra-vocalization value can be inscribed into the projected Token/Value utterance:

THE APPELLANT ARGUES →	THAT THE MAGISTRATE ERRED IN HOLDING →	*That the defendant's conduct*	*did not constitute*	*an assault*
extra-vocalize	extra-vocalize	Token		Value
legal discourse →	legal discourse →	'real' world discourse		legal discourse

This is, in fact, how the issue is framed in Example 9 (Austin v Co: White: 56)

(9) The only ground of appeal is that the magistrate erred in holding that the defendant's conduct did not constitute an assault.

3.4. Reasoning

Legal reasoning has been described as an attempt to engage in dialogue with the purpose to persuade (Goodrich 1986: 179). In order to persuade, legal reasoning enters into two kinds of dialogue: the first mediates between the writer's text and other related texts, between legal discourse and other discourses, between the writer's position and alternative positions (*engagement*); the second kind is not about alternative positions, but a dialogue about degrees of ideational and interpersonal meanings. Reader solidarity with the writer's position is assumed, but at the same time a space for reader alignment is created through scaling meanings, up and down. *Graduation* is the semantic resource for this kind of dialogue.

Graduation is a resource for legal reasoning to negotiate legal issues, rules, categories, precedent and facts. It is constructed as either/or choices (typology of graduation). Graduation is also a resource to negotiate degrees of meaning (topology of graduation). With respect to legal reasoning, graduation makes it possible to frame legal issues as matters of degree. Graduation does not make new meanings, but allows writer and reader to enter into a dialogue about the degree of experiential and interpersonal meanings taken from external texts.

How are external texts incorporated into the writer's own and how does a writer shunt between the topological degrees of incorporation from quoted speech to the case name only? In the social construction of facts (see Section 3.2 above) a dynamic was identified from quoted or reported speech to nominalization: *X said that Y* was nominalised to *statement*, *evidence*, *decision,* which is a way of evaluating the external world. In the Reasoning, the dynamic movement that takes place in the construction of events is generally reversed – from nominalized forms to quoted speech. An external text is first introduced in nominalized forms, which allows the writer to attribute some kind of evaluation to the text such as *authority* to evaluate a text as 'highly relevant' or *statement*, which would evaluate the following text as 'less relevant'. For example:

(10) (D v S: Buckmaster: 17-22):
17 One of the earliest is the case of <u>Langridge v. Levy</u>. […]

21 How far it is from the present case can be seen from the judgment of Parke B., who, in delivering the judgment of the Court, used these words:
22 "We should pause before we made a precedent by our decision which would be an authority for an action against the vendors, even of such instruments and articles as are dangerous in themselves, at the suit of any person whomsoever into whose hands they might happen to pass, and who should be injured thereby" [...]
24 The case of Winterbottom v. Wright is, on the other hand, AN AUTHORITY that is closely applicable [...]
27 It may be noted, also, that in this case Alderson B. said: "The only safe rule is to confine the right to recover to those who enter into the contract; if we go one step beyond that, there is no reason why we should not go fifty."

(11) (D v S: Atkin, 26-33)
26 This appears to me to be THE DOCTRINE OF HEAVEN V PENDER, as laid down by Lord Esher (then Brett M.R.) when it is limited by the notion of proximity introduced by Lord Esher himself and A.L. Smith L.J. in Le Lievre v. Gould.
27 Lord Esher says: "That case establishes that, under certain circumstances, one man may owe a duty to another, even though there is no contract between them.
28 If one man is near to another, or is near to the property of another, a duty lies upon him not to do that which may cause a personal injury to that other, or may injure his property." [...]
31 That this is the sense in which nearness of 'proximity' was intended by Lord Esher is obvious from his own illustration in Heaven v. Pender of the application of THIS DOCTRINE to the sale of goods.
32 "This" (i.e. the rule he has just formulated) "includes the case of goods, etc., supplied to be used immediately by a particular person or persons, or one of a class of persons, where it would be obvious to the person supplying, if he thought that the goods would in all probability be used at once by such persons before a reasonable opportunity for discovering any defect which might exist, and where the thing supplied would be of such nature that a neglect of ordinary care or skill as to its condition or the manner of supplying it would probably cause danger to the person or property of the person for whose use it was supplied, and who was about to use it [...]"

The dynamic movement can be plotted on the cline of extra-vocalization as follows:

Quoted speech	Reported speech	Token/ Value	Nominalization and embedding	Nominalization only	Case name only

In the Reasoning element of a judgment, a new decision needs to be fitted into the existing body of law. To come back to Bakhtin here, any utterance originates in and is part of a social dialogue and any text consists of "varying degrees of otherness or varying degrees of 'our-own-ness'" (1986: 89).

To conclude this section about dialogue in legal reasoning, in the Reasoning element of a judgment, a variety of dialogues is negotiated simultaneously. The dialogues represent a dynamic element that moves the text between 'real' world discourse and legal discourse, between positioning in the writer's own text and other texts, between convergence and divergence of intersubjective positions. It is these dialogic qualities of legal discourse which enable a writer to make evaluations and to appear to be 'objective' and 'impersonal' in doing so, and which enable the common law to fit new problems into the existing body of existing law.

3.5. Declaring winners and losers

Conclusion and Order are typically short and sometimes fused and are therefore dealt with together. Conclusion and Order serve the *declaratory* function of judgments (Maley 1985). In the Conclusion the relevant principle or rule of law that applies to a case is declared, and the Order presents the solution to the problem stated in the Issue. In this element of a judgment, the winners and losers of a dispute before a court of law are declared.

As in a judgment a judge speaks only for himself, giving his own account of the facts and his own reasons for his decision, so the Conclusion and the Order are each judge's individual responsibility. Even joint judgments are presented as though the group speaks with one voice. While declaring winners and losers is an either/or decision – only one party can win a legal dispute before a court – the judge's declaration itself is highly dialogic. In the Conclusion, there is intertextual positioning linking the Conclusion to previous texts. There is dialogue with alternative positions where the alternatives are inscribed in the writer's own words. There is intra-textual dialogue, where the writer positions his/her conclusion in relation to the foregoing Facts, Issue and Reasoning by closing down alternative conclusions which might be drawn from his text. And, finally, in the Conclusion the writer provides the answer to the question about possible alternative legal categories posed in the Issue.

Conclusion and Order are also highly dialogic and dialogues may be conducted on two fronts: (i) writers may align their position with the position in other texts; (ii) writers usually also align their own position in some way – either in convergence or in divergence – with the positions taken by their colleagues.

3.5.1. Alignment with other texts

The Conclusion forms a link in a chain of other texts, and extra-vocalization values are one resource to make these links with other texts. Generally speaking, extra-vocalization values in the Conclusion mirror those in the Issue. The Issue states the problem in legal terms and the Conclusion declares the relevant principle of law to solve the problem. Similarly to extra-vocalization values in the Issue, external texts are brought into the writer's text in nominalized and embedded forms and as case names only. The actual words of the external texts are no longer present in the writer's text.

(12) My Lords, I have come to the conclusion in this difficult case that the decision of Oliver, J., ought to be restored. (D v S: Oaksey)

Further, the facts in the present appeal indicate that the violence threatened was more immediate and likely than Barton v Armstrong. Whether or not a finding of assault in Barton v. Armstrong could be supported at the trial, the assault here was proved, in my opinion, and a conviction for assault occasioning actual bodily harm should have been recorded. (Burton v Mel: White)

In my view, therefore the authorities are against the appellant's contention, and, apart from authority, it is difficult to see how any common law proposition can be formulated to support her claim. (D v S: Buckmaster)

3.5.2. Alternatives inscribed in his/her own text: inter-textual and intra-textual dialogues

Because each judge needs to arrive at his/her own conclusion and make his/her own order, or several judges do so as a group, alternative positions to the writer's own are expressed in his/her own words. Two points will be mentioned here. First, judgments, as an individual's assessment of rights and obligations, are written from the first person perspective. This should not be equated with being subjective as opposed to being objective, or with fact versus opinion. Rather, the first person perspective *I* implies a *you* and, associated with that, are possible alternative positions. The second point is White's (1998) argument that while modality can express genuine uncertainty (*we probably finished at 4*), it also indicates the contentiousness of a particular position and the willingness to acknowledge an alternative view. These two combine effectively in the construction of Conclusion and Order.

(13) For the reasons I have given *I am of the opinion that* the appeal should be allowed, the judgment of the learned judge in the court of first instance should be restored, and the respondent should pay the costs in your Lordships' House and in the Court of Appeal. (D v S: Porter)
I would allow the appeal, accordingly. (Agassi v Ro: Denning)
I think the appeal should be allowed. (D v S: Atkin)
I remit the matter back to the magistrate with the direction that he record a conviction for assault occasioning actual bodily harm, proceed to hear submissions and fix the appropriate penalty, levy and costs of the trial. (Burton v Mel: White)
For the foregoing reasons, *we would dismiss* the appeal. (Austin v Co: Mason et al)

The use of modality in *I would allow the appeal* or *we would dismiss the appeal* does not indicate uncertainty on the part of the writer. That interpretation would be quite inappropriate given the coercive nature of judgments. What is at issue here is the writer positioning himself in relation to his colleagues who may have arrived at a different Conclusion and Order, and acknowledging this divergence. The Orders in all four texts for this study were inscribed in the writer's own words through first person pronouns and modality. Taking explicit responsibility for an order through the first person pronoun and acknowledging alternative possibilities can also be found where all the judges on the bench arrive at the same conclusion and order (D v S), where several judges write a joint judgements (Agassi v Ro), and in cases where there is only one judgment (Burton v Mel).

4. Conclusion

The central concern of this chapter has been the negotiation of tradition and authority in appellate judgments and intersubjective positioning in relation to authority. Appellate judgments provide a public account of the judges' reasoning processes; therefore, I have, first of all, explored the specific forms of negotiating alternative positions used by judges, and secondly, how texts (or rather judges as writers) negotiate past decisions, integrate these texts into their own texts and align themselves with these past decisions.

The basic assumption in this study was that, in an appellate judgment, the writer enters into a number of dialogues with previous texts: with the evidence, argument and submissions made by the litigants in court, with the decision, which is being appealed against, and with similar decisions in the past (precedent). The writer also enters into a dialogue with possible future texts: a possible appeal against his/her decision and judges and lawyers who will be involved in similar cases in the future. And finally, a writer may enter into a dialogue with his/her colleagues on the bench who may decide a case differently.

Furthermore, I have argued that legal reasoning and interpretation is not primarily and exclusively an exercise of conclusive and unassailable logic leading to inevitable outcomes, as claimed by traditional legal theory, but that legal reasoning is an exercise in intersubjective positioning and making choices, although not totally unrestricted choices. Central to these arguments have been the notions of 'dialogue' and 'negotiation'. Legal reasoning has been described as an attempt to engage in dialogue with the purpose of persuading.

It has been found that all structural elements of a judgment are highly dialogic with a persuasive goal, but different elements draw on different systems to different degrees depending on their declaratory or justifying function and on the various dialogues involved in declaring the law and justifying a decision. Graduation and engagement are important resources for legal discourse and the choices made from these two systems are both reflective of and constitutive of legal discourse. Events, behaviour, positions and prior texts can be evaluated as positive or negative without using attitudinal terms, which contributes to the appearance of legal discourse as 'objective'. Those resources for intersubjective positioning also provide the common law with the flexibility it requires to deal with new situations for which no direct authority exists.

References

Bakhtin, Mikhail M.. [1930s] 1981. *The Dialogic Imagination: Four Essays*. Ed. Michael Holquist. Trans. Caryl Emerson and Michael Holquist. Austin, Tx: University of Texas Press.

Bakhtin, Mikhail M. 1986. *Speech Genres and Other Late Essays*. Trans. by Vern W. McGee. Austin, Tx: University of Texas Press.

Bhatia, Vijay K. 1989. Specialist-discipline and the ESP Curriculum. In Tickoo, Makhan (ed) *Language across the Curriculum*. Singapore, SEAMEO Regional Language Centre, 47-63.

Bhatia, Vijay K. 1993. *Analyzing Genre. Language Use in Professional Settings*. London: Longman.

Bhatia, Vijay K. 2004. *Worlds of Written Discourse. A Genre-based View*. London: Continuum.

Cownie, Fiona / Bradney, Anthony / Burron, Mandy 2007. *English Legal System in Context*. Oxford: Oxford University Press.

Fairclough, Norman 1992. *Discourse and Social Change*. Cambridge: Polity Press.

Fairclough, Norman. 1995. *Critical Discourse Analysis. The Critical Study of Language*. London: Longman.

Gibbons, John / Hale, Sandra 1999. Varying Realities: Patterned Changes in the Interpreter's Representation of Courtroom and External Realities. *Applied Linguistics* 20/2, 203-220.

Goodrich, Peter 1984. The Role of Linguistics in Legal Analysis. *The Modern Law Review* 47, 523-534.

Goodrich, Peter 1986. Traditions of Interpretation and the Status of the Legal Text. *Legal Studies* 6, 53.

Goodrich, Peter 1987. *Legal Discourse: Studies in Linguistics, Rhetoric and Legal Analysis*. London: Macmillan Press.

Goodrich, Peter. 1990. *Languages of Law: From Logics of Memory to Nomadic Masks*. London: Weidenfeld and Nicholson.

Maley, Yon 1985. Judicial Discourse: the Case of Legal Judgment. In J.E. Clark (ed.) *The Cultivated Australian*. Hamburg: Buske, 159-175.

Maley, Yon 1989. Interpersonal Meanings in Judicial Discourse. *Occasional Papers in Systemic Linguistics* 3, 69-87.

Maley, Yon 1994. The Language of the Law. In Gibbons, John (ed.) *Language and the Law*. London: Longman, 11-50.

Maley, Yon 1995. From Adjudication to Mediation: Third Party Discourse in Conflict Resolution. *Journal of Pragmatics* 23, 93-110.

THOMAS CHRISTIANSEN

The Concepts of Property and of Land Rights in the Legal Discourse of Australia Relating to Indigenous Groups

1. Introduction

The issues of property and land rights as applied to Indigenous groups in Australia (Aboriginal peoples and Torres Strait Islanders) have received increasing attention in recent years, especially since the landmark Mabo judgement (1992), by which a successful challenge was made to the concept of *terra nullius*, a legal expediency purportedly dating from the early days of colonization whereby, under English law, Australia was classed as an 'uninhabited or barbarous country' and thus open to unrestricted settlement by Europeans.[1]

The concept of property has been the subject of much philosophical reflection (e.g. Cicero, Hobbes, Locke, Proudhon). Land rights in particular have been a point of political contention in most societies and the problem of property is even starker in countries like Australia

1 The notion of Australia as a *terra nullius* – which gave the Crown control over land occupied by Aboriginal peoples – was cited in 1835 by Gov. Bourke of New South Wales in reaction to the unofficial Batman 'Treaty' (a dubious document supposedly signed between the Kulin people in the Port Philip area of what is today Melbourne and one Batman). However, this interpretation was contested at various times even in the 19th century and was of questionable legal value, given that it was not endorsed by the Judicial Committee of the Privy Council until 1889. Connor (2005) has argued that the concept was always obscure outside specialist circles and is hardly relevant as it was rarely cited in the 19th century itself, gaining currency only when reference to it was made by the prominent historian Reynolds (1987), who confused diverse historical, political geographical and legal concepts.

where settlers arrived and constructed a new nation mostly in total disregard of the existing inhabitants, their social structures and systems of law.[2] Attwood (2003: xi-xii) summarizes the changing attitudes that coloured Europeans' perception of the Aboriginal peoples' entitlement to the land that they had occupied for millennia thus:

> In the founding moments of Australia's settler history in 1770 and 1788 the Aborigines' propertorial rights to the land were overridden. It was held, according to European philosophical and legal authorities that drew on historical theories regarding the history of human societies, that Aborigines belonged to a stage of human development, that of hunters and gatherers, who had no concept of property. In the second half of the nineteenth century and the first half of the twentieth century, racially discriminatory laws were enacted on several grounds, many of which also rested on historical assumptions. Under the influence of Social Darwinism, Australian Aborigines were considered to be backward or primitive people and so were deemed to be an inferior and dying race who had no place in a modern democratic nation. As a result, they were deprived or denied civil rights. In the middle decades of the twentieth century campaigners for rights for Aborigines believed that historical progress required that racial groups such as Aborigines should be assimilated into modern Australian society. At the same time as they advocated civil rights for Aborigines, however, they were convinced that the Aboriginality of most Aborigines, in particular those they called 'half-castes', had been so erased and so they overlooked these people's interest in or entitlement to Indigenous rights.

Furthermore, although it is tempting to group all Aboriginal groups together and assume that they all share a common world view, the situation is considerably more complex, as Thieberger and McGregor note (1994: xiii):

---

2 The Aboriginal peoples led a largely nomadic lifestyle in small groups for 40-70,000 years before the British arrived. Traditional Aboriginal social structure all but broke up with the advent of Europeans both through deliberate dispossession and brute force and through the arrival of diseases such as smallpox, measles, and influenza. Consequently, many of the groups that Europeans encountered may well have been mere remnants of more traditional social systems, which may have been far more numerous: in recent years, estimates of the numbers of Aboriginal peoples living in Australia prior to colonization have reached a figure of 750,000 (see Mulvaney/White 1987).

> Before the invasion which began in 1788 Aboriginal people did not belong to a single political unit such as Australia is now; they were divided into something like 700 different political groups that have traditionally been called 'tribes'. There were approximately 250 different languages spoken on the Australian continent when Europeans first arrived on the shores.

It is also important to recognize that the concept of 'Aborigine' is alien to the Indigenous peoples themselves who, prior to the arrival of Europeans, would probably have had little sense of shared identity. As Attwood (2003: xii) states:

> The peoples living here prior to British Colonisation were not a homogeneous group implied by the name 'Aborigines'. Instead they only came to have a common, Aboriginal consciousness in the context of colonisation.

This diversity, coupled with the fact that many Aboriginal societies and cultures, like their languages, have disappeared and left very little trace, means that discussion of Aboriginal concepts is always tentative. One must avoid either overgeneralization or adhering uncritically to any of the numerous unsubstantiated myths that have grown up around the Aboriginal peoples, like, for example, the idea that they could not conceive of the idea of material ownership as alluded to in the first Attwood quote above.

In this chapter, we will examine the issue of how key concepts behind Aboriginal land rights have been framed in Anglo-Australian legal discourse by looking at the lexis and syntactic structures of legal discourse found in a corpus of the *Indigenous Law Bulletin* (until 1997, called the *Aboriginal Law Bulletin*) from 1981-2007. Such a framing does not of course necessarily entail a faithful or true representation of traditional Indigenous attitudes to property and land rights. As Russell (2005: 131) notes, the process of attempting to express Indigenous land rights in terms of Western legal discourse constitutes an act of compromise, including the Westernization and distortion of more traditional concepts:

> Adopting the white man's political means to achieve Aboriginal ends is a deeply ironic process. It means the colonized people's greatest success in reducing, if not completely overcoming, their subjugation is achieved by adopt-

> ing much of the colonizers' political methods and culture. [...] The very vocabulary through which Indigenous leaders come to articulate their aspirations – referring to their societies as 'nations,' asserting an original 'sovereignty', and claiming 'title' to their lands and waters is the vocabulary of the dominant society.

For a true appreciation of Indigenous Australians' attitudes and conceptualization of property and land rights one has to use primary sources and look at discourse (also in a wider semiotic sense) in Indigenous languages as used within the context of the relevant cultural context and social semiotic system. It is, however, in Anglo-Australian legal discourse that one may witness the way that originally Aboriginal concepts are having an effect on mainstream Australian attitudes to property and land rights.

2. The concepts of possession and property in English and Anglo-Australian Law and in Indigenous Australian cultures and societies

The allied notions of possession and property are naturally central to any so-called Western society, which are fundamentally capitalist in nature. This is not to say that such concepts are clear or unambiguous. As Viscount Jowitt (British Lord Chancellor, 1945-51) famously put it, "In truth English law has never worked out a completely logical and exhaustive definition of possession" (Smith/Keenan 1985: 391).

The concept of possession is enshrined in Roman law where a distinction is made between *corpus* (physical control) and *animus* (the intention to exclude others). Similarly, in English law, there are two elements to property: possession and ownership. The former is a *de facto* state of affairs, and the latter, *de jure*. The two aspects may be combined as in an owner/occupier or separate as in a tenant and landlord. Under English Law, ownership is a concept centred on the individual, not on a group of people unless they are treated legally as a single individual (*corporation*). Ownership gives rights to control over possession of a thing, use of it, and access to it.

As far as one can generalize about Indigenous Australian and Aboriginal cultures, traditionally, society is organized around tribes constituting different communities subdivided into so-called 'moieties' with kinship (e.g. patrilineal or matrilineal) determining the relative status of individuals. The economy was that of the hunter-gatherer, and thus based on cooperation and the sharing of labour/resources. In such a context, the group takes precedence over the individual. As regards land, its centrality to the group is clear. Although Aboriginal peoples were 'nomadic' in that they mainly lived in temporary, semi-permanent, or naturally-formed shelters, they did live in defined areas, sometimes moving long distances into other group's areas according to the season.

Knowledge of the area that it inhabits is vital for such a community's survival, and the close bond between the group and a particular area is shown by the fact that Aboriginal languages, although rich in lexis, often only have terms for fauna and natural phenomena found in a particular zone. For instance, groups living inland may lack words for the sea; or those in the north, words for snow (see Thieberger/McGregor 1994: xxii). This attachment to a particular area or territory is reinforced by religious beliefs: creation myths often have it that specific groups are created in a specific place and destined to inhabit that and no other. To cite Broome (2001: 18):

> During the creation time, the ancestral heroes performed great deeds and gave life and form to the tribe's local territory. These ancestral beings still lived in the local community in spiritual form, continually generating life. Across the north of Australia one of the most important ancestors was the Rainbow Snake which was associated with rain, spirit children and fertility. Each tribe believed that its boundaries were fixed and validated by the stories about the movements of their ancestors, and therefore there was no reason or desire to possess the country of another group.

It was the idea that the group was an integral part of a particular territory that was a central tenet of Aboriginal peoples' religious beliefs, as Broome explains (2001: 18-19):

> The essence of this religious belief was the oneness of the land and all that moved upon it. It was a view of the world in which humans and the natural species were all part of the same ongoing life force. In the Dreamtime[3] when the great ancestors had roamed the earth, they were human, animal and bird at one and the same time: all natural things were in a unity. The ancestors still existed in the here and now.

For Aboriginal peoples, 'title' is often equitable to occupancy. Traditionally, title can be both assigned to a corporate group or community or, in some cases to an individual, and passed down according to complex criteria, even now not fully understood by anthropologists (see Hiatt 1996: 13-35) relating, in general terms, to either patrilineal or matrilineal descent. However, such title rarely entails exclusion of others (except in the case of certain religious sites which only the initiated had a right of access to), as Attwood (2009: 49) states:

> They [The Aboriginal peoples] also had a sense of ownership in regard to the land but they conceived of that prerogative as a right to *use* the *resources* on particular parts of the landscape for a particular purpose – to fish, gather, hunt and so forth – and they did not necessarily regard these rights as being exclusive or permanent.

Finally, in Aboriginal culture, ownership is often encoded by a variety of semiotic means such as story-telling, artwork, and ceremonies. For European settlers, as Attwood (2009) notes, title required not only legal documentation but also certain rituals – as incomprehensible to Aboriginal people as the latter's were to Europeans – that signalled the individual's taking possession of the land, such as walking and marking the boundary, or giving names to landmarks.

---

3 This term – an English translation of various terms in different Aboriginal languages – can be used to refer either to the mythological period in which the world was created by ancestral totemic spirits or "a division of an Aboriginal people based on allegiance to a totemic master" (see Yallop *et al.* 2005: 433).

3. Possession as a linguistic concept

When it comes to the concept of possession, it is instructive to examine how it is conceptualized linguistically, firstly in English, the language in which the legal discourse of Australia is encoded, and then briefly and in general terms in Indigenous Australian languages.

3.1. Possession in English

In English what is called the *possessive case* can be used in a variety of contexts, in which it is clear that no single concept of possession holds.[4] Langacker (2000: 175) gives the following examples: *my watch; her cousin; your foot; the baby's bib; his rook; our host; their group; Sara's office; the book's weight; your anxiety; our neighbourhood; its location; my quandary; Lincoln's assassination; Booth's assassination; their candidate; my bus, the cat's fleas.* For Langacker (2000: 176), the common element is that the relationship between the possessor and possessed is asymmetrical:

> I ascribe the basic and universal nature of possessives to the pairing of an essential cognitive ability with a fundamental conceptual archetype, in fact with several such archetypes. The ability is not that of mere association (conceptual co-occurrence) but rather the intrinsically asymmetrical reference point relationship. What all possessive locutions have in common, I suggest, is that one entity (the one we call possessor) is invoked as reference point for establishing mental contact with another (the possessed) [...].

Langacker (2000: 174) represents this basic conceptual archetype by means of a diagram (see Figure 1).

---

4 By coincidence, in the famous Gove Case (1971), Mr Justice Blackburn dismissed the arguments in favour of the Yolngu peoples' land claims that were based on the fact that their language contained possessives, on the grounds that possessives in English express a variety of meanings not all indicative of propertorial relationships (see Hiatt 1996: 29).

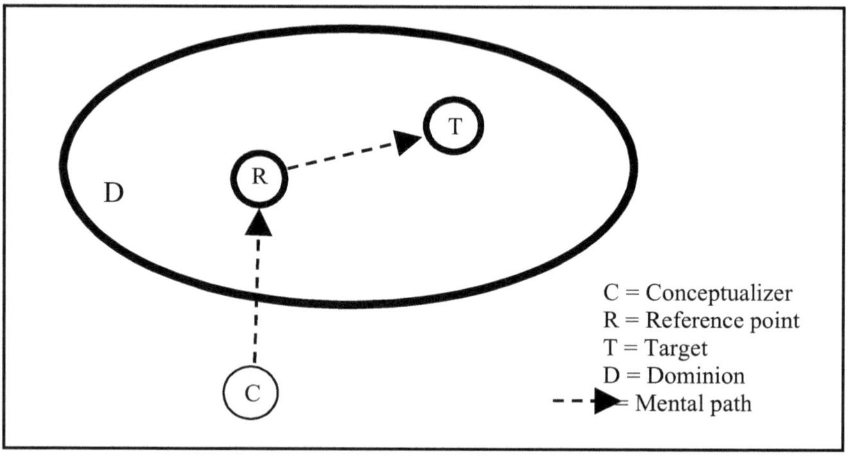

Figure 1. Langacker's diagrammatic representation of the conceptual archetype of possessives (2000: 174).

and a circle represents a thing (in Halliday's terms, a participant in the process represented). In Langacker's analysis, the relationship of possessed to possessor is that the former is accessed via the latter:

> Heavy circles indicate the successive salience, through processing time, of the reference point and target. Initially the reference point has a certain cognitive salience, either intrinsic or contextually determined. It is, of course, owing to some kind of salience that an entity comes to be chosen as a reference point in the first place. (Langacker 2000: 174)

The relationship is thus basically that of locating something within a conceptual frame, by reference to some other element. Langacker (2000: 176) states:

> There are two main diachronic sources of possessive elements, namely locatives (such as spatial prepositions) and verbs of control (with meanings like 'grasp', 'hold', and 'keep'). Their original content involves two experientially basic ways in which we locate objects physically: we either find them because we know their spatial location, i.e. their position within a spatial frame or in relation to some reference object; or else we actively control them and determine their position.

3.2. Possession in Indigenous Australian languages

Many Indigenous Australian languages no longer exist and it is difficult to estimate the precise number that there have been.[5] Today, there is evidence of 250 Australian languages falling into 26 different family-like groupings, one of which, the Pama-Nyungan, covers 90 percent of the continent.[6] Something akin to the distinction between inalienable and alienable possession as found in English and other languages is identifiable in Indigenous Australian languages,[7] and the latter in particular can be equated with ownership. However such distinctions are often encoded with a degree of complexity that discourages simple generalizations; to cite Dixon (2003: 59):

> It is generally said that Australian languages make a distinction between alienable and inalienable possession. This is true, but in a rough and ready way, but such a formula essentially misses the point. Alienable possession is shown by genitive marking of the NP [noun phrase] (which can be just a noun or pronoun) referring to the possessor; the possessor phrase modifies the possessed noun which is head of the whole NP. That is, in '[old woman]-genitive dog' ('the old woman's dog') it is 'dog' which is the head of the phrase and will be cross-referenced on the verbs in languages with cross-referencing.
> Australian languages show a whole-part relationship – this is what is often called inalienable possession – by simply apposing the noun referring to the whole and that referring to the part; the former functions as head of the NP. In Elbl, Yor-Yorunt (Alpher 1991), an NP can be just *pam* 'person' or *pam yor* 'person hand'. Parts of parts can be specified by further apposition e.g. *pam yor wel* 'person hand nail' ('person's fingernail'). Note that the 'possessor', *pam*, is head of each of these NPs.

---

5 During the colonial period, it was only in a few isolated cases that systematic research into Aboriginal languages was carried out, notably in South Australia, by German missionaries, *e.g.* Reuther (1981).

6 For a general overview of Aboriginal languages, see Dixon (1993); Thieberger/McGregor (1994).

7 Such a finding, *contra* linguistic relativity and the so-called Whorfian hypothesis that there are underlying similarities between languages and cultures in general is in line with current thinking in anthropology. Sperber (1982) and Brown (1991) have spoken in terms of *metaculture*, a set of basic concepts, common to all human societies, presumably instinctive.

Complications apart, the examples that Dixon gives are, in essence, similar to the examples from English considered by Langacker and, on the face of it, Figure 1 could be applicable also to them. As regards Langacker's theory that the conceptual archetype of possession is closely linked to location and control, there is evidence that this could also be so in some Indigenous Australian languages at least, for instance, Meryam Mir,[8] whose possessive pronouns we list in Table 1.

PRONOUN	GLOSS IN ENGLISH (Thieberger/McGregor 1994: 347-348)
Kara	my or mine
Kari	me, my: *karidoge* at my place or with me; *karim* to/for me; *kariyalam* from me; *karitkem* with me; *karitkak* without me
Kerbi	us, our (but not you): *kerbidoge* at our place or with us, *kerbim* for us, *kerbiyala*, from us, *kerbitkem* with us, *kerbitkak* without us
Keriba	our (but not including you); ours
Mara	your (when it is just you and no-one else)
Mari	you, your: *maridoge* at your place or with you, *marim* to/for you, *mariyalam* from you, *maritkem* with you, *maritkak* without you
Merbi	us, our (including you): *merbidoge* at our place or with us, *merbim* for/to us, *merbiyalam* from us, *merbitkem* with us, *merbitkak* without us
Meriba	our (including you); ours
tabara, tabra, taba, tara	his, her, himself, herself: *Lezide tabara imus itwi* Les shaved his own beard (as opposed to shaving someone else's beard)
Wába	your (when there is more than one of you); yours
Wábi	us, our (including you): *wabidoge* at our place or with us, *wabim* for/to us, *wabiyalam* from us, *wabitkem* with us, *wabitkak* without us
Wiyaba, yába	their; theirs
Wiyabi, yábi	them, their: *yabidoge* at their place or with them, *yabim* to/for them, *yabiyalam* from them, *yabitkem* with them, *yabitkak* without them

Table 1. Pronouns in Meryam Mir (Thieberger/McGregor 1994: 347-348).

8 This is a Melanesian, non-Pama-Nyungan, language from the Torres Strait on the northern-most tip of Australia. It is particularly relevant because it was people from this area that were successful plaintiffs in the seminal case leading to the Mabo judgment 1992.

As can be seen, the concept of being at "the possessor's place with them" is recurrent and this implies the idea of occupation and/or ownership and of a person being in physical control of some item.

Examination of the other word lists in Thieberger and McGregor (1994), who give words from a sample of 17 different Indigenous languages (including Torres Strait Creole and the so-called 'Sydney Language'[9]), shows that in Pama-Nyungan languages there is not generally such an explicit link between possessive pronouns or determiners and location. The nature of the concept of possession in Aboriginal languages can, however, be examined by looking for the existence of related lexis in the wordlists. Thieberger and McGregor compiled these by inviting selected informants/scholars to list lexis divided into groups of items with similar meanings according, where possible, to a standard grouping of 26 separate categories[10] (Figure 2).

The words that occurred in most separate wordlists (a maximum of 17) were so-called possessive pronouns, and the lexical items, 'hold', 'steal', with 'have' and 'own' in joint-third place. The first of these entails possession but not ownership, but the second does, indirectly.[11] 'Owner' obviously entails the concept of property. The relatively low figure for 'have' is particularly interesting as this is a word in English that has a variety of meanings and functions (not only the denotation of possession, see Christiansen 2009) and is thus relatively frequent. Other words such as 'abandon', 'barter' etc. were found in one wordlist each.

The mean for the group was 3.23 and the standard deviation was only 2.68, indicating that divergence from this average was relatively low. By contrast, the mean for a sample of 72 items taken at random from the wordlists (the first item in the second column of

---

9 This is a reconstruction from records and witness accounts of the language originally spoken in the area that became Sydney.

10 Among these were: body parts and products; kin relationships; human classification; human artefacts; insects and spiders; location, direction and time; interjections and particles; pronouns and demonstratives; and place names.

11 This word may, however, be a concept acquired from almost 200 years of contact with Europeans and may reflect the current status of many Aboriginal people, living on the margins of society.

even-numbered pages)[12] was 7.81 (standard deviation, 6.61). On average, words relating to possession were found less often than words in general in the word lists of Indigenous Australian languages.

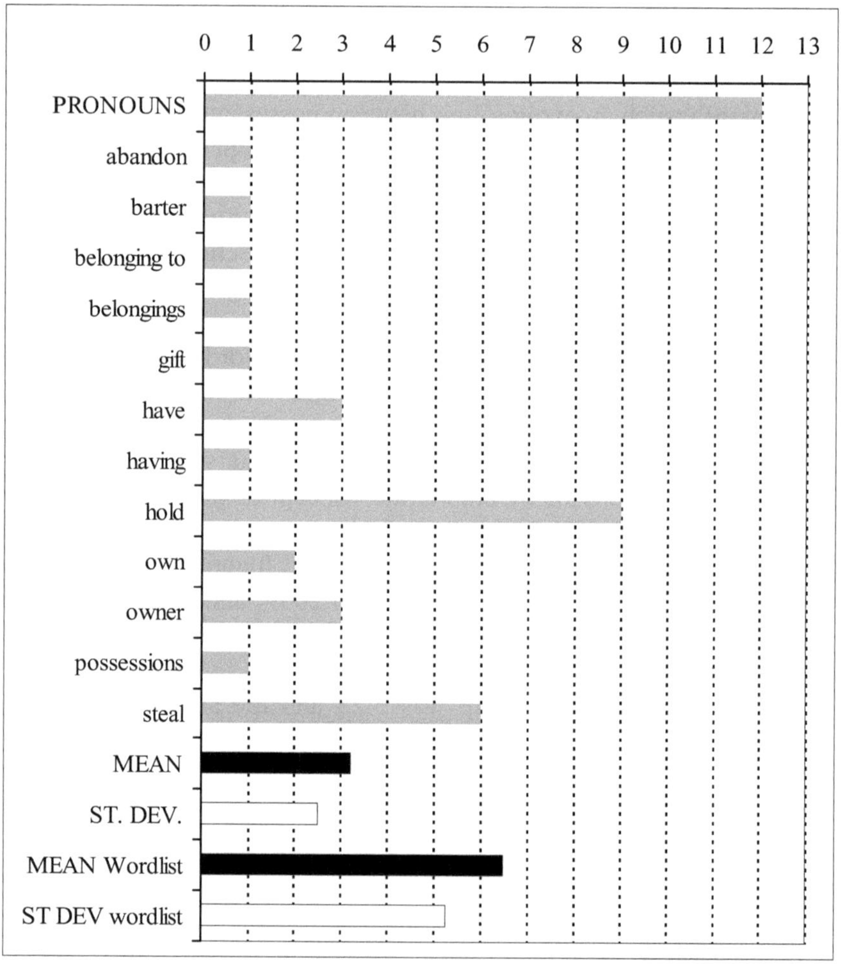

Figure 2. Occurrences of words relating to possession in terms of number of wordlists in Thieberger/McGregor (1994).

12 These included: 'all'; 'blood pudding'; 'frightened'; 'intimate'; 'kill'; 'mud crab'; 'nothing'; 'parrot'; 'rock'; 'smoke'; 'tell'; 'urine'; 'why'; 'yesterday'.

One can draw two conclusions from this: firstly, that a concept of possession, similar in at least some aspects to that found in English, exists in at least some Indigenous Australian languages; secondly, that it is not particularly prevalent, however, in comparison to other concepts in general. The difference then would not seem to be in the semantics or in the linguistic system as such but rather in the importance attached to the concept within the different cultures: Anglo-Australian and Indigenous Australian.

4. Corpora

To examine the concept of property and of land rights in Australian legal discourse relating to Indigenous groups and how this is influenced, albeit it in watered-down fashion, by Indigenous groups' traditional attitudes towards property and land rights, we compiled a corpus of articles taken from the *Indigenous Law Bulletin* (henceforth ILB) published by the University of New South Wales, Faculty of Law.[13] This comprised approximately 2,995,435 words in roughly 1800 files spanning the period from 1981 to 2007. As a reference corpus, we chose the *Harvard Law Review* (HLR) published by Harvard Law School in the USA.[14] This contained approximately 5,788,630 words, in 616 files.

The former corpus is smaller but more specialized, dealing specifically with law pertaining to Indigenous groups in particular land rights which have been one of the most important issues in Indigenous affairs since the 1970s. The latter is twice as large, regards law in general, and covers a shorter but more contemporary period: 2004-2009. It is revealing to compare the frequencies of a selection of terms identified by us in our background reading of the literature as pertaining to legal aspects of Indigenous peoples' land rights in the two corpora (Figure 3).

---

13 Retrieved from <www.austlii.edu.au/au/journals/ILB>.

14 Retrieved from <www.harvardlawreview.org>.

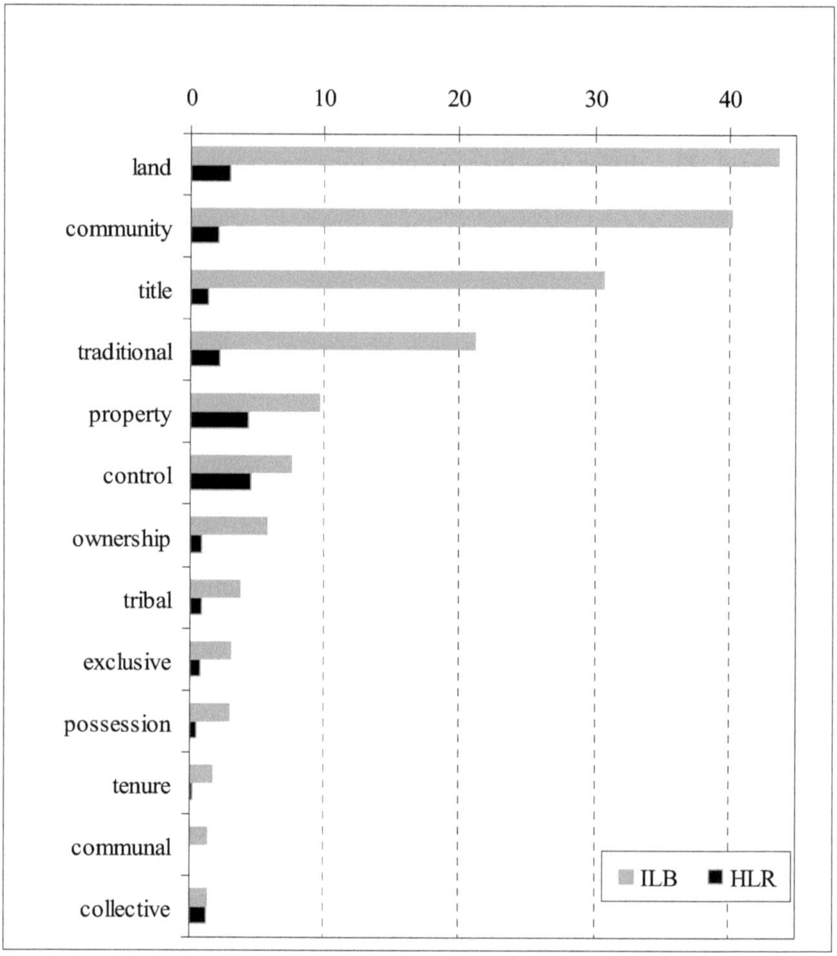

Figure 3. Total ratio selected words in ILB and HLR.

In Figure 3 the bars represent ratios calculated by applying the equation of (X/Y) x 10,000 (X equals the number of items found, Y the words in that corpus and 10,000 an arbitrary figure employed to avoid the inconvenience of using numbers with too many decimal places).[15] In every case, the term in question is found proportionately more in ILB than HLR, notably so for items such as 'land', 'community', 'title', 'traditional'. The one item where there is a more equal balance is 'collective'.

5. Analysis

In our analysis we will look at the lexical items pertaining to Indigenous land rights as featured in Figure 3, as a representative sample for analysis. As a first stage, we will look at these words individually from the perspective of clusters (Section 5.1) then look at the general trends displayed by the same clusters collectively and their component lexical elements (Section 5.2).

5.1. Clusters

Given the differences between the two corpora as outlined in Section 4, direct comparison between frequencies of individual lexical items or expressions is of only partial use. A more productive line of research is to look at lexical clusters. In this regard, Scott (1998: 31) states "[they are] words which are found repeatedly in each other's company. They represent a tighter relationship than collocates, more like groups or phrases". To extract these, we used *Wordsmith v.3* (Scott 1996).[16] We looked at clusters in a range of two to five words for each of the terms listed in Figure 3 (in the same order). The results for the five most numerous clusters are given in the tables below –

15 For example, *land* is found 13,107 times in ILB (2,995,435 words). Our calculation would thus be 13,107 divided by 2,995,435. The result (0.004375655) is multiplied by 10,000 to give the more manageable figure of 43.8.

16 This is not of course the latest version of the program, which is now in its fifth version, but it proved sufficient for our needs.

numbers given are as a ratio as calculated for Figure 3. It should be noted that the top five are a relatively small sample as some of the longer lists ran to hundreds of clusters. However, concentrating on the most frequent in each category provides enough data for a brief preliminary comparison.

ILB		HLR	
land council/s	5.0	land use	0.3
land claim/s	2.8	law/s of the land	0.2
aboriginal land rights	2.2	land assembly	0.2
land rights act	1.8	land assembly districts	0.1
Crown land/s	1.7	religious land uses	0.1

Table 2. Clusters for 'land' in ILB and HLR compared.

In both corpora, the top five clusters for 'land' show little in common apart from 'land council/s' and 'land assembly' both denoting an administrative body. In ILB 'rights' occurs in two separate clusters, in HLR 'assembly' and 'use/s' do.

ILB		HLR	
aboriginal community/ies	2.5	political community	0.08
indigenous community	0.9	international community	0.06
community services	0.7	community lawyering community standards	0.03
community development	0.5		
community member/s	0.5	community-based	0.03

Table 3. Clusters for 'community' in ILB and HLR compared.

In ILB, by far the most frequent cluster is 'aboriginal community/ies', followed by the near-synonym 'indigenous community'. For HLR, there are two that are most prominent: 'political community' and 'international community' (both vaguer terms).

ILB		HLR	
native title act	2.3	exception to title	0.03
title rights	1.9	violate* title	0.02
native title rights	1.9	violation of title	0.02
title holders	1.2	tribal title	0.01
aboriginal title	1.2	actionable under title	0.01

Table 4. Clusters for 'title' in ILB and HLR compared.

The three most frequent clusters in ILB are very similar: 'native title act', 'title rights' and 'native title rights'. In HLR, two are also related to a similar theme: 'exception to title' and 'violate title', 'violation of title'. In both ILB and HLR, the concept of Indigenous title is referred to, but by different terms (ILB 'aboriginal title' and HLR 'tribal title'). It is noteworthy that ILB contains neither 'tribal title' nor 'violation of title'. Revealingly, outside the top five, clusters include 'extinguish native title' and 'extinguishment of native title', which can both be seen as less contentious terms.

ILB		HLR	
traditional owner/s	2.2	traditional approach/es	0.08
traditional aborigines	0.8	traditional rule/s	0.05
traditional language/s	0.6	traditional contours	0.05
traditional law/s	0.5	traditional model/s	0.05
traditional land/s	0.4	traditional view/s	0.04

Table 5. Clusters for 'traditional' in ILB and HLR compared.

By far the most frequent cluster in ILB is 'traditional owner'. In the top five of HLR, clusters relate to praxis: 'approaches', 'rules', 'contours' etc. In ILB, the cluster is linked to more concrete entities ('lands', 'areas', 'owners').

ILB		HLR	
intellectual property	1.1	property rights	0.4
property rights	0.8	intellectual property	0.4
cultural property	0.4	real property	0.3
intellectual property rights	0.3	property law	0.2
property law	0.2	private property	0.2

Table 6. Clusters for 'property' in ILB and HLR compared.

In ILB, the most frequent clusters are ‘intellectual property’, ‘property rights’ and the abstract concept of ‘cultural property’. In HLR, there are also ‘property rights’ and ‘intellectual property’. Revealingly, in ILB, property is viewed predominantly in the abstract (intellectual, cultural) and in HLR in more concrete terms: ‘real property’ (land), ‘private property’.

ILB		HLR	
social control	0.2	control or limit	0.7
aboriginal control	0.2	control over state	0.2
ownership and control	0.1	control of state	0.2
take* control	0.09	benefits associated with control	0.2
right to control	0.06	private benefits of control	0.2

Table 7. Clusters for ‘control’ in ILB and HLR compared.

Three clusters stand out in the top five of ILB: ‘social control’, ‘aboriginal control’ and ‘ownership and control’ (an important concept in the English law conception of possession – see Section 2). In HLR, the most frequent cluster is the general phrase ‘control or limit’.

ILB		HLR	
land ownership	0.3	ownership separation	0.08
aboriginal ownership	0.2	land ownership	0.06
traditional ownership	0.2	ownership and control	0.04
ownership and control	0.1	corporate ownership	0.04
rights of ownership	0.1	dispersed ownership	0.04

Table 8. Clusters for ‘ownership’ in ILB and HLR compared.

In ILB, the most frequent cluster is ‘land ownership’, which comes second in HLR to ‘ownership separation’. In ILB, clusters relating to Indigenous ownership feature in the top five (‘aboriginal’/ ‘traditional’ ‘ownership’), though none occur in HLR. In both corpora, the key concept of ‘ownership and control’ comes in the top five.

ILB		HLR	
tribal government/s	0.2	tribal court/s	0.1
tribal court/s	0.2	tribal sovereignty	0.1
tribal land/s	0.1	tribal authority	0.07
tribal peoples	0.1	tribal land/s	0.06
indigenous and tribal peoples	0.1	tribal member/s tribal jurisdiction	0.04

Table 9. Clusters for 'tribal' in ILB and HLR compared.

In both ILB and HLR, 'tribal' occurs as an attributive adjective referring to institutions ('governments', 'courts'), and in HLR to the associated area of authority ('jurisdiction', 'sovereignty'). In ILB there is reference to groups ('tribal peoples') and in both to territory: 'tribal lands'.

<table>
<tr><th colspan="2">ILB</th><th colspan="2">HLR</th></tr>
<tr><td>exclusive possession</td><td>0.6</td><td>exclusive right/s</td><td>0.2</td></tr>
<tr><td>exclusive right/s</td><td>0.2</td><td rowspan="2">exclusive jurisdiction
exclusive control</td><td rowspan="2">0.04</td></tr>
<tr><td>right/s of exclusive possession</td><td>0.1</td></tr>
<tr><td>right/s to exclusive possession</td><td>0.09</td><td>exclusive review</td><td>0.03</td></tr>
<tr><td>exclusive tenure/s</td><td>0.08</td><td>exclusive review provision/s</td><td>0.03</td></tr>
</table>

Table 10. Clusters for 'exclusive' in ILB and HLR compared.

Revealingly, by far the most frequent cluster in ILB is 'exclusive possession', a concept at the very heart of the issue of native title in Indigenous custom and Anglo-Australian law – see Section 2. This term does not appear at all in HLR. In HLR the most common cluster is the more general 'exclusive rights', which is also in second position in ILB.

ILB		HLR	
exclusive possession	0.6	possession of a firearm	0.03
right/s of exclusive possession	0.1	possession of child pornography	0.02
right/s to exclusive possession	0.1	gun possession	0.02
possession act/s exclusive possession act/s	0.07	possession of firearms felon in possession	0.02

Table 11. Clusters for 'possession' in ILB and HLR compared.

As seen in Table 11, in ILB, as well as with aspects of legal property ('rights', 'confer', 'ownership'), 'possession' clusters predominantly with 'exclusive', which is interesting as it shows that there is a need to underline this aspect of possession which is inherent and not stated at all in HLR. In the latter, 'possession' is associated with controlled or illegal items ('child pornography', 'firearm/s', 'gun').

ILB		HLR	
land tenure	0.3	life tenure	0.05
security of tenure	0.07	tenure protections tenure and salary	0.01
tenure history/ies marine tenure	0.06	salary and tenure enjoy life tenure	0.009
customary marine tenure	0.05		

Table 12. Clusters for 'tenure' in ILB and HLR compared.

In ILB, the most frequent clusters for 'tenure' relate to land or resources ('marine'). In HLR, the focus is on employment ('life tenure', 'salary').

ILB		HLR	
communal native title	0.08	communal violence	0.007
communal land/s	0.07		
communal title	0.06		
communal moral rights indigenous communal moral rights	0.04		

Table 13. Clusters for 'communal' in ILB and HLR compared.

It is with the clusters of 'communal' that transpires to be the most striking difference between ILB and HLR. In the former, it refers to the (mainly Aboriginal) community, whereas in the latter only one cluster, with decidedly negative connotations, occurs: 'violence'. Of further interest is the fact that the most frequent clusters 'communal (native) title', 'communal land' are concepts that would seem to stem from traditional Aboriginal concepts of possession (see Section 2).

ILB		HLR	
collective right/s	0.2	collective action/s	0.5
collective ownership	0.03	state collective action	0.2
collective and individual rights	0.02	collective bargaining	0.1
collective group	0.01	collective action problem/s	0.1
collective past		collective sanctions	0.07

Table 14. Clusters for 'collective' in ILB and HLR compared.

In ILB, 'collective' clusters by far the most frequently with 'rights' then 'ownership'; in HLR most frequently, but not by so wide a margin, with actions. In the former, then, 'collective' is associated with abstract concepts, in the latter with more concrete processes.

5.2. General patterns

As regards general trends that can be discerned from the data represented in Tables 2-14, Figure 4 compares the numbers of lexical items found in each list of clusters with the total numbers of occurrences of all lexical items in that list, not counting the head word from which each cluster is generated. For example, in Table 2, for ILB, excluding 'land', there are six separate items (i.e. 'council/s'; 'claim/s', 'Aboriginal'; 'rights'; 'act'; and 'crown'), which occur together in a total of seven times in the list. The ratio of these two figures is 1: 1.167. This can be compared to the corresponding ratio for HLR: 1: 1.571. The fact that the figure for ILB is lower shows that the term 'collective' in this corpus clusters with a more restricted group of words and thus is used in a more limited range of contexts.

This kind of analysis can be carried out on all the sets of clusters in Tables 2-14. To increase the range of the results, we extend the selection from the top five to the top 25 items in each list. This is still a relatively small sample in the case of many of the clusters but it is certainly more representative than the shorter lists used in Section 5.1. The ratios obtained through such an analysis are summarized in Figure 4.

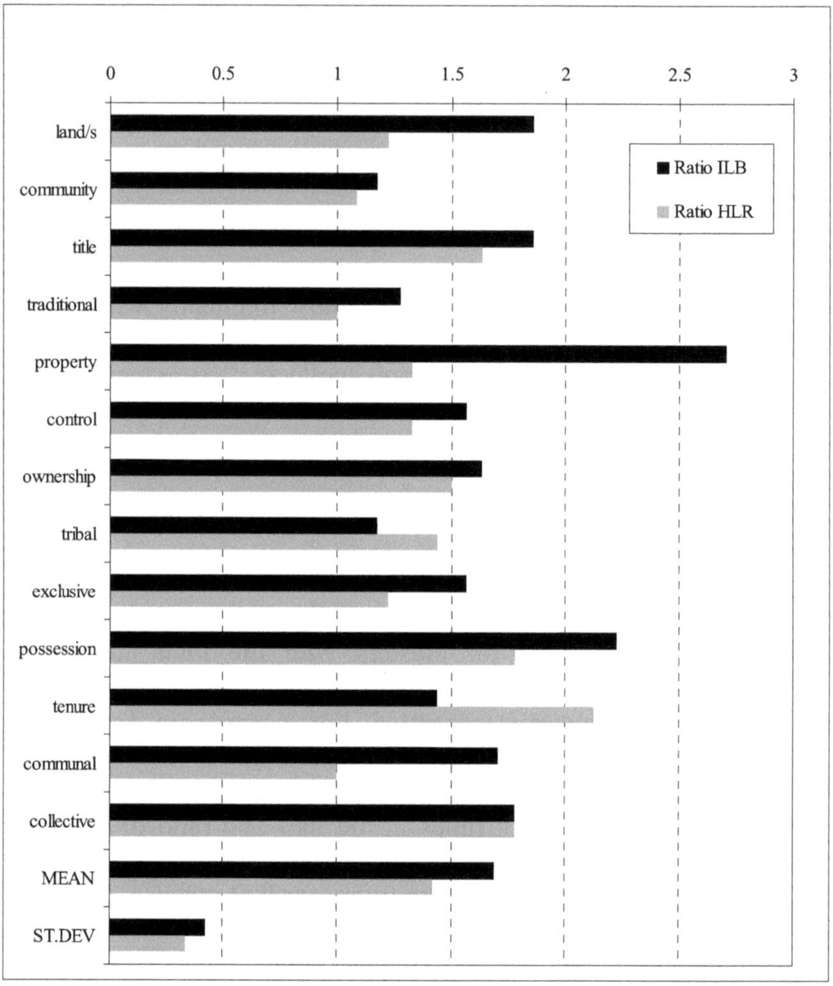

Figure 4. Comparison of ratio of number of items in lists of clusters and number of occurrences of such items in same lists in ILB and HLR.

Looking firstly at the mean, it can be seen that, for ILB, the ratio is generally higher, although there is greater variation within that mean (standard deviation). As regards the cluster heads, the only two out of the thirteen where the HLR ratio is higher than ILB are 'tribal' and 'tenure' while for 'collective' the ratios are equal. For 'land', 'property', and 'communal' the ratio for ILB is notably higher. The indication is therefore that it is in ILB that the sample of words pertaining to Indigenous property rights have the more restricted set of uses and thus more precise meanings. The fact that 'tribal' in particular is an exception is revealing in that in the US context, the history of the treatment of Indigenous peoples, though far from ideal, is different from Australia's: the social structure of Indigenous people was early on recognized and to a degree respected.

Looking at the most common words in the lists of the 25 most frequent word clusters allows one to identify those words that are frequent in the general area of discourse relating to possession and property in both corpora and thus facilitates examination of the underlying concepts or perspectives. In Table 15, we list those items that are found in the various cluster lists for ILB and HLR that occurred three or more times – excluding those items which are cluster heads (e.g. 'land/s'; ''title'; 'collective') except when they occurred as items in the list of which another word was cluster head: As Table 15 shows, marginally more words occur in the various cluster lists for HLR than ILB (33 versus 27), while in ILB there are proportionately fewer content words (24% as opposed to 30%). In ILB, there is a wider spread of words across the different levels of frequency. Eleven items (a third of the total) occur more than seven times, for HLR only three (under a tenth) out of the 33 do. Furthermore, in that group only one item in the HLR list is a content word ('life', occurring only eight times), while in the ILB list eight of the eleven are content words, including three of the five most frequent items (each more than 16 occurrences). Furthermore on the ILB list, the most prominent (content words) are 'rights', 'native', 'title', 'Aboriginal', 'lands', 'exclusive'. All of these, except 'native', are also found in our sample of terms pertaining to legal aspects of Indigenous peoples (see Figure 3), which provides confirmation that elements, at least, of this intuitive list are significant. For HLR, the list is much more heterogeneous: 'life', 'salary', 'right/s', 'interests', 'state', 'actions', 'private', 'guns' and individual items tend to occur at a relatively low level of frequency (over half the total – 18 – occurring only three times).

ILB		*HLR*	
RIGHTS	34	OF	21
OF	25	AND	12
NATIVE	19	LIFE	8
TITLE	18	SALARY RIGHT/S INTEREST/S	7
AND	17	STATE IN ACTION/S	6
ABORIGINAL LAND/S	15	TO PRIVATE GUN/S	5
INDIGENOUS	10	WITH LAW JURISDICTION	4
EXCLUSIVE	9	USE/S TRIBAL SIMPLE SEPARATION RULE/S REVIEW PROJECTIONS OFFICE MEDIA LAND/S FIREARMS ENACT* COURT CONTROL CHOICE BENEFITS BARGAINING AUTHORITY	3
ACT/S TO	8		
INTELLECTUAL POSSESSION	7		
PEOPLE/S	6		
COUNCIL CULTURAL OWNERSHIP	5		
CLAIM/S LAW THE	4		
CONFER GROUP/S NON OR OWNER/S PREVIOUS SYSTEM/S	3		

Table 15. Occurrences of lexical items in selected word cluster lists.

6. Discussion and conclusions

As has been shown, in both English and Indigenous Australian languages, it is possible to identify a concept of possession expressed in various ways that are at least partly consistent with Langacker's cognitive-grammatical analysis. Analysis of wordlists taken from Aboriginal languages showed that words relating to possession were present but relatively less frequently. This indicates that, while a concept of possession and property is not 'foreign' to Aboriginal cultures, it is not so prevalent as it is in Australia at large, which is considered more materialistic.

Looking at clusters and the general trends that these display, it emerges that the words pertaining to possession show different patterns of frequency and cluster tendencies in the legal discourse relating to Aboriginal land rights as exemplified in ILB and in the more general discourse of the HLR. In general, as is expected given the nature of the respective publications, in ILB, items pertaining to property and possession relate mainly to land and in HLR to a wide variety of entities.

In the analysis of clusters, it transpires that many items occur with a more restricted group of items in ILB than they do in HLR, indicating that, in the former, words have a more specialized set of meanings. Particularly illustrative of this are the terms 'exclusive' and 'possession', which show very different patterns and associations in each corpus. In ILB they frequently co-occur, while they rarely do in HLR. This does not mean that in the latter the two are not linked – quite the opposite in fact – rather that the relationship is so established that this precise type of possession, considered the norm, is not specified. Furthermore only in ILB is 'communal' a concept related to property. Similarly, 'collective' shows quite different associations in each corpus.

Overall, it is shown that in ILB the set of items which were intuitively selected as being pertinent to the discourse of Indigenous people's land rights in Australia did indeed show a marked tendency to occur with members of the same set and with a more restricted range of lexical items. These, however, pertain to the very nature of possession, property, and ownership and in particular whether the latter relate to the individual or to the group. In this way, in ILB the general concept of possession, expressed by various means, proves to be a notion which can be qualified in diverse ways and explored from different angles, including that of collective, non-exclusive, ownership and use.

By contrast, in HLR the concept of possession is a given entity, and terms pertaining to it are used to qualify other concepts but are not themselves qualified or a matter of debate. This fact is interesting because it thus emerges that it is in the more specific discourse of ILB that the concept of possession is less stable than in the more general discourse of HLR, where one may have assumed that, given the variety of possible legal topics, the reverse would be true.

From this, we can conclude that in Australian legal discourse as exemplified in our corpus of ILB texts, the concept of possession is not treated as a fixed notion. Instead it takes on different senses reflecting the fact that the concept itself is not atomic but can be broken down into component elements capable of taking on different patterns of relations with each other. This mirrors the way that the English language cognitive profile of possession, as evidenced by Langacker, is itself a configuration of more basic concepts such as location and reference point: it is the element through which the conceptualizer accesses the final entity (the target) – whether it is the occupant, the unobtrusive/non-physical user, or the 'owner', 'obtrusive/physical controller' and 'excluder' in the legal sense.

Such redefinition is caused by increasing contemplation and recognition of the radically different conceptualizations of property rights of Aboriginal peoples that have been acquiring political and legal weight since the 1970s. In essence, in the Aboriginal people's less individualistic, less anthropocentric view of the universe, the roles of the reference point and target are flexible and it may be the occupier that becomes the target and the land the reference point. In such a view, the land and the effect that it has on the person (for example, in terms of traditional affiliations and religious beliefs) becomes the focus, not the person and how they affect the land. This presents an interesting challenge to legislators and commentators, who have to find a way to balance these two different conceptual systems within one workable, and just, legal framework.

References

Attwood, Bain 2003. *Rights for Aborigines*. Crows Nest (NSW): Allen and Unwin.

Attwood, Bain 2009. *Possession: Batman's Treaty and the Matter of History*. Melbourne (Vic): Melbourne University Press.

Broome, R. [3]2001. *Aboriginal Australians, Black Responses to White Dominance 1788-2001*. Crows Nest (NSW): Allen and Unwin.

Brown, Donald E. 1991. *Human Universals*. New York: McGraw-Hill.

Christiansen, Thomas 2009. Possessive and Deontic 'Have' and 'Have Got': Evolution and Migration of forms within the Syntax of contemporary British English. In Dossena, Marina / Torretta, Domenico / Sportelli, Annamaria (eds) *Forms of Migration. Migration of Forms*. Bari: Progedit, 432-448.

Connor, Michael 2005. *The invention of Terra Nullius: historical and legal fictions on the foundation of Australia*. Paddington (NSW): Macleay Press.

Dixon, Robert 1993. Australian Aboriginal languages. In Schulz, Gerhard (ed.) *The Languages of Australia*, Occasional Paper 14, Papers from the Australian Academy of the Humanities Symposium 1992. Canberra: The Highland Press, 71-82.

Dixon, Robert 2002. *Australian Languages*. Cambridge: Cambridge University Press.

Hiatt, Lester R. 1996. *Arguments about Aborigines*. Cambridge: Cambridge University Press.

Langacker, Ronald 1987. *Foundations of Cognitive Grammar*. Vol. I. Stanford: Stanford University Press.

Langacker, Ronald 2000. *Grammar and Conceptualization*. Berlin: Mouton De Gruyter.

Mulvaney, Derek J. / White, J. Peter (eds) 1987. *Australians to 1788*. Broadway (NSW). Fairfax, Syme & Weldon
Reynolds, Henry 1987. *The Law of the Land*. Ringwood (Vic): Penguin.
Reuther, Johann G. 1981. *The Diari*. Australian Institute of Aboriginal Studies, Canberra. (Translated by P. Scherer).
Russell, Peter H. 2005. *Recognising Aboriginal Title: The Mabo Case and Indigenous Resistance to English-Settler Colonialism*. Sydney (NSW): University of New South Wales Press.
Scott, Michael 1996. *Wordsmith version 3*. Oxford: Oxford University Press.
Scott, Michael 1998. *WordSmith Tools Manual version 3*. Oxford: Oxford University Press <http://www.liv.ac.uk/~ms2928/wordsmith.htm>.
Smith, Kenneth / Keenan, Denis [7]1985. *English Law*. London: Pitman.
Sperber, Dan 1982. *On Anthropological Knowledge*. Cambridge: Cambridge University Press.
Thieberger, Nick / McGregor, William 1994. *Macquarie Aboriginal Words*. Macquarie (NSW): Macquarie Dictionary.
Yallop, Colin / Bernard, John R.L. / Blair, David / Butler, Sue / Delbridge, Arthur / Peters, Pam / Witton, Nic (eds) *Macquarie Dictionary*. Macquarie (NSW): Macquarie Dictionary.

ISMAEL ARINAS PELLÓN

How Does a Patent Move? Genre Analysis Has Something to Say about It

1. Introduction

Patents are a genre that combines features of technical and juridical texts. The purpose of this chapter is to identify the rhetorical moves of US patents, more specifically the moves that typically appear in patents of machines, manufactures, compositions of matter and methods. What is being patented affects the rhetorical structure to a certain degree, but the moves described here reflect the structure that prototypically satisfies both the legal requirements and the communication conventions that such a genre demands. To identify the move structure of US patents (which amount to over 7.5 million issued) a corpus of 333 granted patents has been analysed using the freeware program Antconc.[1] The United States Patent and Trademark Office granted 289,479 patents in 2008.[2]

The chapter will begin by providing a brief introduction to the peculiarities of US patents; it will continue with a brief review of the methodology used for the genre analysis and then the rhetorical moves of the patents will be identified based on the corpus data.

1 <http://www.antlab.sci.waseda.ac.jp/software.html>.

2 < http://www.uspto.gov/web/offices/ac/ido/oeip/taf/tafp.html>.

2. Basic facts about patents

The United States and the Philippines are the only countries to determine the priority among competing inventions according to the *first to invent* principle. All the other countries establish this right according to the *first to file* principle (DeMatteis/Gibbs/Neustel 2006: 16). The US patent office currently grants three types of patents: utility, design and plant[3] patents. Utility patents include processes, machines, manufactures and composition of matter.[4] Utility patents have the following two peculiarities:

- After the Supreme Court decision in *Diamond v. Chakrabarty*, 447 U.S. 303, 206 USPQ 193 (1980), microorganisms resulting from genetic engineering are considered as manufactures or composition of matter (Manual of Patent Examining Procedure or MPEP, chapter 2105).
- Since the State *Street Bank v. Signature Group, Inc.* decision in July 1998, business methods have also been considered as patentable matter (DeMatteis/Gibbs/Neustel 2006: 75). This decision served also to consider software as a patentable business method (Hunt/Nguyen/Rodgers 2007: 95).

The first US patent was granted in July 31, 1790 to Samuel Hopkins (Frobert-Adamo 2000: 154). Since then, the US Patent and Trademark Office has granted more than 7.5 million patents. 289.479 patents were granted during 2008. Of these 261,488 were utility patents, 26.750 were design patents, and 1,241 were plant patents. For the purpose of this study, only utility patents were selected and, from these, biotechnology and drug patents were excluded from the collected corpus. See Section 3 below for an explanation.

Each new patent "must be different from all patent documents that have gone before it" and "it has to be completely future proof" or, in other words, the attorney drafting the patent "has to anticipate everything that could go wrong for the next twenty years" (Roberts

3 Plant Patent Act of 1930.

4 < http://www.uspto.gov/web/offices/com/iip/pdf/brochure_03.pdf >.

2007: viii-ix). On the one hand, to obtain a patent inventors must be convincing to "any person skilled in the art to which it pertains"[5] in terms of novelty,[6] non-obviousness,[7] technical adequacy,[8] and usefulness[9] (Frobert-Adamo 2000: 161). On the other hand, patent applicants try to disclose as few details as possible of their discovery[10] while still meeting the requirement that the description should enable a *person skilled in the art* to replicate the invention. Roberts (2007: 4) states that during the granting process there is also a conflict between the patentee's desire of achieving the broadest patent scope and the patent office "who wants to keep it narrow and away from what has been put into the public domain before". These struggles between the *progress of science* and individual reward have consequences not only in the choice of wording, but also in the move structure of the patent genre as will be seen below. The US Patent and Trademark Office (USPTO) is aware of this conflict and in the MPEP, section 724, it advises that:

> wherever possible, trade secret law and patent laws should be administered in such manner that the former will not deter an inventor from seeking the benefit of the latter, because the public is most benefited by the early disclosure of the invention in consideration of the patent grant. If a patent applicant is unwilling to pursue his right to a patent at the risk of certain loss of trade secret protection, the two systems will conflict, the public will be deprived of knowledge of the invention in many cases, and inventors will be reluctant to bring unsettled legal questions of significant current interest for resolution.

Hunt, Nguyen and Rodgers (2007: 7-8) present a table showing that the information in patents is organized as follows: bibliographic data,

---

5 Consolidated Patent Rules, Title 37 – Code of Federal Regulations: Patents, Trademarks, and Copyrights, section 1.57, (c), 1.

6 35 U.S.C. 102.

7 35 U.S.C. 103.

8 35 U.S.C. 112, paragraph 1.

9 35 U.S.C. 101.

10 "The term 'invention' means invention or discovery." (35 U.S.C. 100 Definitions (a))

abstract, specification, claims, drawings[11] and list of cited references. Both the structure of each of these parts and the language to be used are determined by the US Code / Title 35 (35 USC), the US Code of Federal Regulations / Title 37 (37 CFR), and the MPEP.[12] According to an on-line brochure[13] of the World Intellectual Property Organization (WIPO), patents as such are documents containing technical information in their descriptions and drawings, legal information in their claims, and business-relevant information in the bibliographical data. The purpose of this chapter is to describe how the technical and legal information is structured rhetorically within the patents filed in the United States.

From the point of view of Business Management, Pitkethly remarks that: "a patent can be described as an exclusive right of limited duration over a new, non-obvious invention capable of industrial application where the right to sue others for infringement, is granted in return for publication of the invention" (1997: 4). Bazerman has considered patents from the point of view of rhetoric (1999: 90) and he states that ideas become profitable when they are transformed into the property of an individual. The advantage in the case of patents is that the owner of the patent can exclude others from the fabrication, use or sale of the owned invention. The US Constitution in section 8 of its first article establishes that "The Congress shall have power [...] to promote the Progress of Science and useful Arts, by securing for limited Times to Authors and Inventors the exclusive Right to their respective Writings and Discoveries." The protection of a patent can be thus seen as a compensation for the public disclosure of an invention. However, disclosing the details of an inventive idea (Bazerman 1999: 91, 97, 104, 106) is in conflict with the commercial interests of patentees, as they have to reveal secret information to competitors. Myers (1995) equates patents to enclosed land plots. Following

11 "Such application shall include […] (B) a drawing as prescribed by section 113 of this title;" (35 USC, Section 111 Application). "The applicant shall furnish a drawing where necessary for the understanding of the subject matter sought to be patented." (35 USC, Section 113 Drawings).

12 <http://www.uspto.gov/web/offices/pac/mpep/mpep.htm>.

13 <http://www.wipo.int/export/sites/www/freepublications/en/patents/434/wipo pub_l434_03.pdf> (page 7). All the links belong to the USPTO.

Myers's metaphor, it can be said that patent applicants try to claim as much land as possible without trespassing somebody else's property.

3. Methodology used for the analysis of the rhetorical structure

The data analysed consists of a corpus of 333 US patents spanning from 1999 till 2009. All the patents are freely available from <http://patft.uspto.gov/netahtml/PTO/search-bool.html>. Design, plant, genetic material and medical treatment patents were excluded from this corpus. There are many reasons for this exclusion mostly related either to document structure requirements (plant and design patents)[14] or to the degree of precision of their language (genetic material and medical treatment patents). As Roberts (2007: 62) points out: "patenting in relation to most technologies has developed along the same lines as those in mechanical engineering". In any case, the excluded patents represent approximately 10% of the total body of available patents in the USPTO.

The search for patents on the USPTO was based on a list of electromechanical engineering terms chosen from the *Routledge Spanish Technical Dictionary – Diccionario Técnico Inglés*. Those query results coinciding with the following criteria were downloaded in *txt* file format: patents granted later than 1998 and patents regarding manufactures, compositions of matter, methods and processes. After a file cleaning process, each patent in the corpus is shown to contain a title, the number that identifies the document in the USPTO, the date

14 According to Title 37 of the US Code of Federal Regulations, both plant and design patents must only use one single claim and the description is different from the rest of patents (section 1.164 and 1.153 on the following link: <http://www.uspto.gov/web/offices/pac/mpep/consolidated_rules.pdf>). Of a total of 289,479 patents in 2008, only 26,750 were design patents and 1,241 were plant patents (source: statistics of the US Patent and Trademark Office <http://www.uspto.gov/web/offices/ac/ido/oeip/taf/cbcby.pdf>).

of the grant, an abstract, the claims, and the description (technically, *specifications*). The rest of the information is of little or no linguistic value for an analysis with concordancing tools. The specification, as is written and sent to the patent examiners, has typically the following headings:

- Background of the invention;
- Brief summary of the invention;
- Brief description of the several views of the drawing;
- Detailed description of the invention;
- A claim or claims;[15]
- Abstract of the disclosure.[16]

The US patent legislation provides valuable clues as to where the search for expressions linked to rhetorical moves can start. Section 1.75 of 37 CFR indicates how the patent claims have to be written and what language must be used to structure them. Section 2100 of MPEP provides instructions to the patent examiners on how to interpret the scope or breadth of claims in relation to the use of certain phraseology. Therefore, claims can be analysed by searching this phraseology in the corpus with the help of the concordancing software AntConc.

Another strategy consists in searching for the titles of the specification sections with the concordancer and checking the language used immediately before and after. Obviously, a qualitative reading of some patents supplies word combinations with the potential of being pointers to a rhetorical move. Actually, without a POS-tagged corpus the detection of any rhetorical moves located far from patent headings requires the traditional reading of several patents to identify rhetorically promising structures.

The theoretical background that supports this study can be found mainly in the seminal works of Swales (1990) and Bhatia (1993). Although Swales (1990) mentions prototypicality as one cha-

---

15 Claims are of two types: independent and dependent. The latter must always refer to one of the former.

16 This order is required by the above-mentioned laws and rules, but the granted patents available on the US Patent and Trademark Office website place the abstract and claims before the four other sections.

racteristic of genres, it is Paltridge (1997) who develops further the application of this concept from frame semantics in the methodology for the characterization of a genre. The rhetorical move structure presented in this chapter can be considered central to the prototypical idea of US patents. This means that individual patents are more or less prototypical. The factors influencing how close an individual patent is to the genre prototype may be related to individual stylistic preferences, the experience with the genre of the people drafting the application, the age and nationality of the translators of that specific patent, or the restrictions imposed by the specific field of knowledge to which the invention belongs.

Nevertheless, a genre such as that of patents tends to be highly formulaic[17] and since the text of patents is not subject to copyright protection, the recycling of fixed expressions and clusters from other patents seems to be a common practice.[18] Apart from simplifying the task of drafting a patent application, the fact that a structure is used in previously successful applications is a relative guarantee that the recycled phraseology will yield the desired legal consequences. The German academic tradition of *Textlinguistik* describes *Texthandlungsmuster* or *complex text patterns* (Engberg 2001: 59) as linguistic patterns of action used within a specific situation for a communicative purpose that is related to the situation. These text patterns are relatively fixed expressions of which the phraseology mentioned above is a good example.

Bazerman (1999: 102) and Swales (2004: 64) agree on the potential of associating *speech acts* to non-literary genres in terms of greater precision of rhetorical goals and means. Nevertheless, both of them also agree on the fact that relating speech acts to long written genres entails many difficulties. Instead, complex text patterns imply considering multi-word expressions as they are used across genres to

17 Particularly in the *claims* section which is the one containing essentially legal information. Tiersma (1999: 102) indicates that the purpose of this ritualistic and formulaic language is to "signal the parties that this is a legal act with significant consequences".

18 This is not what Tiersma (1999: 59) calls *boilerplate* ("a standard provision that is routinely added to a particular type of document") which would be a case of wordiness.

achieve similar communicative purposes and therefore imply the use of a different approach from that of speech acts.

It has already been mentioned that patents are peculiar in the sense that the disclosure must be *sufficient* to enable a person skilled in the art, but it does not need to go beyond that point (Frobert-Adamo 2000: 160; Roberts 2007: 49-50). Regarding this aspect of sufficiency, Myers (1995: 98) explains that the two inventors in his study "had to leave parts strategically vague, to allow for the unpredictability of applications and competitors". At the same time, each patent tries to set the boundaries of a scientific area in which a finding has been brought to light. These boundaries can neither be so broad as to conflict with other existing patents, nor so narrow as to leave previously unclaimed space free (Myers 1995: 74-75). Both the limited disclosure and the expansive claiming strategies can be achieved by resourcing to *all-inclusive* language (Bhatia 1993: 103). This resource is common in normative texts and contracts to pre-empt potentially new situations. Roberts (2007: 122-124) calls this all-inclusive language *labels* when referring to nouns, and mentions how advantageous this strategy can be for adequately expanding the scope of the invention. Detecting lexical items and action patterns with this all-inclusiveness function has also been essential for the identification of the move structure of patents.

For the identification of lexical items, the software Antconc was used because it is furnished with a *keyword* extraction function. Essentially, extracting keywords from a corpus requires having another corpus as a reference for comparison; Antconc uses an algorithm that first compares the frequency of each word in both corpora and then checks the distribution of the most frequent and least frequent words. The result of these two operations is a list of a maximum of 1,000 words made up of both the most frequent and evenly distributed words and the unusually least frequent words in the corpus analysed.[19] This word-list can be ordered by frequency of occurrence, alphabetically, or in inverse alphabetical order.

---

19 Unusually infrequent in comparison with the corpus used as a reference.

For the present study, the Baby BNC[20] was used as the reference corpus. It consists of a four-million-word sampling of the British National Corpus which is made up of 100 million words. The Baby BNC includes approximately one million words from 25 fiction texts, around one million words from 14 British newspapers, almost 700,000 words from spoken language samples, and the rest consists of 30 academic texts. With a list of keywords available and the phraseology mentioned in the patent legislation, the next step was using Antconc's concordancing function to search for meaningful text patterns.

4. US patent move structure

The moves presented here are arranged according to the order of the sections found in the patents retrieved from the USPTO with the search facility on the website.

Patent sections	*Patent Moves*
Claims	1. Determining scope of property
Background of the invention	2. Determining technical scope 3. Determining gaps in prior art
Brief summary of the invention	4. Summarizing purpose and characteristics
Brief description of the several views of the drawing	5.Physical & functional description
Detailed description of the invention	5. Physical & functional description 6. Warning and referring to claims

Table 1. Distribution of moves in relation to patent sections.

Let us begin with the action patterns that introduce the moves within claims. It has been already observed that, according to the WIPO,

20 <http://www.natcorp.ox.ac.uk/corpus/baby/baby-des.html>.

claims contain information which is legally relevant. The purpose of this section is to lay down the metes and bounds of the intellectual property protected by the patent. After the standard heading *claims* for the section, all patents begin with one of the following sentences closed by a colon:

- What is claimed is: (236 occurrences)
- The invention claimed is: (35 occurrences)
- We claim: (23 occurrences)
- I claim: (22 occurrences)
- What is claimed: (5 occurrences)
- Having thus described the invention, it is claimed: (2 occurrences)
- Having thus described the invention, what is claimed is: (2 occurrences)
- It is claimed: (1 occurrence)
- The invention is claimed as follows: (1 occurrence)
- Having thus described the preferred embodiments, the invention is now claimed to be: (1 occurrence)
- What is claimed as new and desired to be protected by Letters Patent of the United States is: (1 occurrence)
- What is claimed as new and desired to be protected by Letters Patent is set forth in the appended claims: (1 occurrence)
- Having thus described the invention, what is claimed as new and desired to be secured by Letters Patent is as follows: (1 occurrence)
- Having thus described the invention and illustrated its use, what I claim as new and is desired to be secured by Letters of Patent of the United States is: (1 occurrence)
- Accordingly, what is desired to be secured by Letters Patent of the United States is the invention as defined and differentiated in the following claims: (1 occurrence)

This is followed by what 37 CFR, section 1.75, paragraph (e), subparagraph (1) establishes as a *preamble.* Examples (1), (2), (3), (4), (5) and (6) illustrate how this preamble looks in combination with the transitional language (in italics) used to link the preamble with the characterizing text of the claim:

(1) A variable-cycle engine capable of alternating between two-cycle and four-cycle operation, *comprising*: …

(2) A method for generating a tornado *comprising the steps of*: …

(3) A portable hydraulic powered high capacity air compressor system for use with a vehicle, *said vehicle including* a hydraulic power system for delivering pressurized hydraulic fluid to a hydraulically operated device, *said air compressor system comprising*: …

(4) A first entity *including*: a first bit-pattern; a non-volatile memory storing resource data; a first base key for use with at least a first variant key: …

(5) A process for converting a feedstock *comprising* organic compounds to conversion product *which comprises*: …

(6) A terephthalic acid composition *comprising*: …

By analysing these selected examples and the others presented by the concordancer in combination with the information contained in MPEP 2111.03, the following generalization can be made: a preamble has three possible forms which are illustrated respectively by Tables 2, 3, and 4 below.

<table>
<tr><td rowspan="7">Complex nominal group (NG) with a hyperonymic head +</td><td rowspan="2">Capable of + [NG] +</td><td>comprising</td></tr>
<tr><td>consisting of</td></tr>
<tr><td rowspan="2">or
for use + [NG] +</td><td>consists essentially of</td></tr>
<tr><td>group consisting of</td></tr>
<tr><td rowspan="2">or
for + -ing + [NG] +</td><td>having</td></tr>
<tr><td>composed of</td></tr>
<tr><td>or equivalent purpose constructions + [NG] +</td><td>comprising the steps of</td></tr>
</table>

Table 2. First possible form of a preamble and transitional language that follows.

This is followed by a list of steps in a process, and/or a list of structural components of a product, and/or a list of interacting parts in a machine, and/or a list of elements of matter. These lists roughly consist of a complex nominal group modified by either a prepositional phrase or a subordinate relative clause.

Complex nominal group with a hyperonymic head +	Said + repetition of previous nominal group + having + new nominal group	Repetition of the previous structure several times + comprising[21]

Table 3. Second possible form of a preamble and transitional language that follows.

The preambles shown in Tables 3 (above) and 4 (below) are typical of dependent claims which introduce an improvement and further limitation regarding a previous independent claim or claims. Again 37 CFR, section 1.75, paragraph (e), sub-paragraph (2) establishes that the preamble must be followed by a sentence beginning with the word *wherein.*[22] In the context of claims, *wherein* tends to prefer the company of the words *the,*[23] *said*[24] or a combination that includes the word *said*, as (7), (8), (9), and (10) illustrate:

(7) *wherein said* circular blade is a modified disk blade from an earthworking implement, …

(8) *wherein when said* shuttle is in the lower distal position, range (15), …

(9) *wherein each of said* brake lining blocks includes a groove formed within an end face of said block …

(10) *wherein the* operation *of said* wing latch actuator to effect movement of said latch hook from said latching position to said release position, …

21 *Comprising,* or any of the structures in the last column of Table 2, will appear only after the last repetition of the structure.

22 In the context of claims, the word *wherein* appears 895 times.

23 In the context of claims, the combination *wherein the* appears a total of 328 times.

24 In the context of claims, the word *said* in direct combination with *wherein* appears 399 times.

There seems to be a tendency to drop the word *said* when introducing the improvements in the claims. In this case the elements, steps, and/or relationships are written immediately after *wherein a/an/the*[25] or some structure such as *wherein at least + a/an/the/some/[number]* (108 occurrences) or *wherein the + ordinal number* (228 occurrences), or *wherein the at least + cardinal number* (50 occurrences). These alternatives may be motivated by a wish to use a less archaic[26] and formulaic type of language when isolating the elements of the property claimed.

… in accordance with claim + [number] (16 times)	comprising
	further comprising
… claimed in claim + [number] (103 times)	additionally comprising
… according to claim + [number] (256 times)	further including
… of claim + [number] (700 times)	including
… as in claim + [number] (27 times)	in which
	wherein

Table 4. Third possible form of a preamble and transitional language that follows.

Table 4 presents another form of wording the preambles in dependent claims which are used for further restricting the extent of the property claimed in independent claims. Nevertheless, this restriction is kept as vague as possible. Let us illustrate this with one example. In US patent 6768214, one of the elements claimed in claim 70 is "a piezoelectric material disposed proximate the member, [...]"; later claim 72, referring to claim 70, states: "wherein the piezoelectric material is positioned between the portion of the member and the fluid conduit in the recess." In other words, claim 72 is restricting the position of the piezoelectric material (rather loosely, as there are no specifications pro-

25 This structure is harder to analyse without POS tags as the lexical variety of the subsequent elements makes the task of identifying a pattern a manual task. POS tags would allow us to look for syntactic patterns instead.

26 Tiersma (1999: 89) describes *said* as "an ancient legalism".

vided), but it is still including in the property claimed the use for this purpose of both all known piezoelectric materials and those yet to be discovered. Flignor/Orozco (2006: 7), Neifeld (2004: 3), and Gambardella/Giuri/Mariani (2006: 14) indicate that both the length of claims and their number are reliable indexes of a patent's value. The three forms of preamble identified here allow for the construction of long claims that can be further made explicit by a large number of dependent claims. The use of these preamble formats permits the falsification to a certain extent of the purely statistical evaluation of patents.[27]

The following move consists in determining the technical scope of the invention or, in other words, locating the technical region into which the patent is claiming the property and fixing the breadth of specialization inside this region. This move is carried out at the beginning of the section called *Background of the Invention.* In fact, some patents make this explicit by further subdividing the section into two: *Field of the Invention / Field of Invention* (180 patents out of the 333 in the corpus) and *Description of Related Art / Description of the Prior Art* (64 patents out of 333) / *Background Art* (30 patents out of 333) *Description of the Background Art* (1 patent out of 333).

It is in the Field of the Invention that the technical field is demarcated. If the section is explicitly a subdivision, this move is generally indicated by the following collocate structure:[28]

<table>
<tr><td>The present invention</td><td rowspan="4">(generally)</td><td>is concerned with</td><td rowspan="7">(generally)</td></tr>
<tr><td rowspan="2">The invention</td><td>is directed to</td></tr>
<tr><td>is related to</td></tr>
<tr><td rowspan="2">This invention</td><td>concerns</td></tr>
<tr><td rowspan="3">(in general)</td><td>is to</td></tr>
<tr><td rowspan="2">The disclosed invention</td><td>relates to</td></tr>
<tr><td>pertains to</td></tr>
</table>

Table 5. *Determination of technical scope* move.

27 See demo (after 53") at <http://www.patentcafe.com/video/Portfoliodss.wmv>.

28 Optional items between parentheses.

When the section is not explicitly subdivided, the structure shown in Table 5 is alternated with structures such as: *In* + hyperonymic nominal group or simply a hyperonymic nominal group followed by a verb in the simple present (active or passive forms). To further delimit the technical scope, *and more specifically,* or *and more particularly* are used. This move is usually carried out in one single paragraph. Examples of hyperonymic nominal groups are: *centrifuge systems*, *internal combustion engines*, *the trucking industry*, or *the manufacture of integrated circuits*. These are examples of how all-inclusive language performs a rhetorical function in patents.

The third move deals with determining the novelty of the patent. This is achieved by first referring to the state-of-the-art, then establishing the existence of a problem, and finally offering a solution (which should also be proof of utility). It is trickier to identify the action patterns that are used in this move, as the language is less formulaic and 37 CFR is less concerned with the use of the language in this section than with its contents. One query that shows some promise in terms of seeing how the state of the art is introduced, consists in looking at the collocations of *known*. Collocates such as *are known which*, *it is also known*, or *commonly known as* certainly appear in the context of this third move. Unfortunately, they are also frequent in the fourth move.

Looking at what surrounds the expression *prior art* is interesting as it signals what is known and its limitations. The following examples display some of the combinations found which either enumerate the known technology (11) or show also its limitations (12), (13), (14), and (15).

(11) *It is also known in the prior art* to provide toy wheeled vehicles with suspension mechanisms for the wheels, ...

(12) The sucker rods *in the prior art*, therefore, were designed originally to *simply* reciprocate up and down, …

(13) *Although the prior art* discloses engine shutdown systems for conventional ICEs, *they do not meet* the engine shutdown needs of an HEV.

(14) *In view of the above-stated problems in the prior art*, the present invention is concerned with …

(15) … *as well as overcoming* the other above mentioned *deficiencies with the prior art.*

Combinations with adversative conjunctions or with nouns (Table 6), adverbs (*simply, significantly, otherwise*), adjectives (*deficient, unusable, unacceptable*) and verbs (Table 7) provide necessary signposts to identify this move in terms of novelty in the invention and problems in the previous art.

Pointing to the novelty	*Limitations of previous art*
Advantage(s) (538 times)	Problem(s) (271 times)
Solution(s) (463 times)	Failure(s) (173 times)
Efficiency (429 times)	Disadvantage(s) (80 times)
Improvement(s) (180 times)	Corrosion (76 times)
Benefit(s) (175 times)	Limitation(s) (56 times)

Table 6. Nouns pointing to either limitations of previous art or improvements of claimed invention.

Needs improvement	*Results in novelty*
Remove (674 times)	Improve (747 times)
Avoid (220 times)	Achieve (738 times)
Inhibit (133 times)	Enhance (216 times)

Table 7. Verbs pointing to either limitations of previous art or improvements of claimed invention.

The collocates of some verbs can help in determining whether the action pattern is presenting a limitation of the state of the art (16) or the novelty itself (17):

(16) This would greatly *increase the complexity* of construction of the adjustment device, besides *increasing* the *size* and *cost of manufacture*, so militating *against* the use of this transmission.

(17) Some solutions currently adopted to *increase* maximum tractor *speed consist in equipping* the transmission with gears designed to *achieve the desired* velocity ratios, ...

The fifth move is the most technical of all and it involves describing the purpose and relationships of the constituting elements of the invention in at least one *embodiment* (as they are called in patents). Section 1.71, paragraph (b) of 37 CFR, requires that the *best mode* of carrying out the invention be described clearly enough for a person skilled in the art to be able to reproduce it successfully. The *best mode* is usually reflected in the language of the patents as *preferred embodiment*, or by introducing each of the characteristics of the invention with sentences containing *preferably* (2,484 occurrences) as (18) and (19) show:

(18) *Preferably*, the ring gear and the rotary variable load body are coupled to each other through a clutch for reducing an energy loss of the rotary variable load body, when the rotation of the mechanical supercharger is stopped.

(19) The standard error *preferably* comprises a sum of absolute value of differences between desired cam position and measured cam position.

Lists of characteristics of the invention are introduced by combining a relatively small number of lexical items to produce dozens of variations. Searching for the collocation *the present invention* has proved to be particularly productive in detecting these action patterns. The number of variations is considerable, so the following tables provide a general picture of the available combinations.

(by/in) another +	feature + / object +	
(by/in) yet another +	(alternative) embodiment +	
(by/in) still yet another +	arrangement + / aspect +	of the present invention

Table 8. Action patterns to introduce characteristics (I).

<table>
<tr><td rowspan="3">It is yet another +</td><td>object +</td><td rowspan="3">of this invention</td></tr>
<tr><td>feature +</td></tr>
<tr><td>advantage +</td></tr>
</table>

Table 9. Action patterns to introduce characteristics (II).

<table>
<tr><td rowspan="2">According to +</td><td>another +</td><td rowspan="4">aspect/embodiment of this invention there is provided a</td></tr>
<tr><td>still another +</td></tr>
<tr><td rowspan="2">In accordance with +</td><td>yet still another +</td></tr>
<tr><td>a/the [ordinal/cardinal] +</td></tr>
</table>

Table 10. Action patterns to introduce characteristics (III).

The combinations displayed in Tables 8, 9, and 10 can be further elaborated with additions of other less frequent noun heads, or the additional modification of the adjective *exemplary*, or even deictic references such as *described above*. It is worth mentioning that many of the descriptive structures from this move are repeated in the claims, because 37 CFR, section 1.75, paragraph (d), sub-paragraph (1) requires that:

> The claim or claims must conform to the invention as set forth in the remainder of the specification and the terms and phrases used in the claims must find clear support or antecedent basis in the description so that the meaning of the terms in the claims may be ascertainable by reference to the description.

The last move directs the reader to the claims and insists on the fact that the description represents only the best mode[29] as is required by 37 CFR, section 1.71, paragraph (b). It actually hints at alternative legally valid forms of the property claimed without describing them. This move is quite formulaic as examples (20)-(24) show:

29 However, many inventors include several possible best modes in their description of the invention.

(20) Although the present invention has been described and illustrated in detail it is to be clearly understood that the same is by way of illustration and example only and is not to be taken by way of limitation.

(21) The present invention has been described in considerable detail with reference to certain preferred versions thereof, however other versions are possible.

(22) While the present invention has been described in connection with two embodiments thereof, it will be understood that many changes and modifications may be made without departing from the true spirit and scope of the present invention, [...].

(23) Although the present invention has been described with reference to preferred embodiments, workers skilled in the art will recognize that changes may be made in form and detail without departing from the spirit and scope of the invention.

(24) Although the embodiment of the present invention has been described in detail, it will be understood that the present invention is not limited to the above-described embodiment, and various modifications in design may be made without departing from the spirit and scope of the invention defined in claims.

Therefore, the last move consists of a sentence that is a formula placed at the end of the patent (as it appears on the USPTO website). This formula may be a separate paragraph or part of the last paragraph.

5. Conclusion

Bazerman researched patents within a collection of genres that covered the process that extends from invention to commercialization. Myers, on the other hand, studied how two researchers used to writing journal articles adapted to the conventions of the patent discourse community. In contrast, this chapter has focused on the characterization of US patents as a genre taking into account the communicative goals of such documents. US electromechanical patents are the result of the combined knowledge of inventors and lawyers. The former provide the technical expertise regarding the invention seeking a property status, and the latter shape this knowledge in a way that satisfies the commercial interest of the inventors, the legal requirements for patentability and all this without breaching the property rights of other inventors. Roberts and Myers insist on the fact that unpredictability of the actions of competitors forces the patent lawyers to write a 'future proof' document.

The differences in the length and topics of the patents have an important influence on the final move structure of each individual document. There is also some variation in the action patterns used for introducing the rhetorical moves of patents, but this may be due to factors such as the individual stylistic preferences of the patent drafters or the experience and, thus, the familiarity with the linguistic conventions of the genre.

Still, the move structure proposed here can be seen as reflecting the core characteristics of a prototypical patent. The grounds for such an assertion are based on the frequency of the action patterns found. It must be acknowledged that to further refine these results, both a POS-tagged corpus and statistical measurements of co-relation should be performed. Nevertheless, as an initial probe into the genre, this study shows promising expectations. Identifying broader contexts in which action patterns appear will help explain why a specific structure behaves differently in different sections of a patent.

The research on the rhetorical moves of patents can be further improved by tagging the sections of the patent. This would simplify the sorting of concordances as it would introduce the option of searching in the whole corpus or in a specific section. A section such as *claims* tends to be more formulaic as its legal value relies more heavily on the typical features of the language of the law. In contrast, the description of the invention has a fundamentally technical nature and therefore presents the usual organization of information found in technical descriptions. A remarkable peculiarity of the electromechanical patent descriptions is how it achieves clarity in the face of patent examiners and courts while avoiding, when possible, precision in order to achieve a maximum property scope.

A more detailed study of the collocations of the nouns and verbs should provide clues on whether they are used with a positive (innovation) or a negative (technical limitation) meaning in the move that determines the novelty. The application of these results can be useful in several fields: to improve the methods of patent valuation; to improve the methods for legally assessing the invalidation and infringement likelihood of a specific patent; to improve legal research in case of intellectual property conflict; to design teaching materials and tools for academics and engineers in need of help with the writing of their patents; and to construct machine-readable knowledge models or ontologies that would improve semantic searches in patent databases.

References

Bazerman, Charles 1999. *The Languages of Edison's Light*. Michigan: Michigan University Press.

Bhatia, Vijay K. 1993. *Analysing Genre: Language Use in Professional Settings*. London: Longman.

DeMatteis, Bob / Gibbs, Andy / Neustel, Michael 2006. *The Patent Writer: How to Write Successful Patent Applications*. New York: Square One Publishers.

Engberg, Jan 2001. Zeitlicher un kultureller Wandel von Texthandlungsmustern in Geschäftsbriefen. In Eschenbach, Jutta / Schewe, Theo (Hrsg) *Über Grenzen gehen – Kommunikation zwischen Kulturen und Unternehmen*. Festschrift für Ingrid Neumann. Halden/Norway: Høgskolen Østfold, 57-72.

Flignor, Paul / Orozco, David 2006. Intangible Asset & Intellectual Property Valuation: A Multidisciplinary Perspective. At <http://www.wipo.int/export/sites/www/sme/en/documents/pdf/IP_Valuation.pdf>.

Frobert-Adamo, Monique 2000. Influence of Linguistic Patterns on the Transfer of Strategic Information: A Diachronic Study of the Rhetoric of Patent Applications in the United States. In Hager, Peter J. / Schreiber, Howard Jeffrey (eds) *Managing Global Communication in Science and Technology*. New York: John Wiley & Sons, 153-178.

Gambardella, Alfonso / Giuri, Paola / Mariani, Myriam 2006. Study on Evaluating the Knowledge Economy: What are Patents Actually Worth? The Value of Patents for Today's Economy and Society. At <http://ec.europa.eu/internal_market/indprop/docs/patent/studies/patentstudy-report_en.pdf>.

Hunt, David / Nguyen, Long / Rodgers, Matthew 2007. *Patent Searching: Tools & Techniques*. New York: John Wiley & Sons.

Myers, Greg 1995. From Discovery to Invention: The Writing and Rewriting of Two Patents. *Social Studies of Science* 25/1, 57-105.

Neifeld, Richard A. 2004. A Macro-Economic Model Providing Patent Based Company Financial Indicators and Automated Patent Valuations. At <http://www.patentcafe.com/whitepapers/patent_value_whitepaper.pdf>.

Paltridge, Brian 1997. *Genre, Frames and Writing in Research Settings*. Amsterdam: John Benjamins.

Pitkethly, Robert 1997. The Valuation of Patents: A review of patent valuation methods with consideration of option based methods and the potential for further research. *Judge Institute Working Paper* 21/97. Cambridge: The Judge Institute of Management Studies. At <http://www.oiprc.ox.ac.uk/EJWP0599.pdf>.

Roberts, Gwilym 2007. *EIPR: A Practical Guide to Drafting Patents*. London: Sweet & Maxwell.

Routledge Spanish Technical Dictionary – Diccionario Técnico Inglés 1997. London: Routledge.

Swales, John 1990. *Genre Analysis*. Cambridge: Cambridge University Press.

Swales, John 2004. *Research Genres: Explorations and Applications*. Cambridge: Cambridge University Press.

Tiersma, Peter M. 1999. *Legal Language*. Chicago: The University of Chicago Press.

Notes on Contributors

JANET AINSWORTH is John D. Eshelman Professor of Law at Seattle University School of Law. Her research interests centre on linguistic ideology in legal doctrine and practice, and her work has appeared in law reviews such as *The Yale Law Journal* and *The Cornell Law Review* as well as in linguistics journals. She currently serves on the editorial board of *The International Journal of Law and Semiotics* and the Oxford University Press series *Law and Language*. She has also authored *amicus curiae* briefs addressing linguistic issues in a variety of legal contexts for cases pending in the United States Supreme Court.

ISMAEL ARINAS PELLÓN is Lecturer in the Department of Applied Linguistics to Science and Technology at the Universidad Politécnica de Madrid, Spain. His research interests include technical and business genres, corpus linguistics for genre analysis and the teaching of translation, the use of IT for the teaching of LSP and the development of LSP didactic materials. He has been invited twice as PhD researcher by the Language and Communication Department at the Aarhus School of Business, Denmark where he has taught in the Spanish translation master. He was part of the revision committee for the Routledge Technical Spanish-English dictionary (1997).

MARTINA BAJČIĆ is a research assistant at the Faculty of Law of the University of Rijeka (Croatia) where she teaches Legal English and Legal German and is involved in the research project 'Strategies for Translating the EU *acquis*'. She is currently enrolled in a PhD programme in Linguistics at the University of Zagreb. Her research activity lies within the field of legal translation and legal terminology. She previously worked as an interpreter and translator for English and German on an EU-funded Twinning Project at the Croatian Competition Agency.

WILLIAM BROMWICH is a researcher in English linguistics at the Marco Biagi Faculty of Economics at the University of Modena and Reggio Emilia in Italy, where he lectures in English for law and economics. His research interests focus on language and the law, and the linguistic construction of social reality, and his recent work deals with issues of language and disability. In addition he is an expert witness at the Tribunal of Bologna, and English language editor of the *International Journal of Comparative Labour Law and Industrial Relations,* and *Ratio Juris: An International Journal of Jurisprudence and Philosophy of Law.*

SILVIA CACCHIANI is a research fellow in English Language and Translation at the University of Modena and Reggio Emilia, Italy. She holds a PhD in English Linguistics from the University of Pisa, Italy. Her research interests range from the lexical, semantic and discourse-pragmatic aspects of intensifiers and intensifying morphology to lexicology, lexicography and specialized lexicography. She is currently working on pedagogically-oriented law dictionaries for the non-native student and the translator.

Since 1987, THOMAS CHRISTIANSEN has taught in various positions at various institutions in Apulia, Italy, including the universities of Bari and Lecce (now Salento). In 2001, he completed his PhD at the University of Salford (Greater Manchester, UK) on 'Coreference and Noun Phrase Selection in Italian'. He has published a book entitled *Cohesion and the Organisation of Text: A Practical introduction* and a number of articles on various areas of linguistics including systemic linguistics and functional grammar, varieties of English, teaching English, language testing, and analysis of different corpora including spoken discourse. Since 2006, he has been a full-time researcher in English Language and Translation at the Università del Salento (Lecce, Italy).

SNJEŽANA HUSINEC graduated from the Faculty of Philosophy, University of Zagreb (Department of English language and literature and Department of German language and literature). As a lecturer in English and German at the Faculty of Law, University of Zagreb, she teaches legal English to law students and legal German to tax law students, as well as German for social workers to students of social work. Additionally, she teaches legal English courses to legal practitioners. She is currently working on her PhD researching the influence of the German language on Croatian legal terminology. Her main research interests include legal linguistics, contact linguistics and languages for special purposes.

DAVIDE MAZZI is researcher in English language and translation at the University of Modena and Reggio Emilia. His research activity has essentially focused on the following areas: discourse analysis, corpus linguistics, and argumentation studies. In particular, his research interests and the related publications have concentrated on legal and academic discourse. His recent publications include: 'I first have to decide whether there were any notes in the first place. I consider that there *probably* were': Adverbials of Stance in Equity Judges' Argumentation (*Textus*), 2008; and 'His explanation [...] would be discreditable if true; but I am satisfied that it is a lie': Discursive Strategies of Self-projection in Equity Judgments, in L. Sočanac, C. Goddard, L. Kremer (eds) *Curriculum, Multilingualism and the Law*. Zagreb 2009.

CHIARA PREITE is a research fellow in French Language and Translation at the University of Modena and Reggio Emilia, Italy. She holds an MA in Legal Translation from the University of Genoa, Italy, and a PhD in French Linguistics from the University of Brescia, Italy. Her main research interests lie in the fields of legal French, lexicology, lexicography and specialized lexicography. She has published widely on these topics and is the author of the recently published volume *Langage du droit et linguistique. Etude de l'organisation textuelle, énonciative et argomentative des arrêts de la Cour (et du Tribunal) de Justice des Communautés européennes*. She is currently carrying out work on law dictionaries from the jurilinguistic perspective.

GIORGIA RIBONI is a PhD student in English Linguistics and Translation at Università degli Studi di Milano, Italy. She is currently working on her dissertation, which investigates the *genre* of political weblogs. Her research interests include *genre* analysis, multimodality, legal English and Discourse Analysis, which she has combined with the quantitative approach of corpus linguistics. She is involved in local and national projects and has presented papers at international conferences.

JAN ROALD is Associate Professor of The Norwegian School of Economics and Business Administration, Department of Professional and Intercultural Communication since 1983. He teaches economic and legal French. His research interests lie in the field of terminology, terminography, LSP text linguistics and specialized translation. He is co-producer of terminographical products and has conducted a large scale terminographical project in the field of oil and gas production with the aim of elaborating Norwegian terminology. He now focuses on terminology in the economic and legal domains, with an emphasis on comparative and translational aspects of Norwegian and French.

COLIN ROBERTSON is a Scottish lawyer. Married with two children, he has many years' experience in national and EU legal, linguistic and legislative contexts: as lawyer (Commission 1982-3), as legal translator (European Court of Justice 1991-1993) and as legal-linguistic reviser of EU legislative texts (Council of the EU since 1993). While primarily a practitioner, he has produced articles on a range of topics including: the Belgian legal system, international succession law, Scots and English law as two systems with one language (in Italian), multilingual law, lawburrows (in Scots), maills and duties (in Scots) and Scots as a European minority language (in Scots). Current topics include semiotics of EU law, EU legislative drafting and multilingual law and language.

SUSAN ŠARČEVIĆ is Professor and Head of the Department of Foreign Languages at the Faculty of Law of the University of Rijeka (Croatia) where she teaches Legal English and Legal German. At postgraduate level she has taught courses on EU Terminology, Institutions of the European Union and Translating EU Legislation. She has published extensively on legal translation, legal terminology, legal lexicography and multilingual communication in the law (in English, German and

Croatian) and has guest lectured worldwide. She is a legal translator and a reviser of legal texts in English.

LELIJA SOČANAC (PhD in Linguistics) is coordinator of the Centre for Language of Law and head of the Foreign Language Department of the Faculty of Law, University of Zagreb. She teaches Legal English and Legal Linguistics to students of law and Contact Linguistics to students of linguistics. From 2006 to 2009 she was the coordinator of the international Tempus project *Foreign Languages in the Field of Law*. She currently directs the project *Legal and Linguistic Aspects of Multilingualism.* She has co-edited *Curriculum, Multilingualism and the Law* (2009). Her research interests include legal linguistics, contact linguistics and sociolinguistics.

SUNNIVA WHITTAKER is Professor of French Language at the Department of Professional and Intercultural Communication, Norwegian School of Economics and Business Administration, since 2003. Her doctoral thesis *La gradation: Applications aux adjectifs*, was published in 2002. More recently her research has focused on text linguistics, contrastive linguistics and translation studies with particular focus on specialized texts, especially legal texts. She also holds a degree in Conference Interpreting from the Ecole Supérieure d'Interprètes et de Traducteurs in Paris and has contributed to the development of interpreting training programmes.

IGNACIO VÁZQUEZ ORTA is Professor of Applied Linguistics at the Department of English and German Philology of the University of Zaragoza. His research interests include Pragmatics and Discourse Analysis, Systemic Linguistics, Translation and Contrastive Studies (English-Spanish) always with an applied perspective. He is currently responsible for a research group called INTERLAE, which explores interpersonality in academic and professional discourse from a sociopragmatic perspective. He focuses on writer stance in academic and professional discourse. He is particularly interested in the study of professional legal discourse, more specifically, the discourse of arbitration. He is also interested in the translation of English legal documents into Spanish.

Linguistic Insights

Studies in Language and Communication

This series aims to promote specialist language studies in the fields of linguistic theory and applied linguistics, by publishing volumes that focus on specific aspects of language use in one or several languages and provide valuable insights into language and communication research. A cross-disciplinary approach is favoured and most European languages are accepted.

The series includes two types of books:

- **Monographs** – featuring in-depth studies on special aspects of language theory, language analysis or language teaching.
- **Collected papers** – assembling papers from workshops, conferences or symposia.

Each volume of the series is subjected to a double peer-reviewing process.

Vol. 1 Maurizio Gotti & Marina Dossena (eds)
Modality in Specialized Texts. Selected Papers of the 1st CERLIS Conference.
421 pages. 2001. ISBN 3-906767-10-8. US-ISBN 0-8204-5340-4

Vol. 2 Giuseppina Cortese & Philip Riley (eds)
Domain-specific English. Textual Practices across Communities and Classrooms.
420 pages. 2002. ISBN 3-906768-98-8. US-ISBN 0-8204-5884-8

Vol. 3 Maurizio Gotti, Dorothee Heller & Marina Dossena (eds)
Conflict and Negotiation in Specialized Texts. Selected Papers of the 2nd CERLIS Conference.
470 pages. 2002. ISBN 3-906769-12-7. US-ISBN 0-8204-5887-2

Editorial address:

Prof. Maurizio Gotti Università di Bergamo, Facoltà di Lingue e Letterature Straniere,
Via Salvecchio 19, 24129 Bergamo, Italy
Fax: 0039 035 2052789, E-Mail: m.gotti@unibg.it

Vol. 4 Maurizio Gotti, Marina Dossena, Richard Dury, Roberta Facchinetti & Maria Lima
Variation in Central Modals. A Repertoire of Forms and Types of Usage in Middle English and Early Modern English.
364 pages. 2002. ISBN 3-906769-84-4. US-ISBN 0-8204-5898-8

Vol. 5 Stefania Nuccorini (ed.)
Phrases and Phraseology. Data and Descriptions.
187 pages. 2002. ISBN 3-906770-08-7. US-ISBN 0-8204-5933-X

Vol. 6 Vijay Bhatia, Christopher N. Candlin & Maurizio Gotti (eds)
Legal Discourse in Multilingual and Multicultural Contexts. Arbitration Texts in Europe.
385 pages. 2003. ISBN 3-906770-85-0. US-ISBN 0-8204-6254-3

Vol. 7 Marina Dossena & Charles Jones (eds)
Insights into Late Modern English. 2nd edition.
378 pages. 2003, 2007.
ISBN 978-3-03911-257-9. US-ISBN 978-0-8204-8927-8

Vol. 8 Maurizio Gotti
Specialized Discourse. Linguistic Features and Changing Conventions.
351 pages. 2003, 2005.
ISBN 3-03910-606-6. US-ISBN 0-8204-7000-7

Vol. 9 Alan Partington, John Morley & Louann Haarman (eds)
Corpora and Discourse.
420 pages. 2004. ISBN 3-03910-026-2. US-ISBN 0-8204-6262-4

Vol. 10 Martina Möllering
The Acquisition of German Modal Particles. A Corpus-Based Approach.
290 pages. 2004. ISBN 3-03910-043-2. US-ISBN 0-8204-6273-X

Vol. 11 David Hart (ed.)
English Modality in Context. Diachronic Perspectives.
261 pages. 2003. ISBN 3-03910-046-7. US-ISBN 0-8204-6852-5

Vol. 12 Wendy Swanson
Modes of Co-reference as an Indicator of Genre.
430 pages. 2003. ISBN 3-03910-052-1. US-ISBN 0-8204-6855-X

Vol. 13 Gina Poncini
Discursive Strategies in Multicultural Business Meetings.
2nd edition. 338 pages. 2004, 2007.
ISBN 978-3-03911-296-8. US-ISBN 978-0-8204-8937-7

Vol. 14 Christopher N. Candlin & Maurizio Gotti (eds)
Intercultural Aspects of Specialized Communication.
2nd edition. 369 pages. 2004, 2007.
ISBN 978-3-03911-258-6. US-ISBN 978-0-8204-8926-1

Vol. 15 Gabriella Del Lungo Camiciotti & Elena Tognini Bonelli (eds)
Academic Discourse. New Insights into Evaluation.
234 pages. 2004. ISBN 3-03910-353-9. US-ISBN 0-8204-7016-3

Vol. 16 Marina Dossena & Roger Lass (eds)
Methods and Data in English Historical Dialectology.
405 pages. 2004. ISBN 3-03910-362-8. US-ISBN 0-8204-7018-X

Vol. 17 Judy Noguchi
The Science Review Article. An Opportune Genre in the Construction of Science.
274 pages. 2006. ISBN 3-03910-426-8. US-ISBN 0-8204-7034-1

Vol. 18 Giuseppina Cortese & Anna Duszak (eds)
Identity, Community, Discourse. English in Intercultural Settings.
495 pages. 2005. ISBN 3-03910-632-5. US-ISBN 0-8204-7163-1

Vol. 19 Anna Trosborg & Poul Erik Flyvholm Jørgensen (eds)
Business Discourse. Texts and Contexts.
250 pages. 2005. ISBN 3-03910-606-6. US-ISBN 0-8204-7000-7

Vol. 20 Christopher Williams
Tradition and Change in Legal English. Verbal Constructions in Prescriptive Texts.
2nd revised edition. 216 pages. 2005, 2007. ISBN 978-3-03911-444-3.

Vol. 21 Katarzyna Dziubalska-Kolaczyk & Joanna Przedlacka (eds)
English Pronunciation Models: A Changing Scene.
2nd edition. 476 pages. 2005, 2008. ISBN 978-3-03911-682-9.

Vol. 22 Christián Abello-Contesse, Rubén Chacón-Beltrán, M. Dolores López-Jiménez & M. Mar Torreblanca-López (eds)
Age in L2 Acquisition and Teaching.
214 pages. 2006. ISBN 3-03910-668-6. US-ISBN 0-8204-7174-7

Vol. 23 Vijay K. Bhatia, Maurizio Gotti, Jan Engberg & Dorothee Heller (eds)
Vagueness in Normative Texts.
474 pages. 2005. ISBN 3-03910-653-8. US-ISBN 0-8204-7169-0

Vol. 24 Paul Gillaerts & Maurizio Gotti (eds)
Genre Variation in Business Letters. 2nd printing.
407 pages. 2008. ISBN 978-3-03911-681-2.

Vol. 25 Ana María Hornero, María José Luzón & Silvia Murillo (eds)
Corpus Linguistics. Applications for the Study of English.
2nd printing. 526 pages. 2006, 2008. ISBN 978-3-03911-726-0

Vol. 26 J. Lachlan Mackenzie & María de los Ángeles Gómez-González (eds)
Studies in Functional Discourse Grammar.
259 pages. 2005. ISBN 3-03910-696-1 / US-ISBN 0-8204-7558-0

Vol. 27 Debbie G. E. Ho
Classroom Talk. Exploring the Sociocultural Structure of Formal ESL Learning.
2nd edition. 254 pages. 2006, 2007. ISBN 978-3-03911-434-4

Vol. 28 Javier Pérez-Guerra, Dolores González-Álvarez, Jorge L. Bueno-Alonso & Esperanza Rama-Martínez (eds)
'Of Varying Language and Opposing Creed': New Insights into Late Modern English.
455 pages. 2007. ISBN 978-3-03910-788-9

Vol. 29 Francesca Bargiela-Chiappini & Maurizio Gotti (eds)
Asian Business Discourse(s).
350 pages. 2005. ISBN 3-03910-804-2 / US-ISBN 0-8204-7574-2

Vol. 30 Nicholas Brownlees (ed.)
News Discourse in Early Modern Britain. Selected Papers of CHINED 2004.
300 pages. 2006. ISBN 3-03910-805-0 / US-ISBN 0-8204-8025-8

Vol. 31 Roberta Facchinetti & Matti Rissanen (eds)
Corpus-based Studies of Diachronic English.
300 pages. 2006. ISBN 3-03910-851-4 / US-ISBN 0-8204-8040-1

Vol. 32 Marina Dossena & Susan M. Fitzmaurice (eds)
Business and Official Correspondence: Historical Investigations.
209 pages. 2006. ISBN 3-03910-880-8 / US-ISBN 0-8204-8352-4

Vol. 33 Giuliana Garzone & Srikant Sarangi (eds)
Discourse, Ideology and Specialized Communication.
494 pages. 2007. ISBN 978-3-03910-888-6

Vol. 34 Giuliana Garzone & Cornelia Ilie (eds)
The Use of English in Institutional and Business Settings.
An Intercultural Perspective.
372 pages. 2007. ISBN 978-3-03910-889-3

Vol. 35 Vijay K. Bhatia & Maurizio Gotti (eds)
Explorations in Specialized Genres.
316 pages. 2006. ISBN 3-03910-995-2 / US-ISBN 0-8204-8372-9

Vol. 36 Heribert Picht (ed.)
Modern Approaches to Terminological Theories and Applications.
432 pages. 2006. ISBN 3-03911-156-6 / US-ISBN 0-8204-8380-X

Vol. 37 Anne Wagner & Sophie Cacciaguidi-Fahy (eds)
Legal Language and the Search for Clarity / Le langage juridique et la quête de clarté.
Practice and Tools / Pratiques et instruments.
487 pages. 2006. ISBN 3-03911-169-8 / US-ISBN 0-8388-5

Vol. 38 Juan Carlos Palmer-Silveira, Miguel F. Ruiz-Garrido &
Inmaculada Fortanet-Gómez (eds)
Intercultural and International Business Communication:
Theory, Research and Teaching.
2nd edition. 343 pages. 2006, 2008. ISBN 978-3-03911-680-5

Vol. 39 Christiane Dalton-Puffer, Dieter Kastovsky, Nikolaus Ritt &
Herbert Schendl (eds)
Syntax, Style and Grammatical Norms: English from 1500–2000.
250 pages. 2006. ISBN 3-03911-181-7 / US-ISBN 0-8204-8394-X

Vol. 40 Marina Dossena & Irma Taavitsainen (eds)
Diachronic Perspectives on Domain-Specific English.
280 pages. 2006. ISBN 3-03910-176-0 / US-ISBN 0-8204-8391-5

Vol. 41 John Flowerdew & Maurizio Gotti (eds)
Studies in Specialized Discourse.
293 pages. 2006. ISBN 3-03911-178-7

Vol. 42 Ken Hyland & Marina Bondi (eds)
Academic Discourse Across Disciplines.
320 pages. 2006. ISBN 3-03911-183-3 / US-ISBN 0-8204-8396-6

Vol. 43 Paul Gillaerts & Philip Shaw (eds)
The Map and the Landscape: Norms and Practices in Genre.
256 pages. 2006. ISBN 3-03911-182-5 / US-ISBN 0-8204-8395-4

Vol. 44 Maurizio Gotti & Davide Giannoni (eds)
New Trends in Specialized Discourse Analysis.
301 pages. 2006. ISBN 3-03911-184-1 / US-ISBN 0-8204-8381-8

Vol. 45 Maurizio Gotti & Françoise Salager-Meyer (eds)
Advances in Medical Discourse Analysis: Oral and Written Contexts.
492 pages. 2006. ISBN 3-03911-185-X / US-ISBN 0-8204-8382-6

Vol. 46 Maurizio Gotti & Susan Šarcević (eds)
Insights into Specialized Translation.
396 pages. 2006. ISBN 3-03911-186-8 / US-ISBN 0-8204-8383-4

Vol. 47 Khurshid Ahmad & Margaret Rogers (eds)
Evidence-based LSP: Translation, Text and Terminology.
584 pages. 2007. ISBN 978-3-03911-187-9

Vol. 48 Hao Sun & Dániel Z. Kádár (eds)
It's the Dragon's Turn: Chinese Institutional Discourses.
262 pages. 2008. ISBN 978-3-03911-175-6

Vol. 49 Cristina Suárez-Gómez
Relativization in Early English (950-1250): the Position of Relative Clauses.
149 pages. 2006. ISBN 3-03911-203-1 / US-ISBN 0-8204-8904-2

Vol. 50 Maria Vittoria Calvi & Luisa Chierichetti (eds)
Nuevas tendencias en el discurso de especialidad.
319 pages. 2006. ISBN 978-3-03911-261-6

Vol. 51 Mari Carmen Campoy & María José Luzón (eds)
Spoken Corpora in Applied Linguistics.
274 pages. 2008. ISBN 978-3-03911-275-3

Vol. 52 Konrad Ehlich & Dorothee Heller (Hrsg.)
Die Wissenschaft und ihre Sprachen.
323 pages. 2006. ISBN 978-3-03911-272-2

Vol. 53 Jingyu Zhang
The Semantic Salience Hierarchy Model: The L2 Acquisition of Psych Predicates
273 pages. 2007. ISBN 978-3-03911-300-2

Vol. 54 Norman Fairclough, Giuseppina Cortese & Patrizia Ardizzone (eds)
Discourse and Contemporary Social Change.
555 pages. 2007. ISBN 978-3-03911-276-0

Vol. 55 Jan Engberg, Marianne Grove Ditlevsen, Peter Kastberg & Martin Stegu (eds)
New Directions in LSP Teaching.
331 pages. 2007. ISBN 978-3-03911-433-7

Vol. 56 Dorothee Heller & Konrad Ehlich (Hrsg.)
Studien zur Rechtskommunikation.
322 pages. 2007. ISBN 978-3-03911-436-8

Vol. 57 Forthcoming.

Vol. 58 Carmen Frehner
Email – SMS – MMS
294 pages. 2008. ISBN 978-3-03911-451-1

Vol. 59 Isabel Balteiro
The Directionality of Conversion in English: A Dia-Synchronic Study.
276 pages. 2007. ISBN 978-3-03911-241-8

Vol. 60 Maria Milagros Del Saz Rubio
English Discourse Markers of Reformulation.
237 pages. 2007. ISBN 978-3-03911-196-1

Vol. 61 Sally Burgess & Pedro Martín-Martín (eds)
English as an Additional Language in Research Publication and Communication.
259 pages. 2008. ISBN 978-3-03911-462-7

Vol. 62 Sandrine Onillon
Pratiques et représentations de l'écrit.
458 pages. 2008. ISBN 978-3-03911-464-1

Vol. 63 Hugo Bowles & Paul Seedhouse (eds)
Conversation Analysis and Language for Specific Purposes.
2nd edition. 337 pages. 2007, 2009. ISBN 978-3-0343-0045-2

Vol. 64 Vijay K. Bhatia, Christopher N. Candlin & Paola Evangelisti Allori (eds)
Language, Culture and the Law.
The Formulation of Legal Concepts across Systems and Cultures.
342 pages. 2008. ISBN 978-3-03911-470-2

Vol. 65 Jonathan Culpeper & Dániel Z. Kádár (eds)
Historical (Im)politeness.
300 pages. 2010. ISBN 978-3-03911-496-2

Vol. 66 Linda Lombardo (ed.)
Using Corpora to Learn about Language and Discourse.
237 pages. 2009. ISBN 978-3-03911-522-8

Vol. 67 Natsumi Wakamoto
Extroversion/Introversion in Foreign Language Learning.
Interactions with Learner Strategy Use.
159 pages. 2009. ISBN 978-3-03911-596-9

Vol. 68 Eva Alcón-Soler (ed.)
Learning How to Request in an Instructed Language Learning Context.
260 pages. 2008. ISBN 978-3-03911-601-0

Vol. 69 Domenico Pezzini
The Translation of Religious Texts in the Middle Ages.
428 pages. 2008. ISBN 978-3-03911-600-3

Vol. 70 Tomoko Tode
Effects of Frequency in Classroom Second Language Learning. Quasi-experiment and stimulated-recall analysis.
195 pages. 2008. ISBN 978-3-03911-602-7

Vol. 71 Egor Tsedryk
Fusion symétrique et alternances ditransitives.
211 pages. 2009. ISBN 978-3-03911-609-6

Vol. 72 Cynthia J. Kellett Bidoli & Elana Ochse (eds)
English in International Deaf Communication.
444 pages. 2008. ISBN 978-3-03911-610-2

Vol. 73 Joan C. Beal, Carmela Nocera & Massimo Sturiale (eds)
Perspectives on Prescriptivism.
269 pages. 2008. ISBN 978-3-03911-632-4

Vol. 74 Carol Taylor Torsello, Katherine Ackerley & Erik Castello (eds)
Corpora for University Language Teachers.
308 pages. 2008. ISBN 978-3-03911-639-3

Vol. 75 María Luisa Pérez Cañado (ed.)
English Language Teaching in the European Credit Transfer System: Facing the Challenge.
251 pages. 2009. ISBN 978-3-03911-654-6

Vol. 76 Marina Dossena & Ingrid Tieken-Boon van Ostade (eds)
Studies in Late Modern English Correspondence. Methodology and Data.
291 pages. 2008. ISBN 978-3-03911-658-4

Vol. 77 Ingrid Tieken-Boon van Ostade & Wim van der Wurff (eds)
Current Issues in Late Modern English.
436 pages. 2009. ISBN 978-3-03911-660-7

Vol. 78 Marta Navarro Coy (ed.)
Practical Approaches to Foreign Language Teaching and Learning.
297 pages. 2009. ISBN 978-3-03911-661-4

Vol. 79 Qing Ma
Second Language Vocabulary Acquisition.
333 pages. 2009. ISBN 978-3-03911-666-9

Vol. 80 Martin Solly, Michelangelo Conoscenti & Sandra Campagna (eds)
Verbal/Visual Narrative Texts in Higher Education.
384 pages. 2008. ISBN 978-3-03911-672-0

Vol. 81 Meiko Matsumoto
From Simple Verbs to Periphrastic Expressions: The Historical Development of Composite Predicates, Phrasal Verbs, and Related Constructions in English.
235 pages. 2008. ISBN 978-3-03911-675-1

Vol. 82 Melinda Dooly
Doing Diversity. Teachers' Construction of Their Classroom Reality.
180 pages. 2009. ISBN 978-3-03911-687-4

Vol. 83 Victoria Guillén-Nieto, Carmen Marimón-Llorca & Chelo Vargas-Sierra (eds)
Intercultural Business Communication and
Simulation and Gaming Methodology.
392 pages. 2009. ISBN 978-3-03911-688-1

Vol. 84 Maria Grazia Guido
English as a Lingua Franca in Cross-cultural Immigration Domains.
285 pages. 2008. ISBN 978-3-03911-689-8

Vol. 85 Erik Castello
Text Complexity and Reading Comprehension Tests.
352 pages. 2008. ISBN 978-3-03911-717-8

Vol. 86 Forthcoming.

Vol. 87 Carmen Navarro, Rosa Mª Rodríguez Abella, Francesca Dalle Pezze
& Renzo Miotti (eds)
La comunicación especializada.
355 pages. 2008. ISBN 978-3-03911-733-8

Vol. 88 Kiriko Sato
The Development from Case-Forms to Prepositional Constructions
in Old English Prose.
231 pages. 2009. ISBN 978-3-03911-763-5

Vol. 89 Dorothee Heller (Hrsg.)
Formulierungsmuster in deutscher und italienischer Fachkommunikation.
Intra- und interlinguale Perspektiven.
315 pages. 2008. ISBN 978-3-03911-778-9

Vol. 90 Henning Bergenholtz, Sandro Nielsen & Sven Tarp (eds)
Lexicography at a Crossroads. Dictionaries and Encyclopedias Today,
Lexicographical Tools Tomorrow.
372 pages. 2009. ISBN 978-3-03911-799-4

Vol. 91 Manouchehr Moshtagh Khorasani
The Development of Controversies: From the Early Modern Period
to Online Discussion Forums.
317 pages. 2009. ISBN 978-3-3911-711-6

Vol. 92 María Luisa Carrió-Pastor (ed.)
Content and Language Integrated Learning: Cultural Diversity.
178 pages. 2009. ISBN 978-3-3911-818-2

Vol. 93-94 Forthcoming.

Vol. 95 Facchinetti Roberta, Crystal David, Seidlhofer Barbara (eds)
From International to Local English – And Back Again.
268 pages. 2010. ISBN 978-3-0343-0011-7

Vol. 96 Forthcoming.

Vol. 97 Sylvie Hancil (ed.)
The Role of Prosody in Affective Speech.
403 pages. 2009. ISBN 978-3-03911-696-6

Vol. 98 Marina Dossena & Roger Lass (eds)
Studies in English and European Historical Dialectology.
257 pages. 2009. ISBN 978-3-0343-0024-7

Vol. 99 Christine Béal
Les interactions quotidiennes en français et en anglais.
De l'approche comparative à l'analyse des situations interculturelles.
424 pages. 2010. ISBN 978-3-0343-0027-8

Vol. 100 Maurizio Gotti (ed.)
Commonality and Individuality in Academic Discourse.
398 pages. 2009. ISBN 978-3-0343-0023-0

Vol. 101 Javier E. Díaz Vera & Rosario Caballero (eds)
Textual Healing: Studies in Medieval English Medical, Scientific and Technical Texts.
213 pages. 2009. ISBN 978-3-03911-822-9

Vol. 102 Nuria Edo Marzá
The Specialised Lexicographical Approach: A Step further in Dictionary-making.
316 pages. 2009. ISBN 978-3-0343-0043-8

Vol. 103 Carlos Prado-Alonso, Lidia Gómez-García, Iria Pastor-Gómez & David Tizón-Couto (eds)
New Trends and Methodologies in Applied English Language Research. Diachronic, Diatopic and Contrastive Studies.
348 pages. 2009. ISBN 978-3-0343-0046-9

Vol. 104-108 Forthcoming.

Vol. 109 Ángeles Linde López & Rosalía Crespo Jiménez (eds)
Professional English in the European context: The EHEA challenge.
374 pages. 2010. ISBN 978-3-0343-0088-9

Vol. 110 Rosalía Rodríguez-Vázquez
The Rhythm of Speech, Verse and Vocal Music: A New Theory.
394 pages. 2010. ISBN 978-3-0343-0309-5

Vol. 111 Anastasios Tsangalidis & Roberta Facchinetti (eds)
Studies on English Modality. In Honour of Frank Palmer.
392 pages. 2009. ISBN 978-3-0343-0310-1

Vol. 112-114 Forthcoming.

Vol. 115 Giuliana Garzone & Paola Catenaccio (eds)
Identities across Media and Modes: Discursive Perspectives.
379 pages. 2009. ISBN 978-3-0343-0386-6

Vol. 116 Elena Landone
Los marcadores del discurso y cortesía verbal en español.
390 pages. 2010. ISBN 978-3-0343-0413-9

Vol. 117 Maurizio Gotti & Christopher Williams (eds)
Legal Discourse across Languages and Cultures.
339 pages. 2010. ISBN 978-3-0343-0425-2

Vol. 118 David Hirsh
Academic Vocabulary in Context.
217 pages. 2010. ISBN 978-3-0343-0426-9

Vol. 119-122 Forthcoming.

Vol. 123 Vijay K. Bhatia, Christopher N. Candlin & Maurizio Gotti (eds)
The Discourses of Dispute Resolution.
290 pages. 2010. ISBN 978-3-0343-0476-4